THE WEST POINT ROUTE

The Atlanta & West Point Rail Road and The Western Railway of Alabama

BY ROBERT H. HANSON

TLC
PUBLISHING INC.

2006

TLC Publishing, Inc.
18292 Forest Rd.
Forest, VA 24551

This book is dedicated to my mother, Jacqueline Hodges Hanson. In this project, as well as in so many others throughout my life, I have received her unwavering support. Without her support of my interest in railroads – and support in so many other areas as well, especially in my earlier years – this book most certainly would not be possible.

While it is very belated and very inadequate, thank you, Mother.

PREFACE

This project was undertaken to provide a companion volume to my earlier work, *Safety-Courtesy-Service: History of the Georgia Railroad.* As with the Georgia Road project, there has been very little published on the roads which comprised the West Point Route. Richard E. Prince published a volume in 1962 which included brief histories of the Georgia Railroad and the West Point Route, but it was largely a motive power study, with relatively few pages being devoted to the history portion of the book. Other than this, and a pair of brief booklets issued by the West Point Route in the 1950's and 1960's, there was nothing. This volume, again, attempts to fill an informational void.

I knew I would require a great deal of assistance with this work, and the fraternity of rail enthusiasts and historians did not let me down. Each time help was requested, it was readily given.

Little historical information on the West Point Route exists in the archives of CSX Transportation, the successor company to the partners of the West Point Route. For this reason, virtually all information used in this book came from private collections. It is simply amazing how much information and assistance can be forthcoming from the railfan community when the call goes out for help.

Frank Ardrey, of Birmingham, Alabama; Larry Goolsby of Kensington, Maryland, Oscar W. Kimsey of Harlem, Georgia; J. Parker Lamb of Austin, Texas, and David W. Salter, of Greenwood Village, Colorado, all came through nobly with the use of material from their photo collections. In addition, Frank Ardrey, Larry Goolsby and Ronnie Tidwell of High Shoals, Georgia printed most of the photos used in this volume.

A. M. Langley, Nelson McGahee, Ken Waller, Howard Robins, and C. K. Marsh, Jr. also contributed generously of their time, talant, and material.

Al Ward and D. K. Freeman, both West Point Route veterans, allowed me to "pick their brains" in repeated telephone interviews.

C. L. Goolsby, Bill Folsom, Nelson McGahee, Anita Wheeler (my sister), and Jacqueline Hanson (my mother) all very graciously agreed to proofread the manuscript. This was a time-consuming task, and in the case of the ladies, it was entirely above and beyond the call of duty as they had little or no interest in the subject matter being discussed. In all cases I am grateful for the assistance.

No one writes a book alone, and I received a great deal of help on this project. If anyone has been overlooked, the slight was certainly not intentional and your help is no less appreciated.

Robert H. Hanson
Loganville, Georgia
December 10, 2005

INTRODUCTION

The West Point Route. Its diamond – shaped herald was carried throughout the land by boxcars, gondolas, and timetables. It was a component of a major transcontinental passenger route, forwarding trains such as *The Crescent*, and the *Piedmont Limited*, (the former complete with streamlined, round-end observation car) but few people outside the area, or the railroad industry, knew about the two companies that made up what was essentially one railroad.

It was once nominated by *Trains* Magazine editor David P. Morgan as the all-American railroad (but was ultimately rejected by him due to its abbreviated – 225 miles – length). It was, as he termed it, "Pacific, Mikado, eight-wheel switcher railroading."

Although it was controlled by three major railroads (the Atlantic Coast Line, the Louisville & Nashville, and the Central of Georgia) its passenger operations were most closely co-ordinated with another, corporately unrelated carrier (Southern Railway).

The West Point Route was not as well-known as either of its major passenger connections – the Southern or the Louisville & Nashville - but as the last General Passenger Agent (and later Assistant to the President) A. A. Ward once said, "It was a classy little railroad."

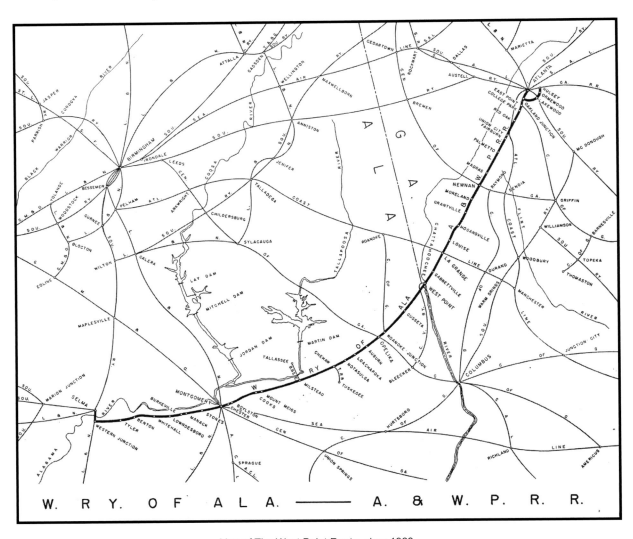

Map of The West Point Route, circa 1963.

TABLE OF CONTENTS

Front Inside Cover: Trains 31 and 32 were all-stops locals between Atlanta and Montgomery. They were at the bottom of the diesel assignment pecking order and thus were the first to give up their diesels when power ran short. No. 32 is shown here at Palmetto, GA, as it heads for Atlanta early in 1953, shortly before the train's demise on March 31 of that year. Credit – Bruce R. Meyer collection.

Back Inside Cover: Western of Alabama 380 and Atlanta & West Point 430 were the last steam power acquired by the West Point Route. Built in 1944, the locomotives were also the last of their wheel arrangement built in the US for a domestic carrier. The 380 has a roll on first 211 (Atlanta-Montgomery through freight) at Red Oak, GA, in March of 1948. Credit – Hugh M. Corner photo, author's collection.

International Standard Book Number:
0-9766201-4-6

Design & Layout by
Megan Johnson
Johnson 2 Studios, Rustburg, Va.

Printed in USA
by Walsworth Publishing Co., Marceline, Mo.

CHAPTER
I

THE EARLY YEARS

Until the 1830's, travel in the United States was an "iffy" proposition. If one was on or near the ocean, or a navigable stream, water travel was most likely the answer. Although slow and frequently circuitous, it was generally far more comfortable than the horseback or stagecoach ride overland. Such rides were generally bumpy, dusty or muddy - depending on the season - and uncomfortable all the time.

Shipping freight was even more unpredictable. Freighters - wagon drivers who hauled freight between cities - were frequently less than reliable, and the freight was loaded and unloaded between companies if it were moving over distances longer than that covered by one company. Each time the shipment was transloaded it would generally shrink in size due to damage and particularly due to pilferage. The latter situation was frequently so bad that merchants routinely shipped anywhere from 10% to 25% more of any item or commodity ordered and hoped that the proper quantity would survive the trip and make it into the hands of the consignee.

With this situation in mind, it was no wonder that whenever business leaders in a given town learned of the success of the Baltimore & Ohio, the Mohawk & Hudson, the South Carolina Railroad and others, they immediately began to lay plans for a railroad to connect their communities to the outside world, or to serve as a trade artery feeding traffic from the hinterlands to their city. The business leaders in Alabama and Georgia were no exception.

THE ALABAMA LINES

The Montgomery Rail Road Company was chartered under the laws of Alabama on January 15, 1834. The purpose of the company was to construct and operate a railroad from Montgomery, on the Alabama River, to a place in Georgia called West Point, on the Chattahoochee River.[20]

The charter stated that John Scott, Jr., Abner MaGehee, George E. Matthews, William B. S. Gilmer, Jesse P. Taylor, John W. Freeman, Thomas M. Cowles, Andrew Dexter, Thomas James, John Goldwaithe, Charles T. Pollard, William Sayre, Edward Hamrick, George Wragg, Benajah S. Bibb, Justus Wyman, Thomas S. Mays, George Whitman, Francis Bughee, N. E. Benson, Joseph Hutchinson, W. P. Converse, John Martin, P. D. Sayre, C. Hooks, Green Wood, J. H. Tharington, and S. W. Goode were appointed Commissioners and that any thirteen of them were competent to act.[21]

In November 1834, the Board held its first meeting, and Abner McGehee was elected president. Shortly thereafter, the Board secured the services of A. A. Dexter as Principal Engineer. Dexter and McGehee made a preliminary inspection of the

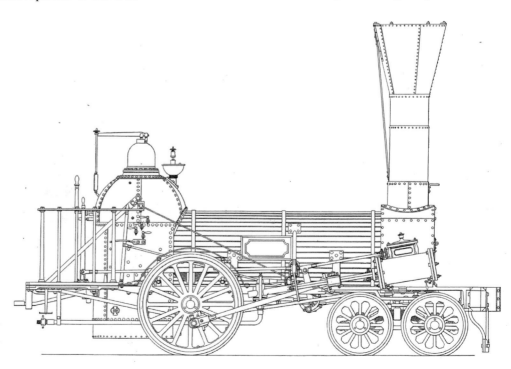

A locomotive of similar construction to the *Abner McGehee* of 1839. (Credit – *Railway Gazette*)

proposed route. On this trip, McGehee secured rights of way and/or timber rights to some of the lands through which the road would pass. [22]

Surveying was begun in 1835. The survey of the first 27 miles was complete by December of that year, and the preliminary survey of the entire line was completed in 1836. The work of clearing and grading was begun on March 1, 1836, with a crew of 40 men. [23]

By 1839, the first segment of the road was nearing completion. Management felt that, with a loan of $50,000, equipment might be purchased and the road pushed to completion as far as Franklin. They felt that two years of operation would demonstrate the road's value as an investment and its contribution to public convenience. [24]

Toward this end, the Board, on October 9, 1839, authorized a bond issue of $50,000 for these purposes. With the proceeds of this loan, construction of the line was expedited.

The road received its first locomotive in 1839. On April 26, the firm of Rogers, Ketchum & Grosvenor of Paterson, NJ, completed work on a 4-2-0 named *Abner McGehee*, and it was delivered shortly thereafter. It bore the builder's construction number 12. [25]

When the first segment of the road was opened to Franklin, 32.4 miles from Montgomery, in June 1840, the company's management was greatly disappointed in its reception by the general public. The receipts from the operations barely covered the expenses incurred, leaving virtually nothing for further construction and the purchase of additional equipment.

In spite of this disappointment, the company took delivery of its second and third locomotives. The *West Point*, was delivered in 1840, and was built by James Brooks. [26] The *General J. Scott* was delivered in 1841, and was built by D. J. Burr. Both engines were of the 4-2-0 wheel arrangement. [27]

By 1841, the financial condition of the company had deteriorated to the point that it had no means with which to continue operations. At this point the road was leased to Abner McGehee.

Mr. McGehee operated the line until July 9, 1842, when it was sold under foreclosure and was purchased by Charles T. Pollard and eight others, including Mr. McGehee, himself. These men then applied for a charter for a new company, the Montgomery & West Point Rail Road Company.

MONTGOMERY & WEST POINT RAIL ROAD

The State of Alabama granted Pollard, McGehee, and their associates a charter for their company on February 13, 1843. By no stretch of the imagination, however, could the situation be called satisfactory, or even stable.

The company did, in the face of all adversity, manage to purchase one additional locomotive; a 4-2-0 named *J. E.*

Thompson. It was constructed by the Baldwin Locomotive Works, bore construction number 210, and was delivered in 1844. [28]

The State of Alabama showed some willingness to extend some financial assistance to the struggling line, but the governor was reluctant to do so without substantial security for the loan. As a result of this insistence, several of the original incorporators of the M&WP sold out leaving, by March 1, 1845, only Abner McGehee, William Taylor, Thomas M. Cowles, Charles T. Pollard, and Alfred V. Scott.[29] These five men pledged, in addition to the corporate assets, their personal property as collateral for a loan from the state. This additional security satisfied the governor and on that date, he authorized the payment to the company of $116,782.64. [30]

With these funds in hand, the advancement of construction became the number one priority. Toward this end, it was decided to invest a portion of the funds in slaves.

According to the 1850 annual report, "An agent was forthwith dispatched to Virginia, who purchased eighty-four negroes, at a total cost of $42,176.20 With these negroes, for several years, the Company had great trouble. At one time as many as ten had run off. Some were found in Kentucky, some in Indiana, some in the mountains of Georgia, and two have never been heard from." [31]

In addition to the slaves, purchases included an additional locomotive, the *John P. King*. This locomotive, a Baldwin 4-2-0, was delivered in 1845.

Even with the loan from the State of Alabama, the company needed even more cash. To alleviate this situation a loan of $250,000 was negotiated. This loan was guaranteed by the Georgia Railroad & Banking Company and the South Carolina Railroad Company.

Charles T. Pollard, President of the Montgomery & West Point Rail Road (Credit – Western Ry of Alabama)

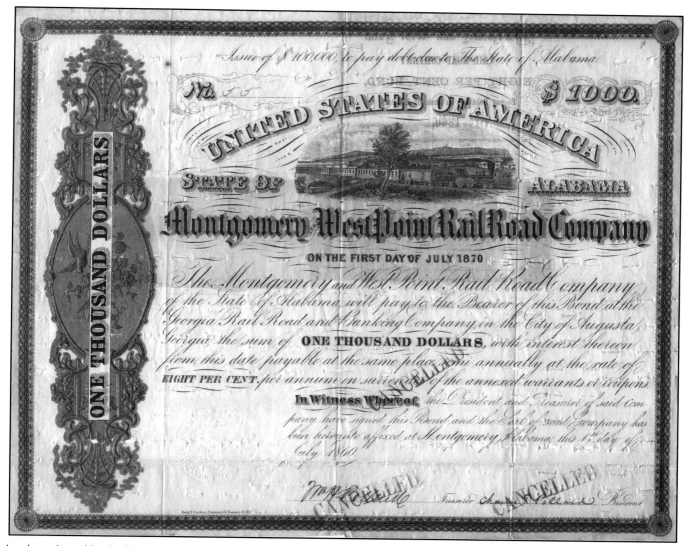

This bond was issued by the Montgomery & West Point Rail Road on July 15, 1860, just months prior to the outbreak of the War Between the States. (Author's collection)

These funds enabled the company to continue its growth. Another locomotive, a Baldwin 4-2-0 named *James Gadsden* was purchased in 1847, and the road was extended from Chehaw to Opelika, a distance of 25.2 miles, in 1848.

In 1850, the company received two new locomotives, the *Macon* and the *Montgomery*, from Baldwin. These locomotives were of the 4-4-0 wheel arrangement, the first of that type on the railroad.

The road was completed to West Point, Ga., on April 28, 1851. A substantial brick depot was built, larger than the warehouse in Montgomery. A temporary shed was built for the accommodation of passengers as the railroad planned to build a more permanent structure on a joint basis with the Atlanta & LaGrange Rail Road when the tracks of that company reached West Point. [32]

Passenger service was inaugurated between Montgomery and West Point with two trains being operated daily in each direction. Connecting service to Palmetto, Ga., the railhead of the Atlanta & LaGrange Rail Road, was provided by stagecoach. [33]

The prospect of additional future revenue was enhanced on July 1 when the company secured a contract to carry the United States Mail. The contract called for a payment of $24,337 per year. [34]

On March 1, 1854, President C. T. Pollard presented to his board a charter for the Western Rail Road, secured at the most recent meeting of the legislature. It authorized the construction of a continuous line of railroad across the state of Alabama, connecting with the Alabama & Mississippi Rivers Railroad at Selma and giving it the authority to purchase the Montgomery & West Point Rail Road. Mr. Pollard was also president of the Western Rail Road.

The Atlanta & LaGrange Rail Road reached West Point on March 15, 1854. Although it was now possible to travel and ship by rail from Atlanta, Ga. to Montgomery, Ala. by rail, there were no through trains or through cars. This was due to the fact that, while the Montgomery & West Point was constructed to a gauge of 4' 8 1/2", the Atlanta & LaGrange was built with the accepted Southern standard gauge of 5' between the rails.

Because of this difference in gauges, a track was laid by the A&L parallel to and 41 feet from the track of the M&WP and a platform 30 feet wide was constructed between the tracks to facilitate the transfer of freight and passengers.

Effective January 1, 1855, it was possible to travel from Atlanta, Ga. to Pensacola, Fla. by train. This was due to the opening of the Alabama & Florida Railroad which operated southward out of Montgomery.

On February 1, 1855, the Montgomery & West Point Rail Road opened a branch extending from Opelika, Ala., to Columbus, Ga., a distance of 29 miles.

At the annual meeting for 1857, a 5% dividend was declared. Also at that meeting, the death of Major Thomas M. Cowles was announced. Major Cowles was one of the original incorporators of the railroad and served on the board of directors from 1835 until the day of his death.

The Montgomery locomotive shop, experienced in locomotive repair, tried its hand at locomotive construction in 1858, when it built a 4-4-0, named the *Native*, from the ground up. Although apparently successful, it was not duplicated.

In 1860, the M&WP gained a feeder line when the Tuskegee Railroad built a line over the route between Tuskegee and a connection with the M&WP at Chehaw, a distance of 5.3 miles. The M&WP had previously surveyed the route in 1855, and sold the company the relay rail it used for construction. For this rail, the M&WP received 50 shares of stock, worth $5000, in the company. [35]

Financial results for 1860 were satisfying. The company showed a net income of $195,960.54. From this income, two semi-annual dividends of 3% were paid in addition to the regular dividend of 5%. [36]

Also in 1860, the M&WP received two new locomotives, the *John Caldwell* and the *John P. King* (the second engine to bear that name), from Baldwin. These locomotives would be the last new power purchased for six years.

THE GEORGIA LINE

The Atlanta & LaGrange Rail Road Company was chartered by the State of Georgia on December 27, 1847, "for the purpose of constructing a rail road communication between the town of Atlanta, in DeKalb (Fulton, after 1853) County or some convenient point on the Macon & Western Rail Road between Griffin and Atlanta, to LaGrange, in Troup County..." [37] The incorporators included B. H. Conyers, Andrew J. Berry, John Griffin, Brittain Sims, Sr., Hugh Brewster, John Ray, John H. Johnson, Willis P. Menifee, Littlebury Watts, Joel W. Terrell, J. V. Davis, Thomas W. Bolten, Joseph Poythress, Henry West, Edward Y. Hill, Robert A. T. Ridley, John Douglas, William Reid, and James M. Beall. [38]

The incorporators held their first meeting on January 13, 1849, in Corinth, Heard County, Georgia, for the purpose of

organization. Several other meetings were held at Corinth and LaGrange. Heard County, which initially showed a great deal of interest in the railroad, was left off the line entirely, and has never had any form of rail service. [39]

After the granting of the charter, no further action was taken until May 24, 1849, when an organizational meeting was held in Newnan. At that meeting John P. King, President of the Georgia Railroad & Banking Company, was elected President of the Atlanta & LaGrange.

That fall, construction began at a point approximately 6.5 miles southwest of Atlanta on the Macon & Western Railroad, now called East Point, Ga. Arrangements were made with the Macon & Western for the use of their track into Atlanta for an annual charge of $3000. [40]

By March 17, 1851, the road had been completed 18.5 miles to Palmetto and train service was inaugurated shortly thereafter. By September 9, the line was complete as far as Newnan, 33 miles.

In mid-1851, the company received its first locomotive, the *Joel W. Terrell*, a 4-4-0 built by Norris Brothers in Philadelphia. [41] Until that time, construction and operations had been conducted with locomotives rented from, most likely, the Georgia Railroad.

By May 25, 1852, construction had advanced to Grantville, 12 miles beyond Newnan and 45 miles from East Point, and had reached Hogansville by September.

Two locomotives, the *E. Y. Hill* and the *F. C. Arms*, were purchased in 1852. The engines, both 4-4-0's, were built by Norris Brothers in May of that year. [42]

John Pendleton King, first president of the Atlanta & LaGrange Rail Road and president of the Georgia Railroad & Banking Company.

Locomotive *Dr. Thompson*, of the A&WP. Delivered by Rogers in 1860, it is shown here in Atlanta in 1868. (Author's collection)

The Georgia Railroad & Banking Company, which had invested in the A&L from the outset, continued to increase its investment in the road. (Its president, John P. King, was also president of the A&L.) By 1852, this investment totaled $279,000, [43] or not quite 14% of the shares. Future investments by the by this company, and later by its lessees, would increase its ownership to approximately 63% of the stock in the A&L and its successor, the Atlanta & West Point, assuring control. [44]

The construction crews reached LaGrange in February of 1853. The Atlanta & LaGrange Rail Road had reached its original intended terminus. In the intervening years, however, the strategy had been changed. The company had requested, and been granted, authority to build beyond LaGrange to West Point, Ga., on the Chattahoochee River. This amendment to the charter was enacted by the Georgia Legislature on December 14, 1849. [45]

Also in February 1853, the railroad took delivery of one new locomotive, the *Patriot*. This engine was a 4-4-0 and was built by Richard Norris & Sons, Philadelphia. [46]

On May 25, 1853, a change was made in the bylaws to relocate the annual meeting of the stockholders from Newnan to Atlanta. From that time onward, the headquarters and principal office of the company would be located in that city. [47]

West Point was reached by the Atlanta & LaGrange tracks on May 15, 1854.

The line now extended 79.92 miles from its junction with the Macon & Western Railroad to West Point, where it made a connection with the Montgomery & West Point Rail Road. [48]

The motive power roster continued to expand as the company purchased new locomotives to handle its expanding business. The *West Point* and the *E. L. Ellsworth* were purchased in 1854; the *Telegraph* and the *Post Boy* were delivered in 1855; and the *George R. Gilmer* was built in 1856. All were 4-4-0's and all were built by Rogers, Ketchum & Grosvenor of Paterson, NJ. [49]

On December 22, 1857, the Georgia Legislature approved an amendment to the charter of the Atlanta & LaGrange Rail Road which changed the name of the company to reflect its actual termini. After that date the name of the company was the Atlanta & West Point Rail Road Company. The amendment also granted the company authority to build branches to Columbus, Ga. and Greenville, Ga. The authority to build these lines was never exercised. [50]

After completion of the line to West Point, the company continued to improve its property. Three new locomotives, the *A. J. Berry*, the *J. McLendon*, and the *John E. Robinson*, were delivered by Rogers Locomotive & Machine Works in 1857 and 1858, and new depots were built at Fairburn in 1858 and in Hogansville in 1859. [51]

The company also faced several problems during this period. The Superintendent recommended that a shop be built in Atlanta. His recommendation was based on the fact that the Georgia Railroad shops in Atlanta and Augusta, which had been performing maintenance work for both roads, were too small to accommodate the increasing demands of both roads. [52]

Another problem was a shortage of labor. The company hired "white hands" (laborers) for the first time in 1859.

This decision stemmed from the fact that the local slave owners were charging a price that the company deemed excessive. [53]

The annual return on investment for the year 1859 was 16.74%. [54] Business continued to grow and the company purchased an additional locomotive to help handle the traffic. The engine, named *Dr. Thompson*, was delivered by Rogers in 1860. [55] It would be the last motive power purchased for six years.

The eve of the War Between the States found both partners of what would be known as the West Point Route established and thriving. The next several years would be a period of trial and hardship for both companies.

[20] Declaration of Incorporation of The Western Railway of Alabama with Copies of Papers and Acts of the Legislature Relating Thereto, and to The Montgomery & West Point Rail Road Company and The Western Railroad of Alabama, to Whose Chartered Privileges It Succeeded, (Montgomery, Ala., 1917). p. 26.

[21] Ibid. p. 24.

[22] Avary, J. Arch, Jr., and Bowie, Marshall L., *The West Point Route*. (Atlanta, 1954). p.3.

[23] Ibid.

[24] Ibid.

[25] Peter Moshein and Robert R. Rothfus, "Rogers Locomotives: A Brief History and Construction List." *Railroad History* 167. Autumn 1992. p. 30.

[26] Richard E. Prince. *Steam Locomotives and History, Georgia Railroad and West Point Route*. Green River Wyoming: 1962. p. 55.

[27] Ibid.

[28] Ibid., p. 58.

[29] Avary and Bowie. *The West Point Route*, p. 4.

[30] Ibid.

[31] Ibid.

[32] S. R. Young. Letter to Dr. Rena M. Andrews, Winthrop College, Rock Hill, SC. September 10, 1945. p. 3.

[33] Avary and Bowie, *The West Point Route*. p. 4.

[34] Young, Letter to Dr. Andrews, p. 3.

[35] Young, Letter to Dr. Andrews. p. 4.

[36] Avary and Bowie, *The West Point Route*, p. 5.

[37] Charter, Amendments and By-Laws of Atlanta and West Point Rail Road Company, Revised by Heyman, Howell & Heyman, General Counsel, 1948. p. 1.

[38] Ibid.

[39] Franklin M. Garrett, *Atlanta and Environs* (Lewis Historical Publishing Co.; 1954, Reprint Edition, Athens, 1969) Vol. 1, pp 258-259.

[40] Macon & Western RR and Atlanta & LaGrange RR. Articles of Agreement, November 26, 1849. Contracts and Agreements, Central of Georgia Railway Co. Vol. 1, p. 2.

[41] William D. Edson, "The Norris Construction Record", Railroad History 150, Spring, 1984, p. 67.

[42] Ibid. p. 68.

[43] Georgia Railroad & Banking Company, Annual Report, 1852.

[44] Robert P. Hanson, editor, *Moody's Transportation Manual - 1980* (Moody's Investment Service, New York, 1980) p. 858.

[45] *Georgia Acts, 1849 and 1850*, p. 238.

[46] Reports of the President and Superintendent of the Atlanta & LaGrange Rail Road Co. to the Stockholders in Convention, July 25, 1856.

[47] Atlanta Historical Society, "Down the West Point Road", paper prepared for the First National Bank of Atlanta. No date. p. 2.

[48] Corporate History of the Atlanta & West Point Rail Road Company, As of the Date of Valuation, June 30, 1918. (ICC Valuation Document). p. 7.

[49] Moshein and Rothfus, Op. Cit. pp. 40-41, 45.

[50] *Georgia Acts, 1857*. p. 66.

[51] Moshein and Rothfus, Op. cit., pp. 46-47.

[52] Avary and Bowie, Op. cit., p. 11.

[53] Ibid.

[54] Ibid.

[55] Moshein and Rothfus, Op. cit., p. 50.

II

THE WAR YEARS

On January 11, 1861, Alabama seceded from the Union, electing to no longer be a part of the United States of America. The state of Georgia followed suit on January 19, 1861.

On February 4, delegates from several Southern states met in Montgomery to form an alliance, now that they were no longer part of the United States. At that meeting they formed the Confederate States of America.

On February 17, 1861, Jefferson Davis arrived in Montgomery on a Montgomery & West Point train,[1] having departed Atlanta on the A&WP and changed trains at West Point. Davis traveled from Atlanta to West Point aboard the private car of A&WP Superintendent George G. Hull. This was the last leg of a long and highly circuitous rail journey (via Corinth, Mississippi, and Chattanooga, Tennessee) from his home near Biloxi, Mississippi.

On April 12, 1861, the United States tried to send supplies to Fort Sumter, in the harbor at Charleston, S.C., in defiance of a warning from the State of South Carolina and the Confederate States of America not to do so. (The fort was on what was considered to be South Carolina soil and the state had politely requested the United States, now a foreign power, to remove its troops and arms.)

In response to this defiance, the fort was shelled and ultimately captured. The War Between the States had begun. It would have a profound effect on the railroads of the West Point Route and the area they served.

THE ALABAMA LINES

On April 9, 1861, M&WP President C. T. Pollard reported net income of $91,725.36 for the fiscal year ending March , 1861. He also reported capital expenditures of $92,317.62 or such items as two locomotives, a supply of replacement ails, additional cars, and the construction of a new car shop n Montgomery to replace an earlier structure destroyed by ire.[2]

On April 8, 1862, President Pollard reported a net ncome of $143,995.46, and the company declared a 6% dividend. In his report, Mr. Pollard also called attention to he enormous increase in prices for "every article necessary or working and keeping up the repairs of the Road and its outfit."[3]

Superintendent Daniel H. Cram reported that the company's freight car ownership totaled 175, down from 06 at the previous report. He was also concerned about the upply of flues and tires for the locomotives.[4] The traditional ources of supply for these items were in the north and herefore could not be relied upon.

In his report of April 8, 1863, President Pollard reported net income of $628,528.56.[5] The high profit figure was misleading, however. It was the result of heavy wear on the oad and equipment and many of the items needed to make epairs or operate the road were either extremely expensive or completely unobtainable at any price.

An example of one such item was lubricating oil. This commodity was in such short supply that the M&WP was able to keep its trains running only by advertising persistently in the local newspapers. These ads urged housewives to help keep the trains running by salvaging cooking fat from the kitchen for use as a lubricant.[6]

Work on the Western Rail Road (Montgomery to Selma) was reported to be progressing satisfactorily. Half of the grading had been completed and the remainder was under contract.

In his report, Superintendent Cram reported that the freight car ownership was down to 147, and that the company had also lost four locomotives.

Mr. Cram was also extremely annoyed with the Confederate Government. The Atlanta Rolling Mill, built and financed by several railroads for the purpose of rolling new rails, had been seized by the Confederate Government and was being used to roll new railroad iron - rails, which were in extremely short supply - into plates for gun boats.[7]

The M&WP carried 286,871 passengers during the fiscal year ending March 31, 1863. Of that figure, 200,160 were Confederate soldiers.[8]

Net income for the fiscal year ended March 31, 1864, was $353,282.57.[9] While the income figure was satisfactory, the numbers were deceptive. Prices for the supplies necessary for the maintenance and operation of the railroad were simply exorbitant, if the needed items were available at all.

Superintendent Cram reported that he had been able to obtain 2 1/2 miles of rail and some locomotive tires from the Atlanta Rolling Mill, now under the supervision of the Confederate States Navy. Cram had nothing but praise for Captain Jackson, CSN, who was in charge of the facility and helped obtain the supplies needed. [10]

The Superintendent also reported a number of difficulties in dealing with the military. In one incident he was threatened with report by a second lieutenant for not moving, via passenger train, a carload of spittoons, but carrying instead a carload of buckshot that Cram knew that General John H. Morgan was waiting for. [11]

Another episode involved a Brigadier General who threatened to arrest Cram when he refused to move a troop train out when there was "an actual certainty" that his train would collide with a downward passenger train. [12]

Federal troops commanded by General Lovell Rousseau attacked the railroad on July 17, 1864, at Loachapoka, Ala. The main line between Chehaw and Opelika was destroyed, along with a portion of the Columbus branch. The troops burned the depots at Loachapoka, Notasulga, Auburn, and Opelika and several cars loaded with military stores were destroyed in the yards at Opelika. The damage was repaired and the line was once again operational by the fall of 1864.

General James H. Wilson, USA, visited Montgomery on April 12, 1865. His visit caused great consternation among Montgomery's inhabitants.

In anticipation of his visit, approximately 88,000 bales of cotton were burned along with the warehouses that held them, to keep the cotton out of Federal hands. The M&WP moved its equipment to Columbus and West Point for safe keeping and continued operations until Wilson reached Montgomery, then gradually contracted the scope of its operations towards West Point and Columbus until Wilson ultimately captured these cities. [13]

Wilson's men destroyed the M&WP's entire fleet of rolling stock. Operations ceased on April 16, 1865, due to the almost total destruction of the railroad and its equipment. All this took place a week after General Robert E. Lee's surrender at Appomattox Court House in Virginia, ending most of the organized Confederate military action east of the Mississippi River.

Superintendent Cram and his forces rebuilt fourteen trestles, several depots, and all shop buildings in Montgomery. They also managed to return to service sixteen of the road's nineteen locomotives.

Because its locomotives and cars did not share the common (5' 0") gauge of the other Southern carriers, but were built to the northern (4' 8 1/2") standard gauge, the M&WP was not able to remove its equipment off-line to distant points and out of harm's way. Cram observed, "The narrow gauge which had during the four years of fearful war had prevented its outfit from being scattered throughout the Southern States, proved in the end to be the certain means of its destruction." [14]

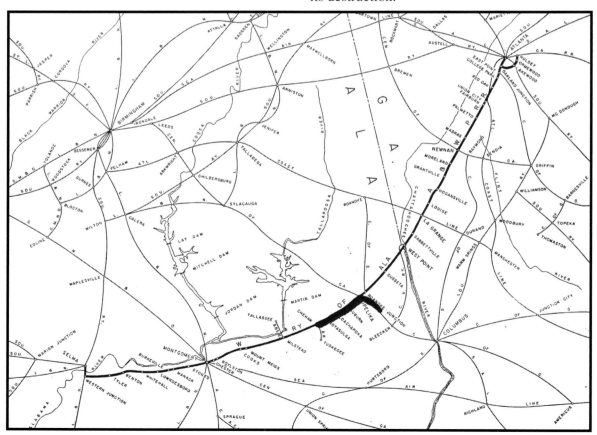

Federal troops destroyed approximately 40 miles of the M&WP. That portion is represented on this map by the bold lines.

THE GEORGIA LINES

The Atlanta & West Point Rail Road did not fare badly in the early part of the war. While shortages were prevalent and high prices were the rule, the line itself suffered no damage due to military action until fairly late in the war.

By 1862, it was reported that some of the rolling stock had been captured by Federal troops at Huntsville, Ala., (on the Memphis & Charleston RR) while loaded with supplies for the Confederate forces. Other cars were off-line on the lower end of the Mobile & Ohio Railroad. A messenger was sent in search of the cars in the earnest hope that some of them would soon be recovered. [15]

Wear and tear were beginning to take their toll on the road and equipment by 1863. Iron rails and repair parts such as locomotive tires were frightfully expensive when they were obtainable at all. Labor was in short supply, owing to the fact that most men were in uniform. To help alleviate this shortage in manpower, the company purchased 24 young Negro men. These men were emancipated with the fall of the Confederacy in 1865. [16]

In the summer of 1864, John P. King, President of both the Atlanta & West Point and Georgia railroads, ordered the movement of as much equipment as possible out of Atlanta, over the Georgia Railroad to Augusta. A small amount of equipment was left on the A&WP and operated on the lower end of the railroad during the occupation of Atlanta by the Federal troops of General William Techumseh Sherman. [17]

The equipment that was stored for safekeeping in Augusta was later seized by the Commander of the Confederate forces. It was used by the Confederate army during the evacuation of Charleston to move troops across the Carolinas.

By July 28, 1864, the only rail lines still intact serving Atlanta were the Atlanta & West Point and the Macon & Western. On August 23, Federal troops cut the A&WP near Fairburn. The soldiers removed the rails, heated them over bonfires of burning crossties, and bent them around trees. The resulting bent rails were dubbed "Sherman's hairpins" and made it impossible to quickly repair the damage. This left the A&WP with nothing more than a bare right of way for 18 miles from Atlanta to Fairburn. [18]

The A&WP's losses in Atlanta included one locomotive and 55 cars, all destroyed by Confederate General John B. Hood to keep them out of the hands of Union forces. The Atlanta passenger depot, called the "Car Shed" was also destroyed by Federal troops. While not owned by the A&WP, it was used by all railroads entering the city.

Sherman's troops left Atlanta on November 16, 1864. The work of rebuilding the A&WP was undertaken by the Confederate government under the supervision of Major John M. Hottel of the Railroad Bureau. [19] Limited operation was restored on January 20, 1865, after the removal of unexploded shells on the right of way and the repair of the tracks.

On April 16, 1865, Wilson's Cavalry raided the city of West Point, Ga., and destroyed the depot, track, and Chattahoochee River bridge of the Atlanta & West Point. No locomotives or cars were involved, having been removed to Atlanta prior to the raid.

The stockholders of the Atlanta & West Point Rail Road met on July 14, 1865, for the first time since 1862. Military op-

General Sherman's troops destroyed 18 miles of the A&WP between Atlanta and Fairburn, represented by the bold line on this map.

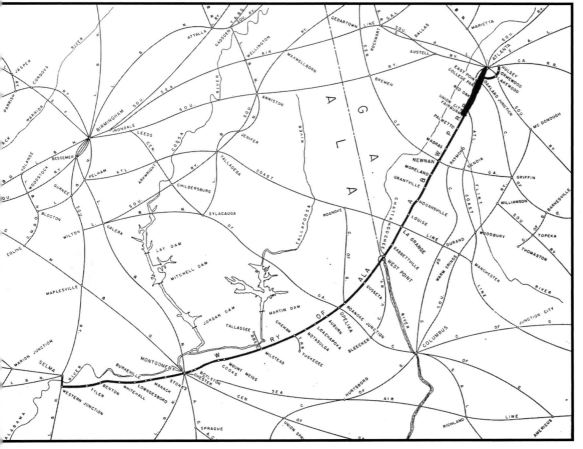

erations and the general disruptions of war had prevented meetings in 1863 and 1864. [20]

Because of this situation, the report to stockholders issued on July 14, 1865, was for a two-year period. The net income for this period was $1,053,617.60, all in Confederate currency. [21]

As a result of the war, the A&WP lost depots at Atlanta, Fairburn, Palmetto, LaGrange, and the joint facility at West Point. It also lost 18 miles of track, the Chattahoochee River bridge, one locomotive 55 cars, 24 slaves and all water stations. The outlook that summer of 1865 was somewhat bleak, to say the least.

A&WP-Georgia Railroad engine house in Atlanta in the fall of 1864, shortly after Sherman's departure. Identified locomotives are (clockwise from foreground): A&WP *Post Boy*, unidentified (behind box car), Georgia Railroad switch engines *South Carolina*, *North Carolina*, and *Rhode Island*, and the *C. A. Bull* of the A&WP is on the turntable. (National Archives photo)

[1] Marshall L. Bowie, *A Time of Adversity - And Courage.* (Atlanta, 1961) p. 6.

[2] Bowie, Op. cit., p. 6.

[3] Ibid. p. 7.

[4] Ibid. p.8.

[5] Ibid.

[6] Robert C. Black III. *The Railroads of the Confederacy.* (Chapel Hill, NC: The University of North Carolina Press, 1952), pp. 127-128.

[7] Bowie. Op. Cit. pp. 9-10.

[8] Ibid. p.10.

[9] Ibid.

[10] Ibid., p. 11.

[11] Bowie, Op. cit. p. 12.

[12] Ibid.

[13] Ibid.

[14] Ibid., p. 13.

[15] J. Arch Avary and Marshall L. Bowie, *The West Point Route.* (Atlanta 1954). p. 12.

[16] Ibid.

[17] Ibid.

[18] Garrett, Op. cit., Vol. 1, p 632.

[19] Robert C. Black III, *The Railroads of the Confederacy.* (Chapel Hill, NC: The University of North Carolina Press, 1952). p. 270.

[20] Avary and Bowie, op. cit., p. 12.

[21] Ibid.

III

RECONSTRUCTION & CONSOLIDATION
MONTGOMERY & WEST POINT RAILROAD

O If General William Tecumseh Sherman said, "War is Hell," then M&WP President C. T. Pollard most likely agreed with him when he reviewed his road's situation at the end of the war.

The company had suffered the destruction of all depot buildings except the depot at Notasulga and the passenger depot at West Point. All shops, water tanks, and bridges on the road as well as virtually all of the cars, locomotives, and machinery had been destroyed or severely damaged as well. The company's total losses due to the war were 1,618,243.[24]

Efforts were immediately undertaken to return the road to operation. Fortunately, one locomotive and five flat cars, which constituted the last train in service on April 16, 1865, were found in a fairly remote location on the road. Although damaged, this equipment was in better shape than the balance of the rolling stock. These pieces of equipment were placed in running order at a makeshift repair shop set up under the train shed at West Point.

The locomotive *Abner McGehee*, long retired and abandoned, was resurrected and placed in work train service. It was in such sad shape that it was passed over by the Union forces as not worthy of the effort required to further disable further. With a week's worth of effort it was again placed in what passed for running order and served ably until the completion of repairs on the Ossinippa bridge on June 16, 1865, when, according to Superintendent Cram, it burst a tire and became "utterly worthless, and was laid up..."[25]

On June 22, 1865, service was resumed between West Point, Ga., and Chehaw, Ala., with the stages of F. C. Taylor & Company providing service over the gap between Chehew and Montgomery. The gap was gradually shortened until it was eliminated completely on August 29, 1865, when the railroad was reopened in its entirety.[26]

As the company had been rendered virtually penniless by the war, financing the rehabilitation presented a problem. Pollard's efforts in this area were aided by General Smith, Commander of the Federal forces in Montgomery. He gave the company authority to issue bills to be used in circulation in an amount not to exceed $50,000, only $30,000 of which was issued. These bills were accepted without hesitation and helped advance the company's rebuilding efforts. President Pollard was also able to arrange a loan of $50,000 from the Southern Express Company under very favorable terms in 1866.[27] The balance of the cost of rebuilding the road was financed through a bond issue of approximately $687,000.

Additional aid was provided by the Central Railroad & Banking Company of Georgia. The company agreed to subscribe to $50,000 in stock and guaranteed $200,000 in bonds.[28]

Five locomotives, all 4-4-0's, were added to the roster. Two were acquired from Baldwin, two from Rogers, and one was constructed from parts of five locomotives of five different builders. Of the latter, Superintendent Cram made the following comment: "Saying nothing as to the beauty, I can testify that its performance has been such as to reflect no discredit upon its eminent makers."[29]

Between the dates of August 8 and August 16, 1866, the gauge of the M&WP was changed from four feet, eight and one half inches to five feet. This was done in order to conform to the Southern standard gauge. The change was made east to west, and the Atlanta & West Point simply extended its passenger service beyond West Point to the break in the gauge, where passengers, baggage, mail and express were transferred to an M&WP train to continue the journey. Freight service was suspended during the change.

The Chattahoochee River bridge at Columbus was completed on September 20, 1866. With this event, the rebuilding of the Montgomery & West Point Rail Road was basically completed. While some work remained to be done on the buildings and rolling stock, the line was now more or less intact as it was prior to the war.

A Montgomery & West Point Rail Road pass for the year 1870. The railroad did not last out the year under that name, but merged with the Western Rail Road of Alabama on September 1 of that year. (Author's collection)

At a meeting of the Board of Directors on March 1, 1867, it was stated that a payment of $8,643.39 had been made to the Western Rail Road. The funds were to be applied to the work then in progress toward making a connection with the M&WP at Montgomery. [30]

Three new locomotives, the *Savannah*, the *Columbus*, and the *Selma*, all 4-4-0's, were shipped from the Rogers works in late August of 1869. They bore road numbers 31-33, respectively. [31]

At the stockholders meeting on June 2, 1870, it was proposed that the M&WP be sold to the Western Rail Road through and exchange of stock. It was reported that the Western would be complete and in operation by September 1, 1870. The proposal was adopted by the stockholders of both companies and the merger took place on September 1. The surviving company was known as the Western Rail Road Company of Alabama. [32]

THE WESTERN RAILROAD OF ALABAMA

The line from Montgomery to Selma was completed in early December, 1870. The Western Rail Road of Alabama now owned a continuous line of railroad that extended from West Point and Columbus, Ga. through Montgomery to Selma, Ala.

The Western received its first four new locomotives in December 1870 and January 1871. No.s 1-4, the *A. M. McGehee*, the *Montgomery*, the *W. S. Holt*, and the *Opelika*, all 4-4-0's, were delivered by Rogers, two in December and

Former Confederate General E. Porter Alexander was elected president of The Western Rail Road of Alabama on September 1, 1875. He served in this capacity for three years. (Western Railway of Alabama).

two in January. [33] They were followed by two 4-4-0's from Baldwin later in the year. No.s 5-6, named *Alabama* and *Georgia* were delivered in November. [34]

In the Annual Report for the year ending August 31 1872, President Pollard reported a new operating income o $150,533.90. [35] This, unfortunately, was not enough to mee the interest payments on the various outstanding loans.

With the heavy debt necessitated by the expenses in curred in rebuilding the M&WP, the road was hard presse to meet the interest payments on the various loans. With th depressed level of rates and fares in the early 1870's, an the depressed state of the national economy as a result o the Panic of 1873, the road was simply unable to make th interest payments on the numerous loans and bond issues.

As a result of the default on thes payments, the Western entered re ceivership on April 1, 1874. It president, C. T. Pollard, was ap pointed receiver.

The receivership lasted only a littl more than a year, for on May 10 1875, the Western Rail Road of Ala bama was sold jointly to the Centra Rail Road and Banking Compan of Georgia and the Georgia Rail road and Banking Company. Th sale was confirmed and the propert was turned over to the purchaser on June 1, 1875.

In buying the Western, the Geor gia and the Central were protectin their investment. They had eithe purchased or endorsed the majorit of the bonds issued by the Wester and its predecessors, and were i the position of having to purchas the property or make good on thei endorsement of the bonds. By pur

The new company wasted no time is raising operating funds by issuing $100,000 in coupon bonds in January of 1871. This bond is No. 2 of that issue. (Author's collection)

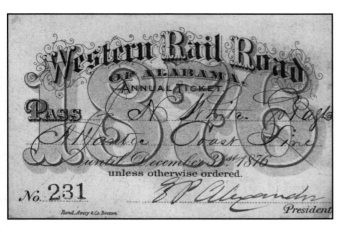

This 1876 annual pass over the Western Rail Road of Alabama was signed by President E. Porter Alexander. (Author's collection)

hasing the property, they at least managed to recover something for their additional investment.

The two purchasers did not form a new corporation immediately. Instead, they chose to operate the property as n unincorporated partnership, doing business as "The Purchasers of the Western Railroad of Alabama". This arrangement lasted eight years.

Former Confederate General E. Porter Alexander was lected president of the organization effective September 1, 875. President (and Receiver) Pollard had stepped down at he end of the receivership.

Central President William Wadley estimated that the Western would need a net income of $204,240 to avoid becoming a financial drain on its wners. In 1874 the Western etted only $60,808. [36] Alexnder had his work cut out for im.

Cecil Gabbett, General Manager of he Western Rail Road of Alabama, as elected to the presidency of the ompany in 1878. (Western Railway f Alabama)

In his annual report for the year ended August 31, 1876, President Alexander reported a net income of $121,088.13. This figure represented a significant increase over that of the previous year, but it was still far short of the amount necessary for the railroad to pay its own way. [37]

The line's net income for the fiscal year 1877 was $100,524.45. This decrease was due to reduction in traffic, both freight and passenger, and the need to spend large amounts of money on repairs and maintenance. [38]

At the annual meeting for 1878, General Manager Cecil Gabbett was elected president of the organization. Porter Alexander had been elected president of the Georgia Railroad the preceding May and did not stand for re-election.

On May 1, 1880, the Western leased the Selma Division - the line between Montgomery and Selma - to the Louisville & Nashville Railroad for a period of five years. The annual rental on the property was $52,000. [39]

Heavy spring rains near Columbus resulted in three stone culverts' being washed out. Two were replaced by wooden trestles and the bridge over Holland's Creek was replaced by an "Iron Combination Bridge placed on Masonry piers." Passengers and freight were transferred around this washout for several days. [40]

Additions to equipment included two locomotives from Rogers, four passenger coaches, and one baggage car. Two older locomotives were retired as being too light for current needs.

The financial performance of the road improved somewhat. Net incomes of $183,994.21 and $276,949.19 were

The Columbus Branch of the WRRofA, shown here as the bold line, was sold to the Central Railroad & Banking Company of Georgia's Columbus & Western subsidiary effective August 31, 1881.

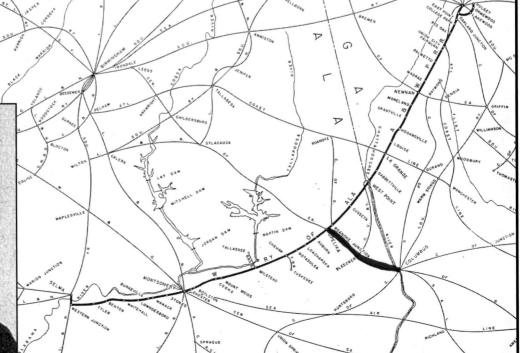

reported for 1879 and 1880, respectively. [41]

On August 31, 1881, the operation of the Columbus branch was transferred under lease to the Columbus & Western Railroad, a subsidiary of the Central Railroad & Banking Company of Georgia. This move had been contemplated for several years.

On March 15, 1883, the Purchasers of the Western Railroad of Alabama chartered a corporation known as The Western Railway of Alabama. It held its first meeting on that same date and elected Lemuel P. Grant, president of the Atlanta & West Point Rail Road, president of the new corporation. The new company took possession of the property on April 1, 1883.

Col. Lemuel P. Grant, president of the Atlanta & West Point Railroad, was elected president of The Western Railway of Alabama on its formation in 1883. Atlanta's Grant Park is named for this gentleman. (Atlanta & West Point Rail Road)

THE ATLANTA & WEST POINT RAILROAD

At the annual meeting of stockholders held on July 25, 1866, President John P. King reported net earnings of $54,648.30 for the year. [42] Although most of the worst of the damage had been repaired, the work of rebuilding continued. Because of the expense involved in repair and reconstruction of the line and its facilities and equipment, no dividend was declared.

Two new locomotives, the *R. Peters* and *F. Phinizy*, were purchased from the New Jersey Locomotive Works. Both locomotives were of the 4-4-0 wheel arrangement and were placed in service in September, 1866. [43] This was the first new motive power purchased since 1860.

President King announced at the annual meeting on July 25, 1867, that the work of rebuilding and repairing the line was essentially finished and that, while no dividend would be declared that year, they would likely be resumed in 1868. [44]

At the 1868 annual meeting, President King announced that the road was now in first class condition and further announced that the board had declared two dividends of four dollars each. Net earnings for the year were $111,667.71. [45]

Superintendent Lemuel P. Grant reported that four new boxcars had been added to the roster and that six more had been ordered from the R. D. Cole Manufacturing Company of Newnan. The company now had a fleet of 99 cars, both freight and passenger.

President King noted that competition for through business was increasing and pointed out that even more competition could be expected with the completion of the line from Dalton, Ga. to Selma, Ala. This would create a new route between Altanta and Selma by way of Kingston and Rome Ga.

Following the War Between the States, the South was flooded with men from the north who came into the area to seek their fortunes. While many of these were honest men who genuinely felt that they were helping rehabilitate the South, a great number of them were men who were less than honest and whose activities would not bear close inspection. Because the majority of these characters - especially the shady ones - carried all their worldly belongings in a valise whose walls were made of carpet, they were given the name "Carpetbaggers." Even today in many parts of the South, the term `Carpetbagger' is an insult. The Southerners who aided and abetted their nefarious activities were called scalawags and were held in even lower esteem than the carpetbaggers. With the loss of suffrage rights by anyone who had served in the Confederate Army, (and remember, no women were allowed to vote at this time), the state government was run by these carpetbaggers, scalawags, and newly-freed and largely illiterate former slaves. The result was simply disastrous.

Part of the increased competition alluded to by Presi-

When this stock certificate was issued in 1869, the financial future of the A&WP seemed uncertain, indeed, due to the many new railroad companies that were being formed with financial aid from the State of Georgia. President John P. King, whose signature adorns this certificate, voiced much concern in his annual report for the year. His fears proved to be unfounded. (Author's collection.)

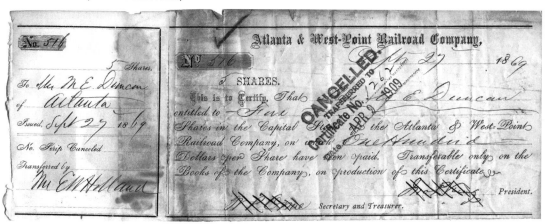

The A&WP was one of five railroads involved in the construction and ownership of the Atlanta Union Depot that was opened in 1871. It is shown here in a post card photograph taken not too many years after it opened. It was used by the A&WP until 1905 and was replaced by Atlanta Union Station in 1930. (Gary Doster Collection)

was followed by four more locomotives in 1870. One 0-4-0, named *Gate City*, was purchased from Baldwin and three 4-4-0's, *LaGrange*, *Fulton*, and *Troup*, came from Rogers. [50]

The A&WP, along with the other roads serving Atlanta, operated out of a makeshift passenger facility after the destruction of the Union Depot - or "Car Shed" - in 1864. In June of 1870, the A&WP, along with the Georgia Railroad, the Western & Atlantic Railroad and the Macon & Western Railroad, entered into a contract with I. P. Stidham & Company of Philadelphia to construct a new Union Depot on the site of the former Car Shed. The A&WP's ownership in this facility was 20%. It was opened for service in the fall of 1871. [51]

In 1872, President King reported that after four years of conducting operations without an accident or without missing a trip, a head-on collision heavily damaged two locomotives, exacerbating an already-tight motive power situation. He made no mention of injuries or death to passengers or crew members. [52]

The A&WP adopted its first locomotive numbering system in 1872. Even though locomotives now carried numbers, they continued to bear names on their flanks as well.

...dent King was the result of the Carpetbagger/Scalawag legislature's policy of state aid to new railroad companies. Part of this aid was in the form of direct subsidy and part was in the form of bond guarantees. As a result of this policy, the state paid for many miles of railroad that were never built and guaranteed bonds for several companies that laid little or no track.

In his annual report for 1869, President King wrote, "No policy could be more unjust and oppressive than the policy of `state aid.' It is a distinguishing feature in this policy that the citizen who has built his own enterprise with his own means, is taxed to build up rival enterprises, by which his own may be ruined." [46] Although it was yet to be seen, his fears were unfounded. Most of the newer roads - those that were actually built, anyway - failed after only a few years. The older lines such as the West Point continued to thrive.

In 1869, the Atlanta & West Point was one of several companies forming the Green Line, a coalition of companies offering an expedited freight service using pool cars in interchange service. Among the other carriers participating in this venture were the Georgia Railroad, the Montgomery & West Point, the Louisville & Nashville, the Louisville, Cincinnati & St. Louis, the Western & Atlantic, as well as several others.[47] By 1872, the A&WP had contributed 25 cars to the pool. [48]

The company was also a partner in the New Orleans & Atlantic Fast Freight Line, and contributed ten freight cars to this operating pool. [49]

The A&WP purchased one new locomotive, a 4-4-0 named *Newnan*, from the Rogers Locomotive & Machine Works. The engine entered service in December, 1869. It

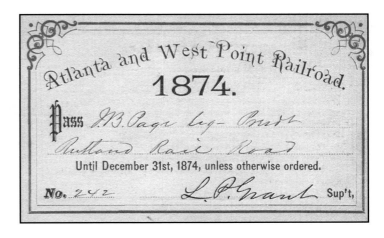

This 1874 annual pass over the Atlanta & West Point Railroad was signed by former Confederate Colonel Lemuel P. Grant as superintendent of the company. He was later elected president. (Author's collection)

W. B. Barry of Newnan, Ga., was elected president of the Atlanta & West Point Rail Road in 1880. He served only one year in this capacity. (Atlanta & West Point Rail Road)

A new freight depot was occupied in Atlanta. These facilities replaced temporary quarters occupied since 1864.

Superintendent Lemuel P. Grant stated in his report to the stockholders that the presence of yellow fever in Charleston had diverted much traffic to Savannah and competing roads. He further reported that the road needed two additional locomotives, one freight and one passenger.

Grant got his wish in 1873. That year, the A&WP took delivery of two new locomotives, the *Dr. John F. Moreland* and the *L. B. Lovelace* from the Grant Locomotive Works. The locomotives, both 4-4-0's, bore road numbers 20 and 21, respectively. [53]

The mid-1870's were kind, financially, to the A&WP. The company reported profits of $69,553, $101,966, and $99,594 in 1874, 1875, and 1876, respectively. [54] These figures represented operating ratios of 78.55, 64.87, and 64.89, respectively for the same years. [55]

The railroad changed locomotive fuel in 1877. Wood, the favored fuel from the outset, was replaced by coal.

The Georgia Railroad, which had performed all locomotive repairs for the Atlanta & West Point, decided to close its Atlanta locomotive shop and concentrate all motive power repairs in Augusta. The West Point, faced with the loss of its only source of locomotive maintenance, leased the Georgia Road shop facility in Atlanta and began performing its own locomotive repairs.

At the annual stockholders meeting of July 23, 1880, John P. King declined to stand for re-election, citing old age and declining health. W. B. Barry of Newnan, Ga., was elected president.

In the late 1870's the Georgia Railroad and Banking Company, which owned a substantial portion of the A&WP's stock, began to cast about for a possible lessee for its railroad properties. This action was taken because the Georgia Road found itself rapidly becoming surrounded by hostile larger systems made up of companies that had formerly been friendly connections.

President King approached several companies regarding a possible lease, but the Central Railroad and Banking Company quickly got the inside track, partially due to th tactic used by its president, William Wadley, of appealing t local pride with the idea that control would remain withi the state.

Wadley, however, ran into a problem when he ap proached his board about the lease. They were extremel reluctant to lease the property and voted against the propos al. Leaving the meeting after his defeat, Wadley filled th air with a string of oaths. If his board wouldn't lease th Georgia, He would lease the property himself! [56]

On May 7, 1881, the stock holdings in the A&WP hel by the Georgia Railroad & Banking Company were leased along with the railroad properties of the company, and th one-half interest in the Western Railroad of Alabama, wer leased, to Colonel Wadley. The lease was retroactive t April 1.

Colonel Wadley then offered the lease once again th Central Railroad & Banking Company which again decline the lease. He then offered a one half interest in the lease t the Louisville & Nashville Railroad which readily accepte it. Wadley then offered the remaining one half interest in th lease to the Central. This time, the Central's board of direc tors, thoroughly alarmed that the L&N might be setting u shop in its back yard, quickly accepted the offer. [57]

After the receivership of the Central in 1893, its ha of the lease was purchased by the L&N. Not wishing to b the sole lessee of these properties, it sold a half interest i the lease to the Atlantic Coast Line Railroad of South Caro lina in 1898. This interest passed to the Atlantic Coast Lin Railroad Company in 1900, and to the Seaboard Coast Lin Railroad in 1967. After 1899, the destiny of the Atlanta & West Point Rail Road and the Western Railway of Alabama along with the Georgia Railroad, was controlled by the L&N and the ACL/SCL. [58]

On July 25, 1881, Lemuel P. Grant was elected presi dent of the Atlanta & West Point Rail Road to succeed W B. Barry. Grant had come up through the engineering an operating departments and had, among other things, bee responsible for the design of the fortifications of the city o Atlanta during the War Between the States and the rebuild ing of the West Point and the Georgia Road following th war.

Also at the same meeting, the A&WP issued, as a divi dend, certificates of indebtedness at 6% interest and du within the next ten years, and callable by management on share for share basis. Never called, the last two shares wer converted to common stock in 1910.

President L. P. Grant of the A&WP was elected presi dent of the Western Railway of Alabama on March 15, 1883 With this act, the route from Atlanta to Montgomery (th Selma Division was still under lease to the L&N) cam under one management for the first time. The West Poin Route was born.

The A&WP issued Certificates of Indebtedness in lieu of a dividend in 1881. Never called for redemption, the last one was converted into stock in 1910. (Author's collection)

24 J. Arch Avary, Jr. and Marshall L. Bowie, *The West Point Route*, (Atlanta: 1954), p. 7.

25 Richard E. Prince, *Steam Locomotives and History, Georgia Railroad and West Point Route,* (Green River, Wyo., 1962), pp. 57-59.

26 S. R. Young. Letter to Dr. Rena M. Andrews, Winthrop College, Rock Hill, SC. September 10, 1045. p. 6.

27 Avary and Bowie, op. cit., p. 7.

28 Avary and Bowie, op. cit., p. 8.

29 Prince, op. cit., p. 59.

30 Avary and Bowie, op. cit., p. 8.

31 Peter Moshein and Robert R. Rothfus, "Rogers Locomotives: A Brief History and Construction List." *Railroad History* 167. Autumn 1992. p. 64.

32 Avary and Bowie, op. cit., p. 8.

33 Moshein and Rothfus, op. cit., p. 67.

34 Annual Report, Purchasers of the Western Railroad of Alabama, August 31, 1880, p. 13.

35 H. V. Poor, *Manual of Railroads of the United States, 1873-74,* (New York, 1873), p. 126.

36 Maury Klein, *Edward Porter Alexander,* (Athens, Ga.: The University of Georgia Press, 1971), p. 154.

37 Annual Report of the Western Railroad of Alabama, August 31, 1876. Montgomery, Ala., 1876, p. 2.

38 Annual Report of the Purchasers of the Western Railroad of Alabama, August 31, 1880, p. 3.

39 H. V. and H. W. Poor, *Poor's Manual of Railroads*, 1886, (New York: 1886), p. 453.

40 Fifth Annual Report of the Purchasers of the Western Railroad of Alabama, 1880, (Montgomery: 1880), p. 5.

41 Ibid.

42 Avary and Bowie, op. cit., p. 12.

43 Reports of the President and Superintendent of the Atlanta & West Point Rail Road to the Stockholders in Convention, July 25, 1868, p. 20.

44 Avary and Bowie, op. cit., p. 12.

45 Annual Report, 1868, p. 11.

46 John F. Stover, *Railroads in the South, 1865-1900,* (Chapel Hill, NC: The University of North Carolina Press), 1955, p. 80.

47 William H. Joubert, *Southern Freight Rates in Transition,* (Gainesville, Fla.: The university of Florida Press), 1949, p. 33.

48 Reports of the President and Superintendent of the Atlanta & West Point Rail Road Co. to the Stockholders in Convention, July 25, 1872, p. 10.

49 Annual Report, 1872, p. 10.

50 Op. cit., p. 16.

51 James Houston Johnston, *Western & Atlantic Railroad of the State of Georgia.* (Atlanta, Georgia Public Service Commission, 1932). p. 175.

52 Annual Report, 1872, p. 6.

53 Richard E. Prince, *Steam Locomotives and History, Georgia Railroad and West Point Route,* (Green River, Wyoming, 1962), p. 64.

54 Henry V. Poor, *Manual of Railroads of the United States, 1878,* (New York:H. V. and H. W. Poor, 1878), p. 497.

55 Ibid.

56 Maurry Klein, *The Great Richmond Terminal,* (Charlottesville, VA.: The University Press of Virginia, 1970), p. 148.

57 Klein, op. cit., pp. 148-149.

58 Lease - Georgia Rail Road & Banking Company to William M. Wadley, May 7, 1881.

THE WEST POINT ROUTE

Although the A&WP and the WofA were united in management as of March 15, 1883, operations were not immediately changed. Operations had been closely coordinated for some time prior to the unification of management, and would be even more closely coordinated in the future. By the turn of the century, the two railroads would be operated virtually as one.

On May 1, 1885, the Western Railway of Alabama once again assumed possession and operation of its Selma Division. The five year lease of that line to the Louisville & Nashville Railroad was not renewed.

The West Point Route, through the Western Railway of Alabama, entered into a traffic agreement with the Cincinnati, Selma & Mobile Railroad effective January 1, 1886. The CS&M was a line which extended westward from Selma to Akron, Alabama, and a connection with the Alabama Great Southern Railway.

As a result of the agreement, the CS&M was operated by the same management as the West Point Route, making it effectively part of the system. For whatever reason, the benefits anticipated from this agreement failed to materialize and it was terminated in 1890.[1]

Traffic on the West Point Route was badly disrupted due to heavy rains in early 1886. Portions of the Western were flooded, often to a depth of five to six feet, for distances of seven and eight miles at a stretch. No trains were run on the Montgomery Division (West Point to Montgomery) from March 29th to April 5th, and no trains were run at night until April 9th.

The situation on the Selma Division was even worse. No trains, other than work trains, were operated between Montgomery and Selma from March 29th until April 26th. [2]

The gauge of the West Point Route was changed from 5' to 4' 9" in May of 1886. This was done so that the gauge of the West Point Route would conform with that of all other Southern roads which made the change at the same time. (The figure of 4' 9" was used to simplify the change. The gauge was later tightened up to the national standard gauge of 4' 8 1/2 ".) The gauge of the Selma Division was changed on May 30; the main line between Atlanta and Montgomery was changed the following day. [3]

On October 7, 1886, the Western entered into an agreement for the use of a Union Station in Montgomery. The agreement called for the rent to be pro-rated based on the number of trains handled by the facility for each of the tenant companies. The Western's eight trains daily amounted to 29 1/2 per cent of the total, and, based on this calculation, the Western's monthly rent on this facility amounted to $466.94.[4] The salaries of the employees were similarly pro-rated.

The West Point Route made several additions to its motive power roster during 1888 and 1889. The A&WP purchased two 4-6-0's, No.s 36 and 37, in 1888 and the WofA also purchased two 4-6-0's, No. 7 in 1888, and No. 11 in 1889. All were built by the Rhode Island Locomotive Works.

The Atlanta & West Point constructed its own track between Atlanta and East Point parallel to that of the Central Railroad & banking Company of Georgia in 1889. This eliminated the trackage rights arrangement with the Central (successor to the Macon & Western RR) which permitted the West Point to use the Central's track between these cities. The agreement was replaced by another that arranged for the two tracks to be operated as double track with all inbound trains of both companies using one track and all outbound trains using the other.

WofA 30 was built by Rogers in 1884. She was later renumbered 15 and was sold in 1905. (Rogers Locomotive Works photo, B. F. Roberts collection.)

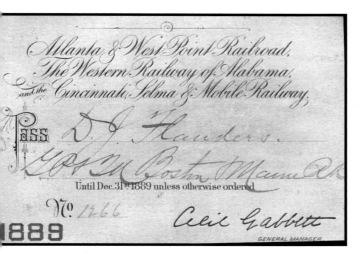

The annual passes issued by the West Point Route for 1889 reflected the operating agreement with the Cincinnati, Selma & Mobile Railway. The agreement was terminated in 1890 and the CS&M later became part of Southern Railway. (Author's collection)

The West Point Route suffered two accidents early in 1890. On February 25, a head-on collision between a freight train and a passenger train near Cusseta, Alabama, resulted in the death of the engineer of the freight. [5]

Almost before the wreckage of this accident could be cleared, train 2 ran into the rear end of No. 6 at Notasulga, Alabama, on February 26. The accident resulted in serious property damage but no serious injuries were reported. [6]

The Montgomery Car Shop was busy during 1890. The facility built one baggage car, one box car, ten flatcars and two cabooses. It also overhauled and varnished eight streetcars of the Montgomery Terminal & Street Railway. [7]

On January 4, 1891, the Richmond & Danville Railroad inaugurated the all-Pullman, extra fare *Washington & Southwestern Vestibuled Limited* between Washington and Atlanta. By September, arrangements had been made for the West Point Route to forward this train between Atlanta and Montgomery and the Louisville & Nashville Railroad to carry the train into New Orleans from Montgomery.

The train, No.s 50 and 53 on the West Point Route, retained its all-Pullman status, but the extra fare was dropped south of Atlanta. The numbers were changed to 37 and 38 to conform with the train numbers on the R&D (later Southern Railway) by 1895.

The Western Railway of Alabama occupied the warehouse of the Montgomery Terminal & Warehouse Company on a rental basis effective March 1, 1891. It was deemed a more advantageous location than the Western's own facility.[8] This arrangement proved to be short-lived, as the agreement was terminated in November. In the Annual Report for 1892, General Manager Edmond L. Tyler reported that the agreement was "eminently unsatisfactory..." and the arrangement was "too bulky and expensive, the plant being insufficient in track and warehouse facilities..." He concluded that "...in all respects this was an unfortunate and embarrassing venture." [9]

More successful efforts in providing station facilities were reported at Selma. In September, the Western occupied a new depot on the site of the naval foundry. The Western also entered into an agreement with the East Tennessee, Virginia & Georgia Railway for the joint use of its passenger depot at Selma. General Manager Tyler reported, "This arrangement has thus far been thoroughly satisfactory, and does away with all transfer of passengers, baggage, etc., heretofore so inconvenient and uncomfortable." [10]

On December 4, 1891, the Savannah, Americus & Montgomery Railway(later to become the Seaboard Air Line Railway), having completed the construction of its tracks to Montgomery, was granted trackage rights over the Western

The L&N's Montgomery station was spared by the flood waters although the approaches to the structure were inundated. The WofA began using this facility in the fall of 1886. (Old Alabama Rails collection.)

The Western Railway of Alabama was struck by floods in March and April 1886. The general offices of the road in Montgomery were flooded, as was a portion of the yard. (Old Alabama Rails collection)

for a short distance in order to gain access to Montgomery Union Station.

The earnings on the Western of Alabama fell from $152,242.48 in 1891 to $140,185.54 in 1892. The decline was attributed to a general business downturn in the Western's service area. [11]

The A&WP fared considerably better. The company earned $126,418.00 in 1891 and $155,649.00 in 1892. [12]

On September 27, 1892, seven freight cars "got loose from train hands" in the Opelika yard and met passenger train 51 two miles west of Opelika causing "a most serious wreck". Two persons, the engineer, and fireman on No. 51, were killed and two mail clerks were injured. One engine, one mail car, one baggage car, and seven freight cars, with contents, were totally destroyed by the collision and the resulting fire. [13]

The business downturn noted by the WofA in 1892 continued into 1893 and spread to the A&WP. The Western's net earnings fell to $121,133.07, and the West Point's profits tumbled to $131,174.00. [14]

Passenger train No. 35 derailed at the Ossinappi Creek bridge on October 6, 1894. The accident caused considerable damage to equipment, but resulted in no deaths or serious injuries.

The West Point Route gained a feeder line in 1895 when the Tallassee Falls Manufacturing Company built a branch railway eight miles in length connecting with the Western at a point two miles west of Cowles.

The car shops of the Western were busy in 1895. In addition to performing routine repairs to various pieces of rolling stock, five Railway Post Office cars (RPO's) were constructed for and delivered to the Louisville & Nashville Railroad.

The West Point Route acquired its first dining car in 1896. It was purchased for through service in conjunction with Southern Railway's *Washington & Southwestern Limited*. The car, numbered 100, was owned jointly by both partners in the West Point Route, but for some reason was carried on the roster of the Atlanta & West Point. Prior to the purchase of car 100, dining car service on the West Point Route was

WofA railway post office car *Opelika* was built by Pullman in 1894. It was converted to baggage car 14 in 1896 and was retired in 1922. (Pullman photo, Frank Moore collection)

Business car *Alabama* was delivered by Pullman in 1894. The name was dropped and the car numbered 100 in 1902 and the car was retired in 1910. (Pullman photo, Frank Moore collection)

provided by the Pullman Company under contract.

In order to enhance their advertising efforts, the Atlanta & West Point Rail Road and The Western Railway of Alabama adopted a new herald, or logo, in 1896. The trade mark adopted consisted of a diamond containing the slogan, "The Atlanta and New Orleans Short Line". The slogan had also been used previously without the diamond logo.

During 1896 and for several years thereafter, the Atlanta & West Point Rail Road operated an experimental tobacco farm near LaGrange. The purpose of this venture was to prove that quality tobacco could be grown in the area. In the several years it operated, it did indeed produce quality tobacco, but did not induce any of the local farmers to grow the crop.

The A&WP was involved in a rather bizarre series of events beginning in December 1896. On December 19, 1896, the charter of the Atlanta & West Point Rail Road was renewed for another 50 years by the Legislature of Georgia.

On December 22, 1896, Levi B. Nelson the owner of five shares of A&WP stock, filed suit in the Superior Court of Fulton County, Georgia, praying for the appointment of a Receiver, payment of indebtedness and distribution of the assets of the company among its shareholders on the grounds that the charter of the company had expired by limitation and had not been, and could not be, legally renewed.[15] While the motive for this suit can only be speculated upon, it might be pointed out that the attorneys for Mr. Nelson were from the firm of King & Spaulding, local attorneys for the Seaboard Air Line System.

The company responded to the suit and a decision was rendered by the Judge of the Superior Court of Fulton County on March 6, 1897. The decision denied the application of a receiver but enjoined the company from carrying out any provisions of the new charter that were not contained in the old, pending final hearing on the case. [16]

The final decision was rendered on December 1, 1897. It upheld the position of the company in every way and ordered Mr. Nelson to pay all costs of the suit.

The Atlanta & West Point inaugurated suburban passenger service on January 31, 1897, between Atlanta and College Park, with some additional service as far out as Newnan. To accommodate this service, the line was double-tracked between East Point and College Park, a distance of 2.11 miles, and a new brick depot was constructed at College Park.

The West Point Route gained another connecting line in 1897. The Chattahoochee Valley Railway, which had been chartered in 1895, was opened between West Point, Georgia, and Riverview, Alabama, a distance of ten miles. It would ultimately be extended to Standing Rock and Bleeker, Alabama, a distance of 44.53 miles, and would provide a valuable connection to the West Point Route for many years.

A fire swept through the Western of Alabama roundhouse in Montgomery on July 31, 1897, completely destroying the structure. Ten locomotives - seven belonging to the A&WP and three owned by the WofA - were badly damaged.

Yellow fever, the plague of the South, struck again in the fall of 1897. As a result, the Selma Division was, for all practical purposes, closed for the period beginning October 18 and ending on November 16, 1897. Operations on the main line were seriously disrupted for about 90 days, mostly due to quarantine regulations.

On January 9, 1898, passenger train No. 35 struck a mule at the entrance of the Cupahatchie River bridge. The train derailed on the structure of the bridge, wrecking the east span, two coaches and a sleeping car. Conductor H. M. Law was killed and numerous injuries were reported. Trains

George C. Smith served as president and general manager of the companies comprising the West Point Route from September, 1894, until November 15, 1900. When he accepted the post, it was with the complete understanding that he would operate the roads for their own benefit, and not that of the parent companies. (A&WP photo)

were detoured over the Central of Georgia Railway while repairs were made to the bridge.

Passenger operations of the Western in Montgomary were moved into a new Union Station on May 1, 1898. The facility was owned by the Louisville & Nashville Railroad and was used by the Western, the Alabama Midland, the Central of Georgia, and the Georgia & Alabama railways as tenants. The Mobile & Ohio Railroad also used the facility after it arrived in Montgomery a few months later.

The Western Railway of Alabama, feeling the need for additional space in its general office building, contracted for a new two-story general office building to be located at the corner of Coosa and Tallapoosa Streets in Montgomery. The R. D. Cole Manufacturing Company, of Newnan, Ga., was the contractor selected to build the structure. It was occupied on June 14, 1899.

At the annual meeting of the stockholders on September 13, 1898, a majority of the A&WP shareholders voted to build a branch line from Oakland City (southwest Atlanta) to Hulsey, site of the Georgia Railroad freight yards, a distance of approximately six miles. The company promptly secured an amendment to its charter to permit it to do so, and spent $39,455.64 on land, surveys and - apparently - some construction. [17]

On December 9, 1898, the Superior Court of the Cit of Atlanta issued a temporary restraining order stoppin all work on the belt line, as the Hulsey branch was know pending a hearing on the legality of the matter. This wa done at the behest of several minority stockholders, Julius M Alexander and the Central of Georgia Railway among them These shareholders maintained that, without a unanimou vote in favor of the project, it was illegal for the company t pursue the project. [18]

The hearing was held on January 25, 1899, and a decisio adverse to the company was rendered on March 9th. Th decision was appealed to the Supreme Court of Georgi the case being argued on May 26-27, 1899. The Georgi Supreme Court upheld the decision on July 20, 1899. [19]

Not to be outdone, a group of Atlanta businessmen, le by A&WP President George C. Smith, obtained a charte for the Atlanta Belt Line Railroad Company on October 17 1899, and proceeded to complete the project. These investor had apparently purchased the completed work from th A&WP and contracted with the company to continue wit the work on their behalf, as the project was completed thre days following the granting of the charter by the State o Georgia.

The Western suffered the derailment of a freight trai at Soapstone Creek on February 14, 1899. The acciden resulted in the destruction of the bridge, but no injurie were reported. The bridge was replaced by using a structur which previously spanned Calebee Creek.

On July 1, 1899, the Western entered into an agreemen with the Central of Georgia Railway to operate a joint freigh agency and yard in Montgomery. The agreement called fo the two companies to operate a joint freight facility largel using the facilities of the Western, but incorporating portion of the Central's facility. The two companies maintaine separate facilities for servicing passenger equipment. Thi arrangement lasted until the Central abandoned its line int Montgomery in the late 1970's.

Both partners of the West Point Route purchase new Ten-Wheelers (4-6-0 typ locomotives) in 1899. The A&W purchased two, numbered 36 an 37, and the WofA bought one, No 17. All were built by Rogers.

In the fall of 1899, al locomotives and cars wer equipped with air brakes an automatic couplers. This wa done in order to comply wit the law that took effect Januar 1, 1900, which required tha all locomotives and cars be s equipped.

A&WP box car 3130 was built by the Ohio Falls Car Company in 1890 and displayed the "Atlanta and New Orleans Short Line" slogan that was later adapted to the diamond –shaped herald.(ACF photo, C. L. Goolsby collection.)

WofA 18 was typical of the passenger power of the West Point Route in the 1890's and early 1900's. The engine was delivered by Baldwin in 1895 and was scrapped in 1923. (H. L. Broadbelt collection, Railroad Museum of Pennsylvania)

The diamond herald with the "Atlanta and New Orleans Short Line" slogan was adopted in 1896. While the slogan would last only until 1902, the herald would last, in one form or another, as long as the company.

ATLANTA & WEST POINT RAILROAD CO.

SUBURBAN TRAIN SCHEDULE No. 26, IN EFFECT JUNE 6, 1900.

STATIONS.	Distance from Atlanta.	Distance Between Stations. Feet.	Miles.	Train No. 11 Daily Ex.Sun	Train No. 13 Daily Ex.Sun	Train No. 19 Daily Ex.Sun	Train No. 21 Daily Ex.Sun	Train No. 25 Daily Ex.Sun	Train No. 27 Daily Ex.Sun	Train No. 29 Daily Ex.Sun
LEAVE				A. M.	A. M.	P. M.	P. M	P. M.	P. M.	P. M.
Atlanta (U. P. Station)......	0	0	0	5 40	8 00	2 30	4 25	6 20	8 40	11 00
Whitehall Street...............	0.11	560	0.11							
Mitchell Street.................	0.54	2275	0.43							
Peters Street....................	0.77	1225	0.23							
Fair Street.......................	0.99	1180	0.22							
Mc Daniel Street	1.31	1692	0.32							
Whitehall Street (West)....	1.77	2319	0.46							
West End	2.03	1464	0.26							
McCall's	2.49	2423	0.46							
Gammage's	2.88	2052	0.39							
Oakland	3.17	1520	0.29							
Perdue's	3.47	1600	0.30							
McPherson........................	4.03	2839	0.56	5 52	8 17	2 45	4 42	6 35	8 53	11 13
McCool............................	4.62	3111	0.59							
Knott's............................	5.11	2595	0.49							
Verbena...........................	5.93	4363	0.82							
Cheney............................	6.15	1129	0.22							
East Point	6.52	1963	0.37	6 03	8 25	2 50	4 50	6 42	9 02	11 20
Taylors............................	7.02	2645	0.50							
Magnesia..........................	7.38	1923	0.36							
Boulevard	7.72	1822	0.34							
Barili's	7.97	1358	0.25							
Gordon Avenue	8.13	802	0.16							
College Park	8.38	1360	0.25	6 10	8 35	3 00	5 05	6 50	9 10	11 28

STATIONS.	Distance from College Park.	Distances between Stations. Feet.	Miles.	Train No. 12 Daily Ex.Sun	Train No. 16 Daily Ex.Sun	Train No. 22 Daily Ex.Sun	Train No. 24 Daily Ex.Sun	Train No. 26 Daily Ex.Sun	Train No. 28 Daily Ex.Sun	Train No. 30 Daily Ex.Sun
LEAVE				A. M.	A. M.	P. M.	P. M.	P. M.	P. M.	P. M.
College Park	0.	0	0.	6 35	9 25	3 15	5 20	7 10	9 20	11 57
Gordon Avenue	0.25	1360	0.25							
Barili's	0.41	802	0.16							
Boulevard	0.66	1358	0.25							
Magnesia..........................	1.00	1822	0.34							A. M.
Taylors............................	1.36	1923	0.36							12 04
East Point	1.86	2645	0.50	6 43	9 35	3 23	5 30	7 22	9 27	12 04
Cheney............................	2.23	1963	0.37							
Verbena...........................	2.45	1129	0.22							
Knott's............................	3.27	4363	0.82							
McCool............................	3.56	2595	0.49							
McPherson........................	4.35	3111	0.59	6 50	9 43	3 32	5 38	7 30	9 35	12 12
Perdue's	4.91	2839	0.56							
Oakland	5.21	1600	0.30							
Gammage's	5.50	1520	0.29							
McCall's	5.89	2052	0.39							
West End	6.35	2423	0.46							
Whitehall Street (West)....	6.61	1464	0.26							
McDaniel Street	7.07	2319	0.46							
Fair Street.......................	7.39	1692	0.32							
Peters Street*	7.61	1180	0.22							
Mitchell Street.................	7.84	1225	0.23							
Whitehall Street...............	8.27	2275	0.43							
Atlanta (U. P. Station)......	8.38	560	0.11	7 05	10 00	3 50	5 55	7 45	9 50	12 25

** A. & W. P. Trains Nos. 12, 16, 24 and 26 will arrive at Central Railway Passenger Station at Whitehall street. All other first-class trains of the A. & W. P. R. R. will arrive and depart from Union Depot, Atlanta.

Suburban trains must not stop at stations not shown on the face of this time table.

GEO. F. HUGGANS, Superintendent.   B. F. WYLY, JR., General Pass. and Ticket Agent.

R. E. LUTZ, Traffic Manager.   GEORGE C. SMITH, President and General Manager.

The A&WP operated a suburban service between 1897 and 1902. This 1900 schedule showed seven suburban trains each way between Atlanta and College Park and two accommodation trains each way between Atlanta and LaGrange, daily except Sunday. (William Stanley Hoole Special Collections Library, University of Alabama)

Montgomery Union Station was opened for operation on May 1, 1898. Its occupants at the time were the Louisville & Nashville (the owner of the facility, Alabama Midland, Central of Georgia, and the Georgia & Alabama. The Mobile & Ohio became a tenant when it began operations into Montgomery in th fall of 1898. (Fouts Commercial Photography, Old Alabama Rails collection)

[1] Fairfax Harrison, *History of the Legal Development of the Lines of the Southern Railway System,* (Washington, DC, 1901), p. 958.

[2] L. D. Hale, "Historical Sketch of The Western Railway of Alabama, 1885-1946", p. 1.

[3] Op. Cit.

[4] Contracts and Agreements, Central of Georgia Railway, Volume 1, pp. 67-70.

[5] Eight Annual Report of the Western Railway of Alabama, August 14, 1890, p. 15,

[6] Op. Cit., p. 15.

[7] Op. Cit., p. 14.

[8] Ninth Annual Report of the Western Railway of Alabama, August 14, 1891, p. 11.

[9] Tenth Annual Report of the Western Railway of Alabama, June 30, 1892, p. 16.

[10] Op. Cit., p. 16

[11] Annual Report, The Western Railway of Alabama, June 30, 1892, p. 3.

[12] Henry V. Poor, *Manual of Railroads of the United States, 1894,* p. 455

[13] Annual Report, The Western Railway of Alabama, June 30, 1893, p 17.

[14] H. V. Poor, Manual of Railroads of the United States, 1894, pp. 454 455.

[15] Annual Report, Atlanta & West Point Railroad, September 14, 1897 p. 15.

[16] Op. cit., p. 15

[17] Annual Report, Atlanta & West Point Railroad Company, Septembe 12, 1899, p. 14.

[18] Op. Cit., pp. 14-15.

[19] Op. Cit., pp. 14-15.

CHAPTER
IV

INTO THE TWENTIETH CENTURY

The 1900's got off to a rocky start. On March 26, 1900, passenger train No. 35 derailed on the Western at Ossinappi Creek. The derailment resulted in the death of Express Messenger Reuben Oslin and injuries to eight passengers and six employees. The accident also resulted in extensive damage to equipment. The cause of the accident remained a mystery, as it could not be traced to any defect in the track or equipment.[1]

During the early part of 1900, the gauge of the West Point Route, which had been changed from 5' 0" to 4' 9" in 1886, was further tightened up to the national standard gauge of 4' 8 1/2 ".

President George Carson Smith resigned his post with Atlanta & West Point Rail Road and The Western Railway of Alabama effective November 15, 1900. He resigned in order to accept the position of General Manager with the Louisville, Evansville & St. Louis Consolidated Railroad, a company considerably larger than either of the components of the West Point Route. [2]

Upon the resignation of Mr. Smith, the board of directors of both the A&WP and the WofA elected Charles A. Wickersham president of their respective companies. Mr. Wickersham was a native of Unionville, Pennsylvania, and began his railroad career as a telegraph operator for the Pennsylvania Railroad at Coatesville, Pennsylvania at the age of 16. After moving to the Chicago, Burlington & Quincy as a dispatcher for 12 years, he moved south as a trainmaster for the Georgia Pacific Railway in 1892. He was named head of transportation for the Cotton States International Exposition in Atlanta in 1895. At the close of the fair, he was appointed superintendent of the Alabama Great Southern Railway in Birmingham. His election as president of the component companies of the West Point Route was effective November 15, 1900. [3]

Charles A. Wickersham was elected president of the A&WP and WofA effective November 15, 1900. He would serve in that capacity until 1947. (A&WP photo)

On November 30, 1900, the Atlanta Belt Line Railroad was leased to the Atlanta & West Point Rail Road for 99 years. The rental on the property was $16,000 per year with the lessee paying all taxes and operating expenses. [4]

The following day, December 1, 1900, the A&WP moved its freight agency and terminals into the Georgia Railroad's Hulsey Yard. Previously they had been operated jointly with the Central of Georgia Railway. [5]

On December 29, 1901, a cloudburst of monumental proportions struck the West Point Route between the hours of midnight and 6:00 AM. On the West Point the rains washed out over a mile of track and disrupted traffic for 36 hours. [6]

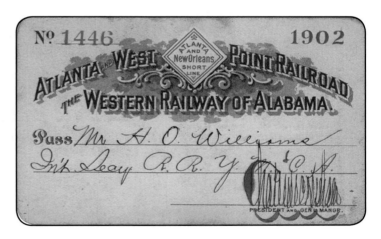

The West Point Route's diamond herald got a new look in May of 1902. Gone was the "Atlanta and New Orleans Short Line" slogan and in its place was the simpler slogan, "The West Point Route". Both heralds are shown in "before" and "after" annual passes for 1902 and 1903. (Both passes, author's collection)

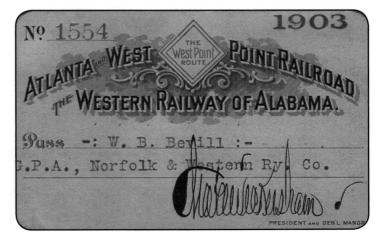

25

Business car 100 was purchased second-hand by the West Point Route (1/2 by each partner) in 1902. The car is said to have been the modified and modernized *Stranraer*, the private car of Helen Gould, daughter of railroad financier Jay Gould. The car is shown here in a much-modernized, steel-sheathed and air conditioned state in the 1960's. (Jay Williams collection)

The Western fared even worse. The downpour washed out the track in several places between West Point and Milstead, suspending traffic for three days and causing $25,000 worth of damage. Train 212, a freight, departed Montgomery at 10:00 PM on the 28th and ran into a washout near Notasulga in the early hours of December 29th. The locomotive turned over, drowning Engineer Russell. [7]

In May of 1902 the A&WP and the WofA once again modified their logo. The diamond motif was retained, but the slogan, "The Atlanta and New Orleans Short Line" was replaced with the legend, "The West Point Route". This herald would serve the companies for over 70 years until it was augmented, but not completely replaced, in the mid-1970's.

On June 8, 1902, A&WP suburban service between Atlanta and College Park was discontinued. The service, which had been inaugurated five years earlier, was rendered unprofitable by the extension of the streetcar lines of the Georgia Railway and Electric Company to College Park . [8]

During the year 1902, the Western's locomotive shop in Montgomery performed repairs to the motive power of the Tuskegee, the LaFayette, and the Union Springs & Northern

railroads as well as servicing the locomotives of the West Point Route.

The Western purchased a cafe-observation car from the Chicago & Alton Railroad in 1902. The car, numbered 672 had been built the previous year.

Other improvements on the Western included a steel water tank and water station in Montgomery and a new passenger station at Selma. The cost of these improvements was $52,743.44. [9]

On November 2, 1902, a new service was inaugurated on the West Point Route. Train 97, a fast mail train between New York and New Orleans, began operations over the West Point Route for the Atlanta to Montgomery portion of the route. The train was handled by Southern Railway to Atlanta and by the Lousiville & Nashville Railroad beyond Montgomery. [10]

While 97 carried no passengers between Washington and Atlanta on the Southern, the West Point Route and the L&N initially provided a single coach for any passenger who might wish to make the trip. (An Atlanta-New Orleans Pullman was added on February 1, 1903.) The train was a mail train first and foremost. Passengers were strictly a secondary consideration. [11]

Those who took the trip were treated to a wild ride. Ninety seven was carded out of Atlanta at 11:15 PM CST (Atlanta was in the Central Time Zone until 1941.) and was scheduled to arrive in Montgomery at 3:1? AM, CST, for a running time of 4 hours, ? minutes, or an averag

A&WP 24 was delivered by Rogers in March, 1903. She was renumbered to 227 in 1907 and sold to the Birmingham & Southeastern Railroad in 1923. (Alco Historic Photos)

eed of 43.4 MPH, including
l stops.[12] This was over a
ngle-track railroad laid
rgely with 70- and 80-pound
il and powered by hand-
red locomotives.

The initial run was made
awlessly. The Southern
ought 97 into Atlanta two
inutes to the good. A&WP
ain 97 departed 10 minutes
ter with a consist of one
PO and one coach behind
/ofA 18, an 1895 Baldwin
-4-0 with engineer L. Z.
IcDonald at the throttle.
he train was in the charge of
onductor G. R. Shockley.[13]

Atlanta Terminal Station, owned jointly by the Atlanta & West Point Rail Road, the Central of Georgia Railway, and Southern Railway, was opened on May 14, 1905. In addition to its owners, it was also used at various times by the Seaboard Air Line Railway, and the Atlanta, Birmingham & Atlantic Railway. It is shown here in June, 1970, the month it was closed and about a year prior to its demolition. (C. L. Goolsby photo)

The union station in
tlanta had by this time, deteriorated to the point that the
ewspapers in the city were beginning to make an issue of its
ondition. The Atlanta Constitution described the depot as,
..an affair whose discomforts and dangers it is impossible
exaggerate. It has bankrupted the vocabulary of epithetical
enunciation and defied cartoonists to a standstill."[14] On
nother occasion, it said, "The present depot is a daily
tensifying nuisance. The place is filthy, unwholesome,
nsightly and perilous to the limbs and life of all who venture
out it. The people have grown utterly disgusted with the
hole dirty and disreputable affair..."[15] This situation had
oviously reached the point that something had to be done.
n November 27, 1902, a group of Atlanta businessmen,
the behest of Samuel Spencer and with the backing of
outhern Railway, petitioned the Georgia Secretary of State
r a charter for the Atlanta Terminal Company.[16]

The charter was issued on February 11, 1903, and
outhern Railway and the Central of Georgia Railway were
e original co-owners. While A&WP President Charles
Vickersham was involved in the discussions regarding the
ew depot almost from the outset,[17] the Atlanta & West Point
id not purchase any stock in the terminal company until
te June of 1903. At that time, the West Point purchased
25,000 of the stock and became the owner of a 1/3 interest

in the company.[18]

The West Point Route's motive power roster received a considerable amount of attention in 1903-05. Ten-Wheelers WofA 9-10 and A&WP 23 and 24 arrived on the property in March 1903. Six-wheel switchers WofA 2-3 and Ten Wheeler WofA 19 followed in June 1903 and Ten Wheelers WofA 11 and A&WP 29 were shipped from the builder in December, 1904. The final locomotive of the lot, WofA 0-6-0 No. 4, was completed in January 1905. All were products of the Rogers Locomotive Works, Paterson, New Jersey.[19]

On February 21, 1904, the Western completed a new line into Selma, using the Lousiville & Nashville's line from a point called Western Junction, about three miles out of town. This arrangement enabled the Western to abandon 8.05 miles of mainline track, including its bridge over the Alabama River. Some of the track was retained to serve local industries, but the bulk of the trackage was dismantled, including the Alabama River bridge.

The Atlanta & West Point ceased using the old Union Depot in Atlanta and moved into the newly completed facility of the Atlanta Terminal Company on May 14, 1905. The company's corporate offices were also moved to this facility from an office building/warehouse near the old Union Depot. A&WP President Charles Wickersham

"A&WP 15" was actually WofA 15 and was relettered properly immediately after delivery by Rogers in 1906. (Rogers Locomotive Works photo, B. F. Roberts collection)

Pacific-type No. 250 was delivered to the A&WP by ALCO's Rogers works in 1907. The engine was sold to the Georgia Railroad in 1934. (America Locomotive Company photo, Harold K. Volrath collection.)

called the new facility, "... the finest and most commodious passenger terminal in the South." [20]

It was about this time (1905) that the Passenger Department of the West Point Route issued a very attractive promotional book called "From Selma to Atlanta." This book, an attractive hard-bound, gold-lettered maroon volume, extolled the virtues of the communities served by the West Point Route. It was a gorgeous piece of promotional work.

On June 6, 1906, Central of Georgia train 15 plowed into the rear coach of an A&WP passenger extra at the West Fair Street crossing at the south approach to Atlanta Terminal Station. The West Point train was a picnic special returning from the company's Pearl Lake picnic grounds near Newnan with crowd composed of the Junior Order of United Mechanics of Atlanta and the Daughters of America. The rear coach of the West Point train was demolished, killing Oscar Cook, a printer, and injuring 19 others. [21]

It was 1910 before the accident investigation was completed and the claims settled. The case was submitted to arbitration and the responsibility for the accident was assigned 2/3 to the Central and 1/3 to the A&WP. The personal injury claims exceeded $101,000. [22]

Train 97 made its last run on January 6, 1907. In spi of its popularity among postal patrons, the train was be known for the spectacular derailment on Southern Railwa at Danville, Virginia, on September 27, 1903, (about whic a well-known folk song was written). This accident ha nothing to do with its demise, however. The mail train wa discontinued due to the failure of the United States Congres to make an appropriation for its continued operation.

On April 1, 1907, the Atlanta & West Point Rail Roa along with the Georgia Railroad and the Louisville Nashville Railroad entered into an agreement to operate joint terminal facility in Atlanta. This facility, an expande version of the Georgia Road's Hulsey Yard, began operatic on July 1, 1907, and had its own operating organizatic known as the Atlanta Joint Terminals. The Louisville Nashville Railroad ceased using the facility in 1956, but th Atlanta Joint Terminals organization lasted until 1983.

The LaGrange Belt Line, a two-mile track connecting th A&WP with the Atlanta, Birmingham & Atlantic Railroa in LaGrange, was completed in 1907. The line was owne jointly by the two carriers and provided access to sever industries, among them the Elm City Cotton Mills.

WofA 151 was built by the Richmond works of the American Locomotive Company in 1910. The locomotive became the Georgia Railroad's No. 252 1934. (American Locomotive Company photo, author's collection)

The West Point Route adopted a new numbering scheme for its locomotives in 1907. The locomotives of the Western of Alabama would occupy numbers in the 100 and 300 series, while those of the Atlanta & West Point would be assigned numbers in the 200 and 400 series. This numbering scheme would endure until steam power was phased out in the mid-1950's.

The West Point Route received its first Pacific, or 4-6-2, type locomotives in 1907. WofA 150 and A&WP 250-251 were delivered by the Rogers Works of the American Locomotive Company.

The Atlanta Belt Line Railroad, after being leased for eight years, was purchased by the A&WP in 1908. The purchase price was $400,000.

Vandals caused the derailment of train 37, The *New York-New Orleans Limited* at Milstead, Alabama on February 28, 1912. Engineer J. D. Smedley was killed in the wreck when the locomotive derailed and rolled down a fill. (Matt Lawson collection)

Four new passenger trains - No.s 17-18-19 and 20 - were inaugurated between Atlanta and Columbus, Georgia, in September 1907. The service was offered in conjunction with the Central of Georgia Railway with the West Point handling the trains between Atlanta and Newnan and the Central handling the trains beyond Newnan to Columbus.

Despite the new trains and the additional $31,956.18 that they generated, passenger revenues for the A&WP were up only $5327.94 for the year ended June 30, 1908. Without the new trains the revenues would have been down by a considerable margin. This was due to a reduction in fares on the A&WP from three cents per mile to two cents per mile ordered by the Georgia Railroad Commission on September 2, 1907. While the decrease covered only intrastate fares, through passenger revenues suffered as well, as passengers to points in Alabama and beyond found that they could save money by purchasing local tickets to West Point and purchasing tickets to their destination from that station. [23]

Passenger revenues for the year ended June 30, 1909, decreased by $28,412.43. It became obvious that the fare reduction ordered by the Railroad Commission of Georgia had failed to stimulate passenger traffic as intended. According to President Wickersham in his annual report, "It however is evident that either the rate per mile must increase or the service decreased." [24]

Mr. Wickersham's annoyance with the Railroad Commission was justified. Besides the A&WP, only the state-owned Western & Atlantic Railroad was required to charge such a low rate. With the exception of the Charleston & Western Carolina Railway, which operated only 15 of its 341 miles in the state of Georgia, and which charged 2 1/4 cents per mile, all other carriers were allowed to charge 2 1/2 cents per mile or better. [25]

In June 1910, a petition bearing the signatures of some eighteen hundred citizens residing along the Atlanta & West Point was presented to the Rail-road Commission of Georgia praying that the company be permitted to increase its maximum passenger rate to two and one-half cents per mile. They gave as their reason for the petition "...superior and satisfactory service for which they were willing to pay as much as permitted on other lines." [26]

Despite all efforts, no relief was forthcoming.

The Western fared somewhat better. When the Alabama legislature ordered freight and passenger rate reductions to be made effective on April 1, 1907, they were delayed by court injunction until June 1, 1909, when they were put into effect for a trial period. After the trial period;, the court ordered the old rates reinstated and this was done on June 20, 1912. While the Western lost, as a result of the rate cut, an estimated $180,616.42, and spent an additional $49,159.14 on litigation to get the rate cuts rescinded, it could have been worse. President Wickersham estimated that, had the rate cuts gone into effect on April 1, 1907, as originally ordered, the WofA would have lost an additional $81,445.56. [27]

On February 28, 1912, train 37, the *New York-New Orleans Limited*, met with a serious accident at Milstead, Alabama. The locomotive, a combination baggage-Railway Post Office car, and the club car derailed and turned over on a fill, "practically demolishing the club car", according to President Wickersham in the annual report for 1912. The wreck resulted in the death of Engineer A. J. Smedley and the injury of two other trainmen and five passengers. [28]

"There is no doubt that the wreck was the work of miscreants," continued President Wickersham, "and two

No.s 201 and 231 were delivered by ALCO's Richmond works in 1912. The 231 was retired in 1936 while the 201 remained on the roster until 1950. (Both photos – American Locomotive Company photos, author's collection)

negroes are now in jail charged with the crime and it would seem from the preliminary trial that they will be convicted." Damage to the equipment was approximately $20,000. [29]

Heavy rains in March and April of 1912 caused washouts in the Carolinas, forcing connecting lines to divert traffic to other routes. A similar situation occurred in May and June in Mississippi and Louisiana, and The West Point Route itself was closed for several days beginning March 14, 1912, by an unprecedented rise in the Chattahoochee River at West Point.

[1] Annual Report, The Western Railway of Alabama, September 4, 1900, p. 16.

[2] T. Addison Busby, editor, *The Biographical Directory of the Railway Officials of America*, (Chicago, 1906), p. 557.

[3] Atlanta *Constitution*, July 14, 1949/ (clipping)

[4] Annual Report, Atlanta & West Point Rail Road Co., September 10, 1901, p. 17.

[5] Op. Cit., p. 17.

[6] Annual Report, Atlanta & West Point Rail Road Company, October 21, 1902, p. 15.

[7] Annual Report, The Western Railway of Alabama, October 21, 1902, p. 16.

[8] "Suburban Trains Are To Come Off", Atlanta *Constitution*, June 7, 1902, p. 8.

[9] Annual Report, The Western Railway of Alabama for the Year Ending June 30, 1902, p. 15.

[10] G. Howard Gregory, *History of the Wreck of Old 97*,(Danville, VA, 1981), p. 1.

[11] *The Official Guide of the Railways*, November, 1904, p. 906.

[12] Op. Cit.,

[13] "Fast Mail Is Greeted By Large Crowd", Atlanta *Constitution*, November 3, 1902, p. 1.

[14] "Now Build A New Station", Atlanta *Constitution*, July 9, 1902, p. 6.

[15] "And Yet Once More - The Depot!", Atlanta *Constitution*, July 14, 1902, p. 4.

[16] Southern Railway Company File 6025, "Atlanta Terminal Company Incorporation Papers, Selection of Officers, etc." November 27, 1902 - June 30, 1903.

[17] "Officials Here To Talk Depot", Atlanta *Constitution*, November 20, 1902, p. 3.

[18] Southern Railway Company File 6025, Op. Cit.

[19] Peter Moshein and Robert R. Rothfus, "Rogers Locomotives: A Brief History and Construction List", *Railroad History* 167, Autumn, 1992, pp. 140, 142, and 147.

[20] Annual Report, Atlanta & West Point Rail Road, October 17, 1905, p. 13.

[21] "Death Follows Railway Collision", Atlanta *Constitution*, June 7, 1907, pp. 1-2.

[22] Annual Report, Atlanta & West Point Rail Road, October 18, 1910, p. 18.

[23] Annual Report, Atlanta & West Point Rail Road, October 17, 1908, pp. 10-11.

[24] Annual Report, Atlanta & West Point Rail Road, October 10, 1909, p. 8.

[25] 38th Annual Report of the Railroad Commission of Georgia (1910), April 1, 1911, p. 279.

[26] Annual Report, Atlanta & West Point Rail Road Company, October 18, 1910, p. 19.

[27] Annual Report, The Western Railway of Alabama, October 15, 1912, p. 15.

[28] "Atlantan Killed in Train Wreck", Atlanta *Constitution*, February 29, 1912, p. 1.

[29] Annual Report, The Western Railway of Alabama, October 15, 1912, p. 15.

CHAPTER

V

THE TEENS & TWENTIES

The A&WP received two new Pacific (4-6-2) type passenger locomotives in 1913 when the Brooks Works of the American Locomotive Company delivered Nos. 280 and 281. These locomotives differed from the earlier examples of this type owned by the West Point Route in that they had piston valves and an outboard bearing trailing truck as opposed to slide valves and an inboard bearing axle on the earlier engines.

On October 1, 1913, President Charles A. Wickersham was named General Manager of the Georgia Railroad by the its lessees. These lessees (the Atlantic Coast Line Railroad and the Louisville & Nashville Railroad) held a 50% interest in the Western as a result of the lease and controlled a majority of the stock of the A&WP through the lease as well as through direct ownership of a number of shares.

This event marked the first time that the President of the A&WP and the WofA had held the position of General Manager of the Georgia Railroad. The reverse had been true when John Pendleton King, president of the Georgia Railroad and Banking company, had also been elected president of the A&WP, but Mr. Wickersham's appointment as General Manager of the Georgia Road marked the first time that all three roads had been under the leadership of the same chief executive officer.

The outbreak of war in Europe in 1914 essentially eliminated the cotton markets there, causing a dramatic downturn in both freight and passenger traffic. The net income for the A&WP for the fiscal year ending June 30, 1915, was $168,902.04, down from $255,451.14 from the previous year.[1]

The Western fared no better. Its net income for fiscal 1915 was $126,006, down from $302,064 in 1914. [2]

The Atlanta Belt Line Railroad surrendered its charter and was formally consolidated into the Atlanta & West Point Rail Road on September 8, 1914. This was strictly a formality as the road had been operated as an integral part of the A&WP under lease since 1900 and had been owned outright by the larger company since 1908.

In order to generally upgrade its passenger equipment, the A&WP purchased five new coaches from American Car & Foundry. The cars, numbered 63-67, were delivered in late 1914 and early 1915. The WofA had made a similar purchase in 1911-12.

Passenger traffic was becoming a sore point. President Wickersham, in his annual report to the A&WP stockholders, lamented the fact that the passenger miles (one passenger hauled one mile) had decreased 13.72 per cent, and the average number of passengers carried per train had decreased from 118 to only 55. He also bemoaned the fact that it was "...not within our power to discontinue a single train." He also pointed out, once again, that the West Point's passenger fares were "...the lowest, with but one exception, of any line in this territory, and clearly unremunerative." [3]

A telephone train dispatching system was installed in 1915. Although this system became the primary method of dispatching, the telegraph key was retained for a number of years as a backup system for use during line failures and other occasions when the phone was out.

The installation of automatic block signals was begun in 1916 and continued into 1917. Interrupted by World War I, the project was completed in 1922.

While the automobile was beginning to make inroads on passenger service, it was beginning to make a positive im-

Pacific-type locomotives 280-281 were delivered by ALCO in 1913. The 280, shown here at the builders, remained on the roster until 1953. (American Locomotive Company photo)

The WofA took delivery of dining car 500 in 1913. The car was built by American Car & Foundry at its Jackson & Sharp plant in Wilmington, Delaware. (ACF photo, George Votava collection)

pact on the freight business. Among the industrial additions and expansions listed in the A&WP's 1917 annual report were a warehouse for the Studebaker Corporation and an assembly plant for the Hanson Motor Company, an Atlanta company which produced autos for a number of years in the 'teens and 'twenties.

At noon on December 28, 1917, the properties of the Atlanta & West Point Rail Road and The Western Railway of Alabama, along with those of most other railroads in the Untied States, were placed under the control of the United States Railroad Administration. The roads were assigned to the Southern Region under the jurisdiction of E. T. Lamb, who had been president of the Atlanta, Birmingham & Atlantic Railway prior to his appointment as Federal Manager.

Mr. Wickersham remained in charge of both properties as president under the direction of the Federal Manager until June 21, 1918, at which time he resigned to accept the position of General Manager for the Federal Manager. This situation prevailed for only a few weeks, for on August 31, 1918, Mr. Wickersham resigned from the position of General Manager for the Federal Manager, and was re-elected president of both companies on September 1, 1918.

During Mr. Wickersham's ten-week tenure as General Manager for the USRA, Milton H. Smith, president of the Louisville & Nashville Rail road, served as president o both the A&WP and WofA.

Each partner in the Wes Point Route received two nev Mikado locomotives in 1918 The locomotives were built b the Lima Locomotive Work and carried road numbers WofA 300-301 and A&WP 400-401 Construction numbers wer consecutive beginning wit 5691.

The United States Railroa Administration assigned to the A&WP two of the Decapo (2-10-0) locomotives which were originally built for th Czarist Russian Government but were diverted due to th Communist revolution of 1917. The locomotives were USA numbers 1011 and 1012 and apparently were not assigne A&WP road numbers. They were apparently not well like and were turned back to the U. S. Government at the end o USRA control. The 1011 was later sold to the Erie Railroa and the 1012 was purchased by circus man John Ringlin for his St. Louis & Hannibal Railroad.

The USRA also allotted one its standard design 0-8- switchers to each partner of the West Point Route. The were assigned road numbers WofA 115 and A&WP 215 an were purchased by their respective roads at the end of fed eral control in 1920.

Among other expenditures for 1920 was the sum o $2200 for the purchase of a Franklin touring car by th A&WP. The purpose served by this auto has not come t light. [4]

With the end of the war and return to private control o March 1, 1920, revenues dropped as wartime traffic evapo rated. Net income on the A&WP fell from $449,254.20 i 1920 and to $154,845.65 in 1921.[5] The Western suffered . similar reduction in profits.

Western of Alabama passenger locomotive No. 150 wa

A&WP 401 was one of four Mikado type locomotives delivered to the West Point Route by the Lima Locomotive Works in 1918. These were the first of th type on the railroad. (Lima Locomotive Works photo, author's collection.)

The Western of Alabama purchased two 4-8-2, or Mountain, type locomotives in 1920. Numbered 180 and 181, they were built by the American Locomotive Company's Richmond works. The 180 is shown here at Atlanta's Terminal Station on July 24, 1934. (B. F. Roberts collection)

ebuilt in the Montgomery locomotive shop early in 1922. t emerged as No. 152 and its rebuilding included the installation of a superheater and piston valves.

The Federated Shop Craft Union struck the A&WP and WofA along with most other railroads in the United States on July 1, 1922, in protest of a reduction in wages authorized by the United States Railway Labor Board. The efforts of the supervisory force, plus the fact that the picket lines were not honored by the operating employees, enabled the operation of the lines until July 6th, when the employment of new men began. This continued until October 1st when a shop force of near normal size was attained. The union, having plainly lost this strike, eventually called it off.

Engineer John McWaters retired after completing 54 years of service with the Atlanta & West Point on January 2, 1923. He was met on the completion of his final run at Atlanta Terminal Station by President Charles Wickersham and General Passenger Agent Joseph P. Billups, a number of newspaper reporters, and at least one motion picture photographer. McWaters had hired out on the West Point in 1869 and was one of the road's more colorful and popular engineers. It was said that he never lost a passenger and he never delayed a train. [6]

The West Point Route acquired three new Mikado-type (2-8-2) freight locomotives in 1923. A&WP 425, WofA 375 and 376 were delivered by the Lima Locomotive Works and bore construction numbers 6730, 6731, and 6732, respectively.

Passenger trains 33 and 34 were radically altered in 1923. The trains, originally Atlanta-Montgomery locals, were transformed into part of a through service between New York and New Orleans in conjunction with the Louisville & Nashville Railroad, Southern Railway, and the Pennsylvania Railroad. The trains were named *The Piedmont Limited* and, on the West Point Route, were second only to No.s 37 and 38 (*The Crescent Limited*) in prestige.

The Courier, a company magazine for the employees of the West Point Route and the affiliated Georgia Railroad, began publication in January 1923. It was a full-sized, slick–paper publication featuring news of the companies, their employees, and on-line industries and cities. L. D. Hale was the editor.

Radio Station WDAJ in College Park, Georgia, was built and operated in 1923 and 1924 by the companies of the West Point Route along with the Georgia Railroad. The broadcasting station was constructed in its entirety by the signal and communications forces of the participating roads. The station was railroad-owned and was built primarily to provide training for the employees and entertainment for the passengers of West Point Route passenger trains. It was the first instance when a railroad installed radios on its trains and entertained passengers from its own station. [7]

The Western's car shops were busy in 1924. In addition to performing routine repairs, the shop forces constructed 50 low-side gondolas, two steel underframe flat cars, 25 steel

A&WP 425 was one of four Mikados built to USRA light 2-8-2 specifications for the A&WP and WofA in 1923. (Lima Locomotive Works photo, author's collection)

underframe ice cars and 25 36-foot box cars.

The service area of the West Point Route was stricken by a severe drought in the summer and fall of 1925. In an attempt to render assistance to those industries and municipalities stricken by the drought, the A&WP and the WofA operated a "Water Train".

This train, consisting of fourteen tank cars, was filled with water from the Chattahoochee River at Lanett, Alabama, and was then run to points along the line where the need was greatest. The train operated twice daily between August 26 and October 2, 1925. [8]

The Western Railway of Alabama Shop Band, which was formed in 1924, accompanied the Atlanta Crackers baseball team to the Little World Series (a minor league equivalent of the World Series) in Ft. Worth, Texas, in 1925. General Passenger Agent J. P. Billups arranged for the band to join the Crackers' special train on the night of September 24, 1925. The band led a parade from the Texas & Pacific station in Ft. Worth to the hotel and was featured on a broadcast over the radio station owned by the Ft. Worth Star-Telegram on the evening of September 27th before returning home to Montgomery on September 28th. [9]

The West Point Route purchased what would prove to be its last new steam passenger locomotives in 1926. A&WP 290 and WofA 190 were delivered by Lima Locomotive Works bearing construction numbers 7008 and 7009, respectively. They were copies of the heavy Pacific design of the United States Railroad Administration (with minor alterations) and were very similar in appearance to the famous Ps-4 class locomotives of Southern Railway. Indeed, their primary assignment was handling trains 37 and 38, the West Point Route's segment of the Southern's *Crescent Limited,* between Atlanta and Montgomery.

The passenger traffic figures of the West Point Route got

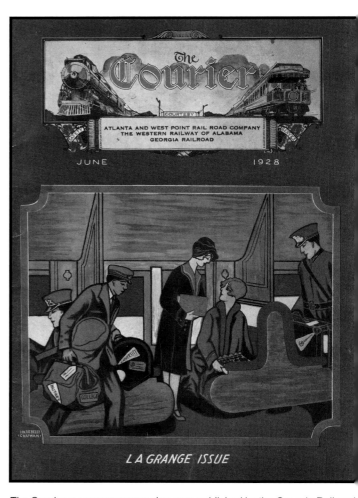

The Courier, a company magazine, was published by the Georgia Railroad and The West Point Route from 1923 until 1930 and was distributed to employees and customers. (Author's collection)

a substantial boost on October 9, 1926, when the A&WP and WofA handled two special trains carrying the football team and boosters of the Tulane Green Wave as they traveled from New Orleans to Atlanta. The two trains, totaling 25 cars, carried 800 passengers to the Georgia Tech-Tulane football game. [10]

The West Point Route Shop Band, along with the A&WP-WofA-GaRR General Office Orchestra and the Georgia Railroad Shop Band of Augusta, performed several concerts which were broadcast over radio station WSB in Atlanta on December 11, 1926. The concerts were apparently enjoyed by the listening public, as numerous favorable telegrams were received, many of which were printed

The West Point Route fielded two bands in the 1920's. The West Point Route Shop Band was located in Montgomery and the Georgia Railroad/West Point Route General Office Orchestra was headquartered in Atlanta. In this photo, The West Point Route Shop Band and the Georgia Railroad Shop Band from Augusta are preparing to march in the Christmas parade in Atlanta in 1926 Note the banner on the left. (*Courier* photo, Nelson Mc-Gahee collection).

The band as it prepares to march in the 1926 Christmas parade. The Drum Major was Miss Margaret Paulin, said by the *Courier* to be "nationally known' and first woman to "wield a baton at the head of a band." The uniforms were apparently red and white. Interestingly, the West Point Route band had no cap insignia but had the logo on the left front of the jacket. The Georgia Railroad Shop band, on the other hand, had cap logos, but no other identification on the uniforms. (*Courier* photo, Nelson McGahee collection)

In a special edition of *The Courier*. [11]

The Atlanta Joint Terminals baseball team was the winner of the industrial league city championship for 1927. Along the way, they defeated teams from Fulton Bag & Cotton Mills, the Coca-Cola Company, and Scottdale Mills.

In his annual report for 1927, President Wickersham called attention to the fact that passenger revenues were decreasing steadily. Indeed, passenger revenues on the A&WP had fallen from $822,989.20 in 1926 to $743,213.54 in 1927. [12] He cited increased competition from bus lines, but placed the greater blame for the decline on the increased use of the private automobile.

The year 1927 marked the opening of the Western's new classification yard in Montgomery. Named Chester Yard (in honor of President Wickersham's grandson, Chester Wickerham Kitchings), the yard contained 15 miles of track space and was illuminated at night by nine 1000-watt floodlights.

Heavyweight boxing champion Jack Dempsey traveled from Atlanta to Montgomery over the West Point Route aboard the Crescent Limited on July 27, 1927, en route to the west coast. He was im-

pressed enough with the service he received at the hands of West Point Route personnel to write a note of appreciation to General Passenger Agent Joe Billups. [13]

On October 15, 1927, the management of the West Point Route and the Georgia Railroad embarked on an unusual experiment. A talent contest was held for the children of employees and as a result, 21 of these children aged six to twelve years received scholarships for lessons in dancing or playing various musical instruments.

At the end of two years, a number of the students had appeared on various radio broadcasts and in live performances in cities up and down the various component rail-

WofA Café-Parlor car 402 was remodeled and reconfigured as a full dining car in 1927. The newly refurbished interior was photographed with the cooks and waiters standing stiffly at their stations. None of the men are identified, but the gentleman seated at the left appears to be Adolph Moritz, the Superintendent of Transportation who died that year. (*Courier* photo, author's collection)

WofA 170 stands on the turntable at the Montgomery Shop after being rebuilt in 1928. The engine's weight and tractive force were both increased in the rebuilding. (Courier photo, author's collection)

roads including theaters in Atlanta, Athens, LaGrange, and Augusta, Ga., and in Montgomery, Auburn, and Selma, Ala., and in such off-line points as Charlotte, NC, and Ft. Worth, Texas. Although the experiment was considered a success, it was not repeated, most likely due to the financial depression which gripped the nation shortly after the conclusion of the initial program. [14]

The Western's locomotive shop in Montgomery rebuilt WofA locomotive No. 170 in 1928, completing the job on October 4. The project included the installation of a super-heater and increased the engine weight from 158,000 lbs. To 185,000 lbs. and increased the tractive effort from 23,000 lbs to 27,072 lbs. [15]

Effective November 1, 1928, the Atlanta & West Point Rail Road granted trackage rights for passenger service only to the Central of Georgia Railway between the end of the paired track at East Point and the junction with the Central's Griffin-Chattanooga line at Newnan. Trains 17-18 and 19-20, which were interline runs between Atlanta and Columbus became Central of Georgia trains at that time, although A&WP tickets were honored on the trains between Atlanta

and Newnan an A&WP operatin employees could b on the runs. [16]

The West Poi Route handled somewhat unusu shipment in Decem ber 1928. A soli train load of pick les from the W&V Pickle Company (Montgomery wa loaded for distribu tion in eastern mar kets. The train cor sisted of 21 cars, totaled 17,172 jars of pickles, and wa reputed to be the first solid train of pickles from any on pickling plant in the United States. [17]

The West Point Route, along with the Georgia Railroad initiated the practice of awarding service buttons, or pin to members of the newly-formed "Old Timers Club". Th initial presentation was made on April 23, 1929, to 250 en ployees of 25 years or more of service. Of the recipient: 120 were Georgia Railroad employees and 130 were en ployees of the West Point Route.

On April 23, 1929, The West Po Route, along with the Georgia R road, began the practice of awa ing service pins to employees v 25 years or more service with th respective organizations. The pr tice was continued until the dem of the companies in 1983. (Nels McGahee collection)

[1]   Annual Report, Atlanta & West Point Rail Road Company, June 30, 1915, p. 5.

[2]   Poor's Manual of Railroads, 1917, p. 194.

[3]   Annual Report, Atlanta & West Point Rail Road Company, 1915, p. 14.

[4]   Annual Report, Atlanta & West Point Rail Road Company, 1920, p. 11

[5]   Annual Report, Atlanta & West Point Rail Road Company, 1921, p. 5.

[6]   "John McWaters, Daddy of All Engineers, Greeted by Officials and Cam eramen As He Completes 54 Years At The Throttle", Atlanta Journal, January 3, 1923.

[7]   S. R. young, "Automatic Block Signals and How They Work", The Courier, December, 1926, p. 15.

[8]   The Courier, October 1925, p. 3.

[9]   The Courier, October 1925, p. 5

[10]   The Courier, October 1926, p. 21

[11]   The Courier, January 1927, pp. 22-24.

[12]   Annual Report, Atlanta & West Point Rail Road, 1927, p. 14.

[13]   The Courier, August 1927, p. 6.

[14]   "The Result of an Unusual Experiment", The Courier, July 1929, p 1-4.

[15]   "Passenger Locomotive Rebuilt Throughout in Montgomery Shops The Courier, November 1928, pp. 22-23.

[16]   Central of Georgia Railway, Contracts and Agreements, Volume XI\ 1929, Document 526.

[17]   "First Solid Trainload of Pickles From South Handled by The West Poi Route", The Courier, Januar 1929, p. 8.

VI

DEPRESSION AND WAR

On July 1, 1930, the Atlanta Joint Terminals Country Club opened its grounds to its members for the first time. The club's facilities included a lake for swimming and fishing, picnic facilities, and a dance pavilion. Membership in the club was open to any employee of the three member railroads of the Atlanta Joint Terminals (A&WP-GaRR-L&N). The price of a membership card valid for three years was a very reasonable $5.00.[1]

In its December 1930 issue, The Courier announced that the last wooden bridges on the West Point Route had been replaced with concrete structures. One of the bridges, over Beech Creek, had been placed in service within weeks prior to publication, and the second span, over Yellow Jacket Creek, had been completed and would be placed in service in January 1931, after the concrete had been properly cured.

The West Point Route saw its earnings dramatically reduced by the onset of the Great Depression. The Western's earnings fell from $411,815.78 in 1929[2] to a net loss of $172,655.72 in 1932.[3]

The A&WP fared no better. From a net profit of $249,877.12 in 1929[4] the financial results deteriorated to a net loss of $296,668,87 in 1932.[5]

The operating ratio – operating expenses stated as a percentage of revenues – of the A&WP went from 77.04 in 1928 to 106.26 in 1932 and the Western's operating ratio soared from 75.26 in 1928 to a hideous 110.46 in 1932.

Passenger revenues, already on the decline, were particularly affected by the economic downturn. Passenger revenues on the A&WP fell from $743,213.54[6] in 1927 to $172,725.56 in 1933.[7] Passenger revenues on the Western plummeted from $695,726.93[8] to $172,725.56[9] during the same period.

Faced with such dismal operating results, particularly in the passenger field, cost cutting measures had to be taken. One such measure was the replacement of trains 41 and 42 on the A&WP by the buses of the Georgia Highway Transport Company. The GHTCo had been formed by the Georgia Railroad in 1928 and the A&WP purchased a 50% interest in this company at about this time. Another measure, this one taken by the

Western, was to convert all passenger trains on the Selma Division to mixed trains, moving passengers and freight on the same train.

Trains 26 and 43 were converted to mixed status effective November 30, 1930.[10] The remaining two Selma Division passenger trains, 32 and 39, assumed mixed status on March 22, 1931.[11] The status of the two freight trains on the division, No.s 209 and 212, remained unchanged.

In June 1934, another step was taken, this one to increase revenues. The extra fare on trains 37 and 38, *The Crescent Limited* was abolished and coaches were added to the train's consist for the first time in the train's history. The train's name was also dropped at this time by all participating carriers.

By 1936, the economic situation had improved to the point that both partners in the West Point Route showed a profit. It wasn't much - $13,964 for the A&WP[12] and $19,189.36 for the Western[13] - but it was a profit. It was the first for either company since 1930.

The Western purchased three locomotives in 1936. The Florida East Coast Railway, in the throes of receivership, defaulted on one of its equipment trust covering some locomotives purchased during the Florida boom of the 1920's, resulting in the sale of some of the locomotives covered by the loan.

Accommodation trains 41 and 42 were discontinued and replaced by the buses of the Georgia Highway Transport Company in 1930. This service lasted only a few years and was discontinued entirely in the mid-1930's. This poor quality image is the only known photo to have been discovered of a GHT bus in service on The West Point Route. The photo appears to have been taken in Atlanta. (Courier photo, Author's collection.)

The Great Depression had a very negative impact on passenger traffic. It is reflected in the abbreviated five car consist of No. 33 as it leaves Atlanta Terminal Station in 1934. (Hugh M. Comer photo, Author's collection)

In 1940, the Army Air Corps established an air base near Selma. Craig Field opened at Felix Spur (MP 219) and remained a source of traffic until its closure in the 1970's.

Additional sources of revenue were created when Chrysler Motor Parts Company and Sears Roebuck & Company each established warehouses on the A&WP in the Atlanta area in 1941. The Army established an Air Corps Advanced Flying School on the WofA at Cloughs, Alabama, near Tuskegee. This school was made famous by the Home Box Office movie, *The Tuskegee Airmen*.

The Western, needing passenger power and seeing the opportunity to obtain a bargain, went shopping and purchased three 4-8-2's – FEC No.s 402, 418, and 419. These engines were built by the American Locomotive Company's Schenectady works in 1924 and were renumbered WofA 185, 186, and 187, respectively.

Passenger comfort took a great stride forward with the installation of air conditioning on A&WP diner 402 in 1936. The air conditioning program continued in 1937 with the installation of the equipment on A&WP coaches 63, 64, 66, and 67, and WofA coaches 102-105 and diner 500.

The West Point Route's flagship passenger train regained its name in 1938. No.s 37 and 38 were re-christened *The Crescent* in May. Although it regained its name and retained its premier status on the West Point Route, the train did not regain its all-Pullman status. Coaches continued to be included in the consist between Atlanta and New Orleans.

This industrial development, along with the general economic upturn and the military buildup, had a very salutary effect on the profits of the West Point Route. In 1940, the A&WP posted a profit of $28,790.20,[14] while the Western showed net earnings of $138,848.88.[15] For 1941, the figures were $220,166.80[16] for the West Point and $259,238.26[17] for the Western.

With the entry of the US into World War II in December 1941, and the rationing of tires, gasoline, and automobiles, the West Point Route, in common with all other railroads, suddenly found themselves with more passengers than they had handled in years. The number of passengers carried by the West Point Route rose from 254,716 in 1938 to 1,490,930, an increase of over 550%.

The WofA purchased three Mountain-type passenger locomotives from the Florida East Coast Railway in 1936. Overhauled and converted from fuel oil to coal, they were numbered 185-187 and served the road until the end of steam in the 1950's. No. 186 is shown in Montgomery on April 24, 1951, towards the end of her career. (C. E. Rutledge photo, author's collection)

The *Crescent*, (No.s 37 and 38) had regained its name but not its all-Pullman status by 1940. This is evidenced by the coaches trailing WofA 181 as it leaves Atlanta with No. 37 in 1940. (Hugh M. Comer photo, author's collection)

Freight tonnage also soared. The A&WP's freight volume jumped from 1,075,604 tons in 1938[18] to 3,839,451 tons in 1944.[19] The Western also experienced a similar upsurge.

To handle this traffic, the partners in the West Point Route requested and received approval from the War Production Board to purchase

The Western purchased 8-0 No. 120 from the Birmingham Southern Railroad 1943. It was the only locomotive of its type on The West Point Route, somewhat d in that the Consolida-on (2-8-0) type was the ost common of all types the U. S. The engine is own here in Montgomery March, 1950. (Harold K. ollrath collection)

a total of 125 box cars, two second-hand 0-8-0 switchers (A&WP), one second-hand 2-8-0 locomotive (WofA), two baggage-express cars (WofA), on second-hand coach (WofA), two new heavy 2-8-2, or Mikado locomotives (one

A&WP 218 came to the road from the Detroit Terminal Railroad in 1943. It was built by ALCO in 1923 and was one of the last steam locomotives to retired when the A&WP dieselized in 1954. (C. E. Rutledge photo, author's collection.)

Baldwin delivered two Mikado type locomotives to The West Point Route in 1944, one to each partner. No.s 308 and 430 were the last new steam locomotives purchased by The West Point Route, and the last of their wheel arrangement built for a U. S. carrier. (H. L. Broadbelt collection, Railroad Museum of Pennsylvania.)

for each partner) and four diesel-electric locomotives, purchased by the Western. The equipment was received between late 1943 and 1945.

The Mikes and the diesels merit special attention. The 2-8-2's were built in 1944 by the Baldwin Locomotive Works and were of a modernized USRA design. They were the last steam locomotives purchased by the West Point Route and were also the heaviest locomotives owned by either company. In addition, they were the last specimens of their wheel arrangement constructed in the United States for a domestic carrier.

The diesels (the first on the West Point Route) were

1000-HP Model VO-1000's, also built by Baldwin. The[y] were numbered 1-4 (later renumbered 621-624) and we[re] delivered in October and December 1944. No's 1-3 were a[s]signed to service in Montgomery's Chester Yard while No.[ ] handled switching duties in Selma.

The West Point Route suffered a management loss o[n] July 13, 1944, with the death of Lyman Delano. Mr. Delan[o] a cousin of President Franklin Delano Roosevelt, was Chai[r]man of the Board of Directors of both the Atlantic Coa[st] Line and Louisville & Nashville railroads, and a long-tim[e] director of both the Atlanta & West Point Rail Road and Th[e] Western Railway of Alabama.

The first diesels pu[r]chased by either pa[rt]ner of The West Poi[nt] Route were four Bal[d]win VO-1000 switche[rs] delivered by that buil[d]er in 1944. They bo[re] road numbers 1-4 an[d] were initially assigne[d] to duties in Montgo[m]ery and Selma. No.[ ] is shown at the builde[r]. (H. L. Broadbelt colle[c]tion, Railroad Museu[m] of Pennsylvania.)

[1] "Atlanta Joint Terminals Country Club Given Official Dedication", *The Courier*, August 1930, pp. 1-3

[2] Annual Report, The Western Railway of Alabama, 1929, p. 5.

[3] Annual Report, The Western Railway of Alabama, 1932, p. 5.

[4] Annual Report, Atlanta & West Point Rail Road, 1929, p. 5

[5] Annual Report, Atlanta & West Point Rail Road, 1932, p. 5.

[6] Annual Report, Atlanta & West Point Rail Road, 1927, p. 20.

[7] Annual Report, Atlanta & West Point Rail Road, 1933, p. 20.

[8] Annual Report, The Western Railway of Alabama, 1927, p. 20.

[9] Annual Report, The Western Railway of Alabama, 1933, p. 20

[10] Atlanta & West Point Rail Road and The Western Railway of Alabama Time Table No. 2, November 30, 1930, p. 8.

[11] Atlanta & West Point Rail Road and The Western Railway of Alabam[a] Time Table No. 1, March 22, 1931, p. 8.

[12] Annual Report, Atlanta & West Point Rail Road, 1936, p. 5.

[13] Annual Report, The Western Railway of Alabama, p. 5.

[14] Annual Report, Atlanta & West Point Rail Road, 1940, p. 5.

[15] Annual Report, The Western Railway of Alabama, 1940, p. 5.

[16] Annual Report, Atlanta & West Point Rail Road, 1941, p. 5.

[17] Annual Report, The Western Railway of Alabama, 1941, p. 5.

[18] Annual Report, Atlanta & West Point Rail Road, 1938, p. 22.

[19] Annual Report, Atlanta & West Point Rail Road, 1944, p. 22.

With the end of hostilities in 1945, traffic – both freight and passenger – plummeted. Net income, while staying in positive numbers, plummeted as well. The A&WP's profits dropped from $353,304.88 in 1945 to $106,105.85 in 1946.[1] The Western did not fare quite as badly, its net income dropping from $347,556.42 in 1945 to $231,551.08 in 1946.[2]

In 1946, the West Point Route, along with the other operators of the train, placed an order for enough lightweight, streamlined passenger cars to completely re-equip *The Crescent*. The total car order was for $11,500,000 and included cars to re-equip several other trains operated as part of the Southern Railway fleet (of which *The Crescent* was a part). Manufacturer's order backlog delayed delivery of the cars for several years.

Charles A. Wickersham, President and General Manager of both the Atlanta & West Point Rail Road and The Western Railway of Alabama since 1900 retired on April 15, 1947. Selected to replace him as President was S. R. Young, who had been promoted from chief engineer to assistant general manager some time earlier.

Samuel Rollo Young entered the service of The West Point Route and the Georgia Railroad on May 28, 1916, as an assistant engineer in the office of the chief engineer. He eventually rose through the ranks to the position of chief engineer before being appointed assistant general manager.[3]

Both partners in the West Point Route participated in the consortium of railroads which purchased the Pullman Company from Pullman, Incorporated. Mandated as a result of antitrust action taken by the Justice Department, the sale took place on June 30, 1947. For $21,645 each, the West Point and the Western each got 585 shares of stock in the Pullman Company. They also received several heavyweight sleepers at a later date.

The first road diesel on the West Point Route entered service in May 1948 when Western of Alabama 501 was delivered by the Electro-Motive Division of General Motors. The unit, a Model F-3, was rated at 1500 HP and was initially assigned to the Selma Division. A series of minor fires plagued the unit initially, but these problems were quickly solved and the unit performed satisfactorily thereafter.

Additional diesel power was acquired in April, 1949, when the A&WP took delivery of two Baldwin switchers. The units, No.s 676 and 677, were Model DS4-4-1000, and were assigned to service at Atlanta's Hulsey Yard.

Diesel power for *The Crescent* was delivered in 1949

In 1946, the several railroads that operated *The Crescent* ordered millions of dollars worth of streamlined, lightweight passenger cars to re-equip the train. Delays in production postponed the modernization, and in the meantime, the train continued to operate in what many consider to be "The Grand Fashion" with heavyweight equipment behind steam power. Train 37, raising dust as it accelerates past Fort MacPherson behind the 290 in 1946 illustrates. (C. . Marsh, Jr. collection)

as well. A&WP 551 and 552 were delivered from EMD in August and September, followed by WofA 502 and 503 in November. The units were EMD FP-7's and were rated at 1500 HP. The management of the West Point Route opted for FP-7's rather than its straight-passenger companion in the EMD catalog, the E-8, because they intended to - and did – use the units in freight as well as passenger service.

Shortly thereafter, the West Point Route received several new GP-7 locomotives from EMD. A&WP 571 and WofA 521 were delivered in March, 1950, and assigned to general service. These units were followed very closely by A&WP 572 and WofA 522-523 in September.

The new equipment ordered for *The Crescent* was delivered in 1949 and early 1950. The West Point Route's contribution to the pool was as follows:

WofA 87	RPO-Baggage-Express
A&WP 68	Coach
A&WP 69	Coach
WofA 106	Coach
A&WP 501	Diner
WofA *Alabama River*	10Rmt –6 DBR Sleeper
A&WP *Chattahoochee River*	10 Rmt -6 DBR Sleeper
WofA *Royal Palace*	5 DBR-Lounge-Observation

The new *Crescent* entered service gradually as the cars were built and placed in operation. The new trains were made complete in March 1950 when the observation cars were delivered. The streamlined *Crescent* was – as its advertisements claimed – "A grand new train with a grand old name."

Additional diesel units were acquired in 1951 as the West Point Route continued its transition from steam to diesel power. In February, two FP-7s (A&WP 553 and 554) were received to dieselize the West Point Route's portion of

the operation of Trains 33-34, the *Piedmont Limited*. It was pointed out in the request for authority to make the purchase that the West Point Route's segment of the run was the only one still operated by steam power.

On March 15, 1951, General Superintendent A. T. Miller requested authority to purchase a 1200 HP switcher for use on the A&WP at LaGrange, GA. In his request, he cited an increase in the number of switching hours at LaGrange, the age of the steam switcher then in use, and an estimated annual return on investment of 20.99 per cent as points in favor of the purchase.[4] The purchase was approved ,and A&WP 678, a Baldwin-Lima Hamilton model S-12, was shipped on July 20 and placed in service on July 27, 1951.

With the delivery of this unit, Superintendent Miller reported that all regularly scheduled operations on the West Point Route were dieselized. Multiple sections and extras such as troop trains required the retention of some steam power on a standby basis, and some local passenger trains continued to be operated by steam when freight traffic rose above normal levels. But there were enough diesels on the property to handle all regularly scheduled day-to-day operations at normal traffic levels.

Samuel Rollo Young was elected president of the Atlanta & West Point Rail Road and The Western Railway of Alabama following the retirement of President Charles A. Wickersham in 1947. (A&WP photo)

The West Point Route lost two of its new streamlined coaches on November 29, 1951, on the Southern Railway when the *Crescent*, detouring over the Southern via Birmingham, Alabama, and Meridian, Mississippi, rather than its usual Montgomery-Mobile route due to floods in Alabama on the L&N, collided head-on with the *Southerner* at Woodstock, Alabama, killing 19 people. The A&WP's two coaches, No.s 68 and 69, were in the consist and were destroyed.

Between April and July of 1952, representatives of the Electro-Motive Division of General Motors (EMD) and the Alco

Although the newest Mikados on The West Point Route were most definitely freight engines, they could, and occasionally did, lend a hand in passenger service. A&WP 430 brings train 38, the northbound Crescent, into Atlanta in March, 1946, in this Hugh Comer photo. (Hugh M. Comer photo, author's collection)

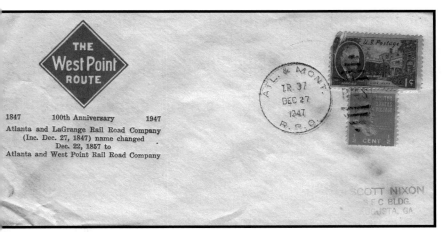

The year 1947 marked the 100th anniversary of the charter of the Atlanta & LaGrange Rail Road, the predecessor to the Atlanta & West Point Rail Road. To commemorate this occasion, a philatelic cover was issued and postmarked aboard train 37, the southbound *Crescent*. (author's collection)

Products (Alco) conducted studies on both the Georgia Railroad and the West Point Route in order to determine just how many units would be needed to complete dieselization of these lines. The Alco representative recommended an additional seven units each for the Georgia Railroad and the West Point Route. The EMD team recommended an additional 14 units for the Georgia Road and 12 for the West Point Route.

After studying the reports, it was recommended by General Superintendent A. T. Miller came to the conclusion that neither report was accurate. He recommended to President Young that the West Point Route purchase an additional nine units which would, in his opinion, would complete dieselization. (It should be noted that even his more conservative estimate was high. The job was accomplished with six additional units.)

Miller pointed out that more units were needed than originally thought due to the fact that the diesels then on the property had – almost literally – the wheels run off of them with 95-plus per cent availability rates. He also pointed out that the units were not held at terminal points long enough to do any but the most basic maintenance and this fact was beginning to show up in increased engine failures. The additional time necessary to perform this maintenance would require the purchase of additional units. Young passed the report to President Champion McDowell Davis of the Atlantic Coast Line and President John E. Tilford of the Louisville & Nashville with the comment to the effect that he felt that even Miller's more conservative estimate was too high. (It should be noted that the ACL and the L&N, which held controlling interest in the West Point Route – and the Georgia Railroad – routinely approved major expenditures such as equipment purchases.)

Miller requested authority to purchase two new GP-7's (one each for the A&WP and the WofA) on July 21, 1952. In support of his request, he cited the fact that the switching unit then being used on the Atlanta-Fairburn turn (called the Atlanta Belt Line assignment) was deemed too light for local freight service. It would be replaced by a GP-7, and it, in turn, would replace two Mikado-type steam locomotives in switching service at Hulsey Yard in Atlanta. The WofA unit would be assigned to local freights 5-6 between Montgomery and Opelika, replacing a Mikado in that service. Trains 5-6 had been dieselized until its unit was reassigned to the Selma Division to alleviate the need for doubleheading passenger diesels on that run. (The diesels were doubleheaded

The West Point Route obtained its first road diesel unit with the delivery of Western of Alabama 501. The 1500 horsepower model F-3 was delivered by the Electro-Motive Division of General Motors in May of 1948. The unit is shown here in Atlanta in 1961. (E. A. Ellis photo, F. E. Ardrey, Jr. collection.)

with several cars between them, not MU'ed, because of light load restrictions on trestles between Montgomery and Selma which did not permit two units to be on the bridges at the same time. This necessitated the use of two engine crews) The higher tonnage rating of the GP-7 enabled the use of only one unit on the run.[5]   The purchase was approved on July 24 and the units, A&WP 575 and WofA 524, were delivered in early November 1952.

From time to time in the late 1940's, the West Point Route had occasion to lease locomotives from its eastern affiliate the Georgia Railroad. Georgia Road engine 255 is shown here on just such an occasion with train 31 near Red Oak, Georgia, in October of 1948. (Hugh M. Comer photo, author's collection.)

Miller shortly requested authority to purchase more diesels. On January 6, 1953, he wrote to President Young recommending that the West Point Route – specifically the Western of Alabama – purchase two more GP-7's. In support of this request, he cited tonnage figures that required the use of three units on the through freights, extra passenger movements such as the Sugar Bowl football specials operated in December 1952 (behind steam) and the need to remove some of the older units from service for routine maintenance, a luxury not permitted by the short terminal times allotted each unit.

Unlike previous requests which had been almost routinely approved, this one hit a snag with Champion McDowell Davis, President of the Atlantic Coast Line. Davis felt that the only purpose of these units would serve would be to prevent the mechanical forces from exerting any major effort to obtain maximum utilization from the existing units.

Miller responded with a supplemental letter dated January 20, 1953, in which he reiterated the need for additional units in order to hold units out of service long enough to perform preventive maintenance and to protect rising traffic levels. (He cited a gravel pit, which would reopen shortly shipping 30 cars a day.) He also noted that Atlanta-Montgomery local passenger trains 31-32 operated behind steam more often than not in the first half of January 1953 due to the need to use the assigned diesels elsewhere – usually in freight service – for lack of sufficient diesels.

Miller also pointed out that the steam locomotives used for protection power would require extensive repairs if they were to remain in service much longer than six to eight months. He summarized his case by earnestly requesting that the West Point Route place an order for two units and seriously consider the purchase of two additional units. Even then, he felt that the road would be short of power in extreme situations.

In the face of these arguments, Davis capitulated.   Authority

Georgia Railroad engine 254 wheels A&WP train 31 past the semaphore signal at Red Oak, Georgia, in March 1948. The engine was on loan to The West Point Route at the time. (Hugh M. Comer photo, author's collection.)

The huge backlog of orders for passenger equipment further delayed delivery of the new cars for *The Crescent* into 1948 and beyond. The train continued to be operated by steam power in the interim. WofA 185 has the train in tow here on February 28, 1948, near Hogansville, Georgia. (David W. Salter photo)

In November, 1953, James Clyde Mixon was named General Manager of the Atlanta & Wset Point and The Western Railway of Alabama. Mr. Mixon came to the West Point Route from the Atlantic Coast Line, where he had come up through the ranks to be General Superintendent of its Northern Division.

One of Mixon's first projects was to make an assessment of the motive power situation. On January 12, 1954, he reported to President Young that, while there were sufficient diesels on the West Point Route to handle all road assignments, the A&WP was still short one unit at the Atlanta Joint Terminals.

He pointed out, however, that there were absolutely no diesels available to use as relief power. A number of units were approaching 750,000 miles, a point at which they would be requiring a complete overhaul. As this would necessitate their removal from service for several weeks, some sort of relief power would obviously be needed. He further advised that with the ongoing development of a gravel pit at Cooks, Alabama (MP163), a fourth unit would likely be needed on train 210 between Montgomery and Atlanta. In addition, Mixon pointed out another reason to buy sufficient diesels to retire the final steam locomotives.

As long as they were serviceable and on the property,

or the purchase of the WofA units was granted on February , 1953. The units, WofA 525 and 526, were delivered in ay. The units, steam generator-equipped GP-7's, had wa-r tanks mounted under the frame where the air tanks were ormally placed, forcing the air tanks to be placed atop the ng hood. The appearance was not unlike that of torpedo bes on a destroyer or PT boat, giving the units, and all like em, the nickname "torpedo boats".

Despite all efforts, passenger traffic continued to decline n the West Point Route. The hrough trains such as the *Cres-ent* and the *Piedmont Lim-ed* did well enough, but local rains 31 and 32 many times ere hauling more crew than assengers. In the face of this ituation, the West Point Route etitioned to discontinue the ervice. Approval was granted n March 24, 1953, and the rain was discontinued shortly hereafter.

The West Point Route re-eived its last new piece of pas-enger equipment in 1953 when he Budd Company delivered oach 120. This car was intend-d to replace the two coaches estroyed in the Woodstock ac-ident in November 1951.

A&WP 677 was delivered by Baldwin in April, 1949. Its initial assignment was as a Hulsey Yard switcher and is shown here at that location on June 10, 1952. (O. W. Kimsey photo)

Diesel power for The Crescent was delivered in the form of A&WP 551-552 and WofA 502-503 in 1949. WofA 502 is shown here in her blue and aluminum dress in Montgomery in March of 1952. (Harold K. Vollrath collection)

the remaining steam locomotives would be included in the planning of the operating personnel. If they were not there, they could not be used and the heavy operating and maintenance expense would be avoided. In light of these findings, Mixon recommended the purchase of two General Motors GP-9 locomotives for the WofA.[6] President Young concurred in the recommendation and the final approval was given on January 18, 1954.

The units, WofA 530-531, were completed in May and delivered in June, 1954. The West Point Route was, by this time, de-facto dieselized, with enough diesel power to handle all traffic except for extra movements and periods of heavy traffic. These units permitted the retirement of all remaining steam power. This was done officially on July 1, 1954, when all remaining steam locomotives on the West Point Route were retired and written off the books. Only two steam locomotives survived – A&WP 290 of which more anon, and WofA 104 which had been sold to the Milstead Railroad years before.

With improved roads and telephone communications, the management of the West Point Route felt that it was no longer necessary to have an open agency every five to ten miles along the railroad, and steps were taken in the 1950's to reduce the expense involved in maintaining these freight and ticket offices that were no longer needed, either by the railroad or by the traveling and shipping public.

The agency at Palmetto, Georgia, (MP 28.6) was closed in 1952. It was followed in 1954 by the closing of the freight office at Lakewood Station, Georgia (MP 4.3) and in 195 by the closing of the agency at Grantville, Georgia (M 54.36). The functions at these locations were transferred to nearby agencies.

Labor unrest, something not commonly found on the West Point Route, erupted in the form of a strike on Marc 16, 1955. At 4:00 PM on that date, 85% of the non-operating employees went on strike, and the operating employees honored the picket lines. For 56 days, the West Point Route was essentially shut down. No passenger service was operated and only a very limited number of freight trains were run.

The strike was actually centered on the Louisville & Nashville Railroad, but the companies of the West Point Route, being affiliates of the L&N were also targeted. The issue, which involved the employees' insurance program was ultimately resolved by arbitration.

Although there were incidents of violence and sabotage – including the derailment of the *Dixie Flyer* near Nashville on April 15th; none of the incidents occurred on the West Point Route. This is not to say that the strike left no bitterness between the adversaries on the West Point Route. The phrase, "a damned scab during the '55 strike" was used as late as the 1970's to describe one of the men who crossed the picket line.

S. R. Young retired as president of the A&WP and WofA (and General Manager of the affiliated Georgia Railroad) in 1956. Upon Young's retirement, J. Clyde Mixon, Genera

Manager of both roads, was elected president of the West Point Route and General Manger of the Georgia Railroad.

The West Point Route, continuing to react to the reduced patronage on its passenger trains, petitioned the Public Service Commissions of Alabama and Georgia on May 9, 1958, to discontinue trains 35 and 36, the by-then unnamed remnants of the *Washington-Atlanta-New Orleans Express*. The carriers' petition stated that the westbound train (No. 35) carried an average of 10 passengers daily while the eastbound train (No. 36) carried only 20. It was further pointed out that many of these would be lost due to a break in connections with the Southern Railway trains of the same number at Atlanta. The commission approved the petition on July 31, 1958, and the trains came off effective August 15th. [7]

On July 31, 1958, A&WP Train 38, the eastbound *Crescent*, derailed at Red Oak, Georgia, while traveling at a speed of between 45 and 50 miles per hour. The two diesel units and seven cars left the tracks. No one was killed or seriously injured, although several crewmen received treatment for cuts and bruises before being released from local hospitals.

The West Point Route received its first diesel road switchers in 1950. WofA 521 and A&WP 571 were delivered in March, followed by A&WP 572 and WofA 522-523 in September. The 521 is shown at Atlanta Union Station in September 1954, while the 572 is shown switching at Atlanta Terminal Station in April, 1953. (O. W. Kimsey, Jr. photo, author's collection) (R. D. Sharpless photo, F. E. Ardrey, Jr. collection.)

The cause of the accident was not determined and the line was reopened by the following day. [8]

Despite the accident and the minor injuries related to it, the A&WP and the WofA each received an E. H. Harriman Certificate of Commendation from the American Museum of Safety for outstanding safety performance for the year 1958. The award was made on September 16, 1959.

The 5-double bedroom, lounge observation car *Royal Palace* was part of the WofA's contribution to the lightweigh *Crescent* pool of 1950. Renamed *Charles A. Wickersham* in 1953, the car carries the markers of the northbound *Crescent* on the Southern in 1954. (author's collection)

After the West Point Route dieselized in 1954, Pacific type locomotive No. 290 (said to have been the last steam locomotive to operate out of the city of Atlanta) was not immediately scrapped and was stored for some time at the Hulsey Yard. Word of the continued existence of the engine got around and a "Save 290 Club", spearheaded by retired Southern Railway engineer E. M. Ivie and Atlanta *Constitution* columnist Leo Aikman, was formed.

Prompted by this group, A&WP President J. Clyde Mix on presented the engine to the City of Atlanta in 1958. The city arranged to have the 290 displayed in a small railroac museum called "Railroad Town" operated at Lakewood Park site of the annual Southeastern Fair, by the Atlanta Chapte of the National Railway Historical Society, the outgrowth of the "Save 290 Club". The museum opened October 5 1959. Dignitaries on the platform that day included A&WI

The *Crescent*, the flagship of the West Point Route's passenger service, was re-equipped by its operators (Pennsylvania RR, Southern Railway, The Wes Point Route, and Louisville & Nashville RR) with lightweight, streamlined equipment in 1950. The result is shown here as WofA 503 and A&WP 554 have train 37, the westbound *Crescent*, in tow just west of Auburn, Alabama in December, 1955. (J. Parker Lamb photo)

AWP 573 and 574 were delivered by EMD in January 1951. They are shown here on train 211 (Atlanta-Montgomery through freight) in December of that year. (O. W. Kimsey, Jr photo)

in 1960. The blue and silver scheme the road diesels wore on delivery (and had since been applied to the yard switchers) gave way to a scheme of solid blue with silver lettering and a red "West Point Route" diamond logo.

Nineteen-sixty also saw the beginning of trailer-on-flat-car (TOFC) or piggyback service on the West Point Route between Atlanta and some of the Gulf ports. This was apparently a joint service with the Louisville & Nashville Railroad and the trailers were apparently loaded on the flatcars at the L&N's Tilford Yard intermodal facility as the West Point Route had no facilities of its own at that time.

The West Point Route was plagued by floods in February and March of 1961 causing extensive damage to the roadbed and interruption of service. The most spectacular incident involving the floods occurred when train 33, the westbound *Piedmont Limited* plunged into a washout.

The two diesels and two lead cars (one being the railway Post Office) went into the Tallapoosa River near Milstead, Alabama in the early morning hours of February 25, 1961. Fireman Jack Vinson, despite suffering cuts and bruises, was able to crawl out of the mostly submerged lead unit

President Clyde Mixon, Southern Railway Vice President [.] W. Bondurant, Leo Aikman, and a Southern Railway Pe-[?]ram Shop foreman named Bill Purdie (who would in later [y]ears become Southern Railway's Master Mechanic – Steam [P]ower under President W. Graham Clator, Jr., and would be [t]he driving force behind its steam program).

The year 1960 saw the West Point Route receive 30 new [st]andard 50-foot box cars and 20 new specially equipped [5]0-foot box cars. In addition, five stock cars were converted [in]to pulpwood racks to reflect the increased traffic in that [c]ommodity.

The diesels of the West Point Route got a new dress

[Th]e units delivered in 1951 were equipped with steam generators that enabled the units to be used in passenger service. The placement of the water tank [fo]r this apparatus forced the air tanks to be located on top of the unit, making them look much like torpedo tubes on a PT boat. This appearance gave them [th]e nickname "torpedo boats". The 574 illustrates this look at Hulsey Yard on June 15, 1952. (O. W. Kimsey, Jr. photo.)

Baldwin delivered A&WP 678 in July 1951. The unit was purchased by the A&WP for yard service at LaGrange, Georgia, and entered service on July 2[?] 1951. It is shown here at the builder. (H. L. Broadbelt collection, Railroad Museum of Pennsylvania)

and walk two miles to summon help. Engineer J. W. Smith was trapped inside the locomotive cab while the waters of the Tallapoosa River continued to rise around him. He was pulled from the cab after being trapped for about four hours and was admitted to a Montgomery hospital with a broken leg and possible internal injuries. Fireman Vinson was also hospitalized for treatment and observation. [9]

On October 4, 1961, a freight train was struck by a tractor-trailer truck at a grade crossing just east of West Point, Ga, causing the the train to derail. Two diesel units and 33 cars left the tracks causing damage to equipment, tracks, and lading of approximately $300,000. Fortunately, no one was injured, and the A&WP filed suit against the trucking company for recovery of damages. [10]

The steam locomotive made a comeback of sorts on the West Point Route in 1961 and 1962. In cooperation with the Atlanta Chapter of the National Railway Historical Society, the company operated a number of fan trips to various points on the line behind Chattahoochee Valley Railway No. 21 and the Atlanta Chapter's ex-Savannah & Atlanta Railway 4-6-2 type No. 750. The trips were run from Atlanta to La-Grange, Newnan/LaGrange, and West Point, with an additional trip south down the connecting Chattahoochee Valley Ry, from there.

The dispatching functions of the West Point Route were consolidated with those of the Georgia Railroad effective February 1, 1962. Under this arrangement, one dispatcher worked both lines from a central dispatching office located in general office build-

ing in Atlanta.

The limited use of two-way radio was begun by the Wes[t] Point Route in the late 1950's. In late 1962, a program t[o] equip all locomotives, cabooses, yard offices, and road wor[k] crews with radios was implemented and completed in earl[y] 1963. This was considered to be a supplementary communi[-] cation system and a safety aid. All primary communication[s] continued to be carried out via telephone and , in the case o[f] train communications, train orders and messages handed u[p] by operators at various locations.

On April 27, 1964, the U. S. Supreme Court rendered [a] decision upholding an award by Arbitration Board No. 28[2] which permitted the elimination of firemen on diesel loco[-] motives in freight and yard service. On May 7, the A&WP [&] WofA began operating some yard engines and freight train[s] without a fireman and by year's end approximately 50% o[f]

A&WP 554 was part of a diesel purchase made in 1951in order to dieselize the West Point Route[s] segment of the *Piedmont Limited* (Tr.s 33-34). The 554 is shown at Atlanta Terminal Station in April o[f] that year. (Author's collection)

eselization of the West Point Route did not occur overnight. Even as new studies for complete dieselization were being conducted and as new units were being ordered, steam continued to work many assignments on the West Point Route. A&WP Mikado 425 works the Montgomery-Opelika local at Opelika the spring of 1952. (J. Parker Lamb photo)

A&WP 575 was delivere[d] by EMD in November 19[..] and was assigned to the A[t]lanta-Fairburn turn, repla[c]ing a switching unit that w[as] deemed to be too light for t[he] service. The 575 is show[n] here much later in her care[er] in Montgomery on Septe[m]ber 2, 1967. (O. W. Kimse[y] Jr. photo)

these jobs had been eliminated.

On December 1, 1964, the freight office of the Atlanta & West Point and Georgia Railroads in Atlanta was consolidated with those of the Atlantic Coast Line and Louisville & Nashville Railroads. The A&WP and Georgia discontinued local parcel, or less-than-carload (LCL), freight operations at that time, although interline operations with the L&N and ACL continued with the use of TOFC trailers in lieu of boxcars for this traffic.

Several staff changes were made in the year 1965. Donald D. Strench was appointed to the newly-created position of Executive Vice President-Assistant General Manager e[f]fective June 1, 1965. John E. MacCarthy was appointed t[o] the position of General Auditor in October, on the death o[f] B. A. Culpepper who had served as Comptroller for over 4[0] years.

Because of rising traffic levels, there never seemed to be quite enough diesels to go around in 1952 and 1953. As a result, Atlanta-Montgomery passeng[er] locals 31 and 32 were operated with steam power more often than not as late as January 1953. No. 32 is at Palmetto, Georgia, behind Pacific 280 short[ly] before the train's demise in 1953. (Bruce R. Meyer collection)

[1] Annual Report, Atlanta & West Point Rail Road, 1946, p 5

[2] Annual Report, The Western railway of Alabama, 1946, p. 5

[3] C. B. Tevenner, ed., *Who's Who in Railroading in North America*, Thirteenth edition, (New York, 1954), p. 802.

[4] Letter, March 15, 1951, A. T. Miller to S. R. Young, ACL File 425, Purchase of Equipment.

[5] Letter, July 21, 1952, A. T. Miller to S. R. Young, ACL File 425, Purchase of Equipment

[6] Letter, January 12, 1954, J. C. Mixon to S. R. Young, ACL File 425, Purchase of Equipment

[7] 86th Annual Report of the Georgia Public Service Commission (1958), (Atlanta, 1959), p. 44.

[8] "79 Spared as Train Leaps Tracks in South Fulton", Atlanta *Constitution*, August 1, 1958, p. 1

[9] "Engineer Jerked From Death in Piedmont Limited Wreck", Atlanta *Journal*, February 25, 1961, p.1

[10] Annual Report, Atlanta & West Point Rail Road, 1961, p. 4.

While the highest speed limit anywhere on The West Point Route was 70 MPH (and that in Alabama), the word was that it was widely ignored on some of the fairly long straight stretches just between College Park and Newnan. That is easy to believe as 551 raises dust as it roars into a slight curve near Red Oak, Georgia, with *The Crescent* on June 1, 1953. (O. W. Kimsey, Jr. photo)

Coach 120 was purchased in 1953 as a replacement for two coaches destroyed in a wreck on the Southern in 1951. It is shown here in Atlanta on March ?, 1969. (O. W. Kimsey, Jr. Photo, author's collection)

As dieselization progressed, more and more steam locomotives were rendered surplus. Some of these engines were not retired immediately but were held in reserve as a hedge against a sudden upsurge in traffic. This view of the Montgomery roundhouse, taken on April 21, 1954, shows three Mikados, two Mountains, and an eight-wheel switcher being stored there, if the numbers on the tanks are any indication. (C. E. Rutledge photo, author's collection)

By the spring of 1954, dieselization was virtually an accomplished fact. Even the lowliest of locals rated diesel power, barring abnormal traffic levels. GP-7 574 is shown here as it leaves Auburn with a three-car local for Montgomery. (J. Parker Lamb photo)

The two units that complete dieselization of the West Poin Route in 1954 were two GP-9' delivered in June of that yea With the purchase WofA 53(531, there were finally enoug units to cover all operations ar permit the retirement of the la of the steam locomotives o the system. Nearly new Wof 531 leads sister unit 530 pa the semiphore mast just west Loachapoka in February 1955.(Parker Lamb photo)

ter years of declining patronage, trains 35 and 36 were discontinued on August 15, 1958. In its later days the train was not much more than a local. ofA 501 leads No. 35 west of Auburn in the fall of 1954. (J. Parker Lamb photo)

Train 38, the eastbound *Crescent*, derailed at Red Oak, Georgia, on July 31, 1958. While two diesels and seven cars left the rails, miraculously no one was killed or seriously injured. (Howard L Robins photos)

A&WP 290 was donated to the City of Atlanta in 1958. The locomotive was displayed, along with several other pieces of equipment, in a small, but well presented, railroad museum maintained by the Atlanta Chapter of the National Railway Historical Society at Lakewood Park. (B. F. Roberts photo.)

Though some of the secondary passenger trains had been discontinued, *The Crescent*, the West Point Route's flagship, continued to be operated in first class fashion. FP-7 554 leads No. 38 with an impressive consist near Hogansville in 1959. (David W. Salter photo)

A&WP 50008 was one of 30 new 50-foot box cars built by Pullman-Standard in 1960. The letters "SEL" on the side indicate that the car is equipped with Spartan Easy Load cargo bracing equipment. (Pullman-Standard photo)

The diesels of The West Point Route got a new dress in 1960. The blue and silver scheme worn since delivery on the road diesels gave way to a solid blue with silver lettering and frame stripe. The 503 is shown in Atlanta on September 30, 1961. (E. A. Ellis photo, author's collection)

The use of four logos on the Geeps, two on each side, was continued after the adoption of the solid blue scheme. The logos, as well as the "Radio Equipped" sign are made of sheet metal and attached with screws. The 572 is shown in Atlanta on January 21, 1967. (J. H. Wade photo. E. Ardrey, Jr. collection.)

A&WP 678 displays the switcher version of the solid blue scheme in Atlanta in 1961. (Rick Jowers photo, C. K. Marsh, Jr. collection.)

The Atlanta & West Point operated a number of steam fan trips for the Atlanta Chapter of the National Railway Historical Society in 1961 and 1962. The train shown here is an April, 1961 trip to West Point with a trip down the Chattahoochee Valley Railway. The train was not turned (although the locomotive – Chattahoochee Valley No. 21 – was), so the markers and the chapter's drumhead sign were moved to the combine, now on the rear of the train, for the return trip. (A. M. Langley, Jr. photo)

VIII

FAMILY LINES & SEABOARD SYSTEM

Clyde Mixon retired as President of the Atlanta & West Point Rail Road and the Western Railway of Alabama (and as General Manager of the Georgia Railroad) in 1966. He was succeeded in these posts by Donald D. Strench, who was promoted from Executive Vice President and Assistant General Manager.

Passenger business continued to decline, both in number of passengers carried and in revenue. To help stem the losses, the West Point Route, on May 13, 1966, filed notices to discontinue trains 33 and 34, the *Piedmont Limited*, effective June 18, 1966. The states of Georgia and Alabama filed protests, and the Interstate Commerce Commission postponed the discontinuance. It was ordered that the trains be run for an additional period not to exceed four months from June18, 1966, and that public hearings be held regarding the proposed discontinuance.[1]

It was shown that the passenger count on the trains in question had dropped to an average of 24 passengers per day each way, and the trains lost $16,990 for the first five months of 1966. Based on these figures, plus the fact that the Louisville & Nashville was planning to discontinue the connecting train from Montgomery, and the fact that the Southern Railway connection in Atlanta had already been broken, eliminating through service, the ICC had little choice but

to approve the application. The decision was handed down on October 14, 1966, and the trains came off in November, after the required interval following posting of notification of discontinuance.

At almost the same time, the Post Office Department delivered another blow to the West Point Route's passenger train revenues. As part of the shift from manually sorted mail to electronically sorted mail, the Post Office Department began shifting the mails from the Railway Post Office cars (RPO's) to bulk transportation via highway and air, using ZIP codes to sort the mail either before or after transportation, rather than en route. The last RPO's on the West Point Route ran on October 18, 1966, on trains 37 and 38, and the already living-on-borrowed-time 33 and 34.[2]

Effective with the issue of December 18, 1966, the operating timetable of the Atlanta & West Point Rail Road and The Western Railway of Alabama was consolidated with that of the Georgia Railroad. The timetables of the two members of The West Point Route had been combined many years earlier.

The West Point Route received its first new motive power in 13 years in 1967 when EMD delivered two GP-40's . The 3000-hp units , WofA 701 and A&WP 726, were delivered in May.

Automobile traffic became increasingly important to The West Point Route in the 1960's. Baldwin switcher 676 leads an interchange cut of brand new 1967 Ford Fairlanes (produced at Ford's Hapeville assembly plant) from the Central of Georgia at Oakland City on April 2, 1967. (O. W. Kimsey, Jr. photo)

The new units also introduced a new paint scheme to the West Point Route. Instead of the familiar solid blue with silver lettering, the new units wore a coat of gloss black, relieved only by white lettering , a red "West Point Route" diamond logo, and a white frame stripe. Instead of the full name of the railroad being spelled out along the side of the unit, the locomotives were lettered simply, "A&WP" or "WofA". This scheme was applied to the older units on the roster as they came due for repainting.

A&WP 726 was part of a two unit order received by the A&WP/WofA in 1967. These were the first locomotives purchased by The West Point Route in 1 years. The four month old 726 is shown in Montgomery on September 2, 1967. (J. H. Wade photo, F. E. Ardrey, Jr. collection)

On October 29, 1967, the *Crescent* lost a sleeping car from its regular consist when a Washington-New Orleans Pullman car was cut back to Washington-Atlanta. This left only one sleeping car line in service on the West Point Route.

Changes in the executive ranks in 1967 included the promotion of Albert A. Ward to the post of general passenger agent, succeeding A. P. McElroy, who retired. Kenneth C. Dufford was appointed general superintendent-chief engineer, succeeding J. B. Wilson, who retired as genera superintendent. E. J. Haley moved from the post of chie engineer to become chief mechanical officer.

The *Crescent* on the West Point Route lost its last Pull man service on February 15, 1968, when the New York-New Orleans sleeper was cut back to New York-Atlanta. All din ing and lounge service was terminated effective the sam date. As a result of these actions, trains 37-38 offered trans portation in coaches only west of Atlanta.

This action was followe closely, on February 25, by th removal of express traffic fron these trains by the Railway Ex press Agency. As a result, train 37 and 38, which as late as 196 ran as much as seven or eigh cars in length, was now down t two, or at most, four cars – usu ally a baggage car and a coach.

In the spring of 1968, D. D Strench left the post of presiden of the A&WP and WofA (an general manager of the Georgi Railroad) to become Vice Presi dent, Operations, of the Louis ville & Nashville Railroad. O June 1, 1968, Chester R. Lapez was elected president of the At lanta & West Point Rail Roa

The West Point Route dropped its blue paint scheme for solid black in 1967. The full-name lettering was replaced by the more austere initials at the same time. WofA F-3 501 illustrates the new scheme at the Montgomery shop on September 2, 1967. (O. W. Cimsey, Jr. photo)

What a difference a year makes! Train 38, *The Crescent*, arrives in Atlanta Terminal Station on February 13, 1967, with an impressive consist including a diner and a Pullman. (O. W. Kimsey, Jr. photo)

and The Western Railway of Alabama, and General Manager of the Georgia Railroad.

Mr. Lapeza was an alumnus of the Atlantic Coast Line, having served as assistant to the Vice President, Operations, for several years. However, he came to the West Point Route and the Georgia Railroad following a stint as General Manager of the Clinchfield Railroad, another ACL-L&N controlled property.

In July 1968, the A&WP and WofA each took delivery of a new GP-40 locomotive from EMD. The arrival of WofA 702 and A&WP 727 brought the total of these locomotives on the West Point Route to four units. Four additional units were purchased in 1969, with A&WP 728 and 729 being delivered in January and WofA 703 and 704 arriving on the property in February.

The last public timetable to bear the names Atlanta & West Point Rail Road and The Western Railway of Alabama (and Georgia Railroad) was issued with an effective date of March 1969. The information contained in this folder remained in effect until the discontinuance of passenger service on the West Point Route and on the Georgia Railroad until the early 1970's.

The discontinuance of passenger service on the West Point Route was not long in coming. After Pullman and diner-lounge service were discontinued in 1968, the only two remaining trains, No.s 37 and 38, the tag-end remainder of *The Crescent*, had only coaches to offer the traveling public. That, plus the fact that the Post Office Department had discontinued the Railway Post Office cars on this run, left the train with very little revenue.

By this time, 37 and 38 had been reduced to local train status. They carried

no through cars and any passengers traveling to or from point beyond Atlanta or Montgomery had to change trains in those cities. The normal consist – or makeup – of the train by this time was a steam-generator equipped GP-7 (the F's had largely been traded in to EMD for newer power by this time) a baggage car and a coach or two.

In light of this situation, the West Point Route had but little choice to discontinue the train and application was made with the various regulatory bodies (the Interstate Commerce Commission and the Public Service Commissions of Alabama and Georgia) to do so. After studying the situation, permission was granted and the trains were discontinued on January 7, 1970.

The modernization of the motive power fleet continued with the receipt of six new GP-40's from EMD. WofA 705-707 and A&WP 730-732 were delivered by the builder in May of 1970.

On September 5, 1972, the A&WP suffered a fairly substantial derailment when train 211, the westbound through freight, went "on the ground" at College Park, GA. Two diesel units and seventeen cars derailed while the train was moving at a speed estimated by engineer Roy Brake at 25 MPH. Fortunately, no one was injured and the accident was cleared, the track repaired, and the line re-opened by the next day. [3]

During 1972, the Louisville & Nashville Railroad, the Seaboard Coast Line Railroad, and their subsidiaries (including the components of the West Point Route) announced

A bit over a year later, on April 4, 1948, No. 37 passes Fort McPherson with only two coaches behind the head-end equipment after The West Point Route discontinued all dining, lounge, and sleeping car service on February 15, 1968. (O. W. Kimsey, Jr. photo)

WofA 702 was one two GP-40's received by The West Point Route in 1968. The unit is shown at Milledgeville, GA, (on the Georgia Railroad) in Octobe of that year. Although the unit is only three months old, it had accumulated a fair amount of road grime in that short period. (E. A. Ellis photo, author' collection.)

the formation of the Family Lines. This was a marketing strategy which emphasized the relationship of the companies involved. It was not a merger, and the companies involved retained their corporate entities, but it did entail some loss of individual identity.

The most obvious loss of individual identity, although not immediately implemented, resulted from the adoption of a common paint scheme for locomotives and rolling stock of the participating carriers. The only clue to actual owner- ship would the reporting marks, as the equipment would be painted in a common scheme and carry a prominent Family Lines logo.

In November of 1973, President C. R. Lapeza of the A&WP and WofA was appointed Vice-President, Operations of the Louisville & Nashville Railroad. James L. Williams was named to fill the positions of president of the A&WP- WofA and general manager of the Georgia Railroad.

Mr. Williams came to the West Point Route-Georgia Railroad from the Seaboard Coast Line. Beginning in 1950, he had worked his way up through the ranks on the Atlantic Coast Line, his most recent assignment (on the successor SCL) had been Superintendent, Florence Division. [4]

In the early 1970's the nation was preparing to observe the bi-centennial of the American Revolution, and the na- tion's railroads were no exception. They were painting lo- comotives and cars in special schemes which featured red, white, and blue paint and patriotic symbols and slogans.

Not to be outdone, the West Point Route, at the sugges tion of W. P. Silcox, an engineering department employee painted two cabooses in a special bi-centennial scheme o red, white, and blue. (The Georgia Railroad also had fou cabooses painted in this scheme.) The cabooses were in th general pool and were used from one end of the system t the other.

The West Point Route received two new locomotives i November of 1974. WofA 708 and A&WP 733, GP40-2's were delivered by EMD that month and were the last loco motives on the West Point Route to be delivered wearin the black paint scheme with white lettering and the red Wes Point Route diamond herald.

In November of 1974, the announcement was made tha the accounting and traffic departments of the West Poin Route and the Georgia Railroad would be consolidated wit those of the controlling roads. The accounting function would be assumed by the Louisville & Nashville Railroa and would be performed in Louisville, Kentucky. The traf fic department would be consolidated with that of the Sea board Coast Line in Jacksonville, Florida.

Simultaneously, it was announced that the remaining of fices would be moved from the brick building at 4 Hunte Street, S.E., in Atlanta to a building 1590 Marietta Boule vard. Located at Tilford Yard, this building was shared wit fellow "Family Lines" members Seaboard Coast Line an Louisville & Nashville. The consolidations and move wer

ccomplished in the late spring
nd early summer of 1975. The
ormer General Office Building
as razed shortly thereafter to
ake way for a state office build-
g and a MARTA station.

With these changes, the
est Point Route was reduced
o the status of not much more
an an operating division of
e Seaboard Coast Line or the
ouisville & Nashville. Its traf-
c solicitation was handled in
cksonville, and its accounting
as done in Louisville. Its new
comotives and rolling stock no
nger bore the familiar diamond
go so long identified with the
ute. In its place was a slogan
nd a trademark which brought to
ind, depending on one's orien-
tion, either a genealogist's newsletter or a Mafia-run orga-
ization – The Family Lines.

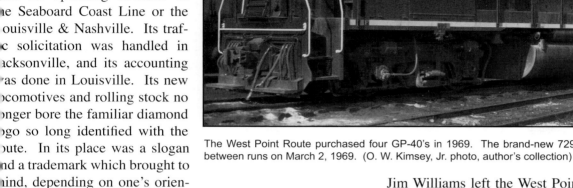

The West Point Route purchased four GP-40's in 1969. The brand-new 729 sits in Atlanta's Hulsey Yard between runs on March 2, 1969. (O. W. Kimsey, Jr. photo, author's collection)

Jim Williams left the West Point Route in 1976 to become Vice President – Operations for the Seaboard Coast Line Railroad. He was replaced in the office of President and General Manager of the West Point Route and Georgia Railroad on May 1 by Millard S. Jones. Mr. Jones would be the last person to hold the office of President of the A&WP-WofA and General Manager of the Georgia Railroad as a separate entity. He would be succeeded in the office in 1981 by Richard D. Spence, who also held the position of president of the Louisville & Nashville Railroad.

The West Point Route received its first new power in five years when four new GP38-2's were received from EMD in 1979. A&WP 6007-6008 and WofA 6045-6046 wore the new Family Lines paint scheme of French gray with a red and yellow stripes and a red, white, and blue "Family Lines" logo with white A&WP or WA sublettering. The 6000-series numbers conformed to a system-wide "Family Lines" numbering scheme. The A&WP units were delivered in April while the Western

Thank you for riding the Georgia and West Point Routes.

PASSENGER TRAIN SCHEDULES

ATLANTA & WEST POINT RAILROAD

W. RY. OF ALABAMA

GEORGIA RAILROAD

The West Point Route (along with the Georgia Railroad) issued its last public timetable in March, 1969. Its cover featured a Santa Fe F-unit and a dome observation car, neither of which was featured on the remaining passenger trains. (Author's collection)

Following the discontinuance of the sleeping, lounge, and dining services, little remained of *The Crescent*. Even the streamlined F-units were traded in on newer motive power, leaving the train to be powered by steam generator-equipped GP-7's. *The Crescent*, or what is left of it, approaches the camera of Oscar Kimsey in Atlanta on June 28, 1969. (O. W. Kimsey, Jr. photo)

Railroad & Banking Company, which owned approximately 46% of the shares in the Atlanta & West Point Rail Road and 50% of the shares of The Western Railway of Alabama, was no longer interested in the railroad business. With changes in the banking laws, the banking business appeared much more lucrative. The bank entered into merger discussions with a bank in Columbus, GA, and needed additional capital with which to pursue this venture. The Georgia Railroad & Banking Company began to cast about for a possible buyer for its railroad properties, which included

units followed in August and October.

The Atlanta & West Point Rail Road and The Western Railway of Alabama, along with the Georgia Railroad, jointly issued their last operating timetable in 1981. It was approximately one-half the size of the previous issues and had an effective date of July 5, 1981. Beginning the following year, the West Point Route would, for operational purposes, be a part of the Atlanta Division of the Louisville & Nashville Railroad while the Georgia Railroad would, operationally, be a part of the Seaboard Coast Line's Florence Division.

As part of a general "Family Lines" upgrading of motive power, the West Point Route received four "GP-16's" in 1981 and 1982. These units were GP-7's from various sources (A&WP, WofA, and SCL) that had been rebuilt with chopped noses and increased horsepower at SCL's Uceta Shops in Tampa, Florida. The units were numbered 4976-4979 with the A&WP receiving the even numbered units and the WofA receiving the odd numbered ones. The 4976 and 4977 were rebuilt in June and July, 1981, respectively and the 4978 and 4979 were shopped in November, 1982, and were the last diesel units received by the West Point Route. [5]

By the late 1970's it was becoming apparent that the Georgia

this stock, as well as the Georgia Railroad. (As mentioned earlier, the railroad properties – including the stock in the A&WP and WofA - were leased jointly to the Louisville & Nashville Railroad and the Seaboard Coast Line Railroad.)

It was reported by sources within the bank that Southern Railway had made a very attractive offer, even larger than the offer finally accepted, but the offer was to be paid partially in cash and partially in Southern Railway stock. As the bank wanted out of the railroad business and wanted to improve its cash position, this offer was declined.

On November 4, 1982, the lessees of the Georgia Railroad, by now themselves subsidiaries of the CSX Corporation, purchased the railroad properties of the Georgia Railroad & Banking Company. The purchase price was $16.5 million,[6] which must rank as one of the great bargains of all time, considering that this was almost exactly the value placed by the Interstate Commerce Commission in 1916

"The Family Lines" was a marketing slogan used by the SCL, L&N and its affiliated lines (including those of the West Point Route) beginning in the early 1970's. A&WP box car 51444 reflects the paint scheme used on freight equipment under this marketing plan. Atlanta, 1978. (O. W. Kimsey, Jr. photo)

n the Georgia Railroad alone, not
king into account the value of
e West Point Route stock. [7]

Having secured outright con-
ol of these companies, the CSX
orporation undertook to con-
olidate all its southern operating
ompanies into one system, and
d so on January 1, 1983. On that
ate, the Atlanta & West Point Rail
oad and The Western Railway
f Alabama lost their operating
entities and became part of the
tlanta Division of the Seaboard
ystem Railroad, which had been
corporated a few days earlier.

In 1986, the Seaboard System
self was merged with the Chessie
ystem (the northern half of the
SX Corporation's railroad em-
ire) to form CSX Transportation,
hich still operates over the tracks
f the former West Point Route.
he corporate charter of the Atlanta & West Point Rail Road
ompany was surrendered and the company was dissolved
n June 26, 1986. For legal reasons, the corporate shell of
he Western Railway of Alabama still exists, although all
perations are conducted by CSX Transportation.

The West Point Route was well engineered and con-
tructed, as witnessed by the fact that virtually none of the
ain line between Atlanta and Montgomery has been relo-
ated, although much of the alignment of the Selma Divi-
ion was revised to alleviate problems caused by the flood-

In the early 1970's, many railroads painted various pieces of equipment in red, white and blue schemes in honor of the Bi-Centennial of the American Revolution. The West Point Route was no exception, painting two cabooses in these colors. WofA caboose 150 is dressed in red, white, and blue at Union Point, Georgia, on the Georgia Railroad in 1978. (C. R. Tidwell photo)

ing of the Alabama River. The Atlanta Belt Line has been
removed for a short distance just south of the former Hulsey
Yard (later an intermodal terminal), although this track may
be replaced if commuter service is inaugurated as has been
discussed by the governor, the general assembly, and the
Georgia Department of Transportation. The traffic created
by the commuter trains would make it advisable to route
freights down the former belt line rather than through the
downtown area.

That the West Point Route was economically viable is
attested to by the fact that
it is still a very active main
line for CSX Transporta-
tion. A substantial num-
ber of through freights
use this route daily, and
from a distance, when
the sound of the air horns
drifts over the landscape,
its not too hard to listen
and imagine that Train 37,
the Crescent, is headed for
Montgomery with its sil-
ver consist behind a pair
of blue and silver FP-7's,
each emblazoned with a
red diamond on the nose
proclaiming "THE WEST
POINT ROUTE".

he final units to be delivered wearing the paint scheme and lettering of the Atlanta & West Point Rail Road and The
estern Railway of Alabama were A&WP 733 and WofA 708, delivered in November of 1974. The one month old 733
ts at Hulsey Yard in Atlanta in December, 1974. (Felix Brunot photo, author's collection)

The motive power of the affiliated companies also began showing up on The West Point Route as well. WofA 702 leads a mixed bag of SCL, L&N and West Point Route power through Opelika, Alabama in the early 1970's. (Carl Ardrey photo)

As the Family Lines concept took root, motive power began to be pooled and West Point Route units were seen in off-line locations. WofA 705 leads an SCL freight in Greenwood, SC, in October of 1972. (J. H. Wade photo, F. E. Ardrey, Jr. collection)

1 Interstate Commerce Commission Finance Docket 24155, "Atlanta & West Point Rail Road Company and The Western Railway of Alabama – Discontinuance of Passenger Trains No.s 33 and 34 Between Atlanta, Ga. And Montgomery, Ala.", Decided October 14, 1966.

2 *Directory of Railway Post Offices,* by John L. Kay, Mobile Post Office Society, 1985, p 21.

3 "17 Rail Cars, Engines Derailed", *Atlanta Constitution,* September 6, 1972, p. 15-A.

4 *Who's Who in Railroading and Rail Transit,* 18th edition, (New York, 1977), p. 427.

5 *Extra 2200 South,* Issue 85, July-August, 1986, p. 30.

6 "Banking Firm to Sell its Railroad Properties", Augusta *Chronicle,* March 23, 1982.

7 *Forty-first Annual Report of the Interstate Commerce Commission,* (Washington, DC, U. S. Government Printing Office, 1927), p. 241.

A&WP 6007 was one of four GP38-2's received by The West Point Route in 1979. They were delivered wearing the Family Lines paint scheme of gra[y] with red and yellow striping and were the last new power to be purchased by either the A&WP or the WofA. The 6007 is at Hulsey Yard in 1980. (R. C[.] Thomason photo)

WofA 4977 was one of fou[r] "GP-16"s produced by the Uce[le]ta Shop of the Seaboard Coas[t] Line for the West Point Route i[n] 1981. They were rebuilt GP-7['s] and 9's and were rated at 160[0] horsepower. The unit is at Unio[n] Point on the Georgia Railroad i[n] 1982. (C. R. Tidwell photo)

IX

SANDHOUSE STORIES

This chapter consists of personal reminiscences and stories that became part of the lore of the West Point Route. They were gleaned from newspapers, contributed by various former employees, and one or two are firsthand experiences of the author.

It is the belief of the author that stories such as these are every bit as important to history as a carefully documented text because in many cases, the storyteller was either personally involved in the tale, or knew someone who was so in many cases, these are eyewitness accounts.

Because the contributors took no notes and were relying on their memories to span the years, there are no footnotes in this chapter.

THE GOOD BOOK

We had an agent in LaGrange, some years ago, named Smith who talked slow and moved slow. One of my first trips out on the road, around 1953, was with W. W. Snow, the General Passenger Agent for the West Point Route. When we visited the LaGrange agency Mr. Smith was shocked to see three men - Mr. Snow, A. P. McElroy, and myself - walk in the door.

Mr. Snow introduced himself as the Passenger Traffic Manager and asked Mr. Smith about some troubles he had been having with his paperwork. Did he, Snow asked, have an agency manual handy?

Now, Mr. Snow was real big on instruction manuals. If there was a function to be performed, he put out a manual on it. In addition to manuals covering specific duties, there was a manual of general instructions to agents. It was this manual that Mr. Snow had refernce to.

Mr. Smith fumbled around in his desk, the file cabinets and the several other cabinets in the agency. After several minutes of searching, he was able to locate the manual, filled with miscellaneous documents and covered with dust. After wiping a substantial amount of dust from the cover, he laid it on the desk.

Mr. Snow asked, "Do you refer to the manual often?"

Mr. Smith replied, "Just like the Bible, sir. Just like the Bible!"

A. A. Ward

Atlanta and West Point Rail Road Company
The Western Railway of Alabama
Georgia Railroad

MANUAL OF INSTRUCTIONS

TO

STATION AGENTS

ISSUED UNDER AUTHORITY OF THE
GENERAL MANAGER

JANUARY 1, 1955

The agent at LaGrange treated the agency manual "…just like the Good Book, sir. Just like the Good Book." (courtesy Nelson McGahee)

PROFESSIONAL OPINION

The West Point Route operated a number of special trains for various special events. One such train was operated around 1967 to the Cotton Bowl in Dallas, with a layover in New Orleans.

This particular train had a consist of twenty cars - 15 sleepers, two diners, and two club cars and one rider coach for crew members.

A Doctor Taylor from East Point made a reservation on this train for himself and for his traveling companion, a Mr. Johnson. The check bounced.

Dr. Taylor was notified by telephone, and gave assurances that he would be at the passenger office with the cash at 4:00 PM that afternoon. He did not show. When he did appear the following day, the space was sold.

When the date of departure arrived, A. P. McElroy and I were on hand to check the passengers in and direct them to their space on the train. Dr. Taylor and Mr. Johnson showed up, expecting their space. Upon being told that his space had been sold, he produced his doctors bag and asked if he could be the train doctor. This was deemed to be a good idea, and the doctor and his companion were sold seat space in one of the lounge cars.

No sooner had the train departed, than doctor set up a casino in his corner of the lounge with all sorts of action taking place. The good doctor was also imbibing somewhat heavily. This continued virtually non-stop all the way to New Orleans.

Somewhere between New Orleans and Dallas, a passenger fell and sustained a fairly bad bump on his head. Doctor Taylor was summoned. Although inebriated, the doctor brought his bag and looked the injured passenger over carefully.

"Un-HUH!" was his only comment.

With that, he closed his bag, got up and left.

The train conductor, Jim Bentley (Manager, Mail and Express for the West Point Route, who was along to help with the crowd) and I were left to put the passenger to bed.

A. A. Ward

JOHN MCWATERS - BALLAST SCORCHER

John McWaters served the West Point Route as an engineer from 1869 until 1923. On the occasion of the completion of his last run, reporters from the Atlanta newspapers asked him if he had made any notable runs. His response was as follows:

"From Opelika to Montgomery, this distance is 66 miles. It's almost dead level and almost dead straight. I drove it one night in 52 minutes. The fastest running time in that drive was 84 miles an hour. They registered that speed in old man Harahan's private car, which was on the train."

"I made another run that the boys talked about a right smart. It was Dr. Crenshaw, the dentist, wanted to make a special run to Montgomery to catch a train for New Orleans to reach the bedside of a member of his family who was dying."

"He chartered a car and an engine, and the boss put me on it with orders to ball the jack. We had a clear track and no stops to make, and we balled the jack."

"From Atlanta to Montgomery is 175 miles. I took Dr. Crenshaw there in two hours and 50 minutes. ...Its an average of about 60 miles an hour, including slow running through the yards."

"Dr. Crenshaw caught his train to New Orleans."

But there was another run that that Mr. McWaters didn't tell the reporters about - perhaps for the reason that it resulted in his getting a speed limit put on his run. Joe Billups [J. P. Billups, General Passenger Agent] told the reporters about it.

"Mr. Mack" (this being the name the old engineer goes by on the West Point) "was handling one his runs on the *New York-New Orleans Limited*. Engineer McDonald had started out of here late one night and made the run to Montgomery in three hours and fifteen minutes. The news of that run spread all over the road. The boys were all talking about it. Pretty soon afterwards, Mr. Mack left out of here one night about an hour late from waiting on a connection."

"The old man took that monster train from here to Montgomery in 2 hours and 58 minutes, arriving there practically on time. That was an average of about 69 miles an hour, including slow running through the yards and including all stops."

"The boss decided he'd better put on a speed limit."

John McWaters and J. P. Billups, as related in the Atlanta *Journal*, January 3, 1923.

TIDYING UP

About the time of the end of World War II in 1945, freight train 209 derailed on a Sunday afternoon in Hoganvsille, GA. Some of the derailed cars contained various flammable liquids and produced some rather spectacular pyrotechnics. Fortunately no one was injured although the derailment created a rather large mess.

After the dust had settled and it was determined that all the train crew had survived, Conductor Sid Howard walked forward to the engine, looked up to the fireman and said, "Lad," – he called everyone "Lad" – "Lad, hand me the coal scoop. We'll spread a little sand around down here and no one will ever know we've been on the ground!"

At the height of the fireworks display, a group of local fellows looked up from their fishing in a nearby stream. One of them was said to have told the others, "Ah done tol' you that we hadn't oughta gone fishin' on a Sunday!"

D. K. Freeman

PRIORITIES

For a number of years, when Georgia Tech played Auburn at Auburn, the West Point Route would run football specials to carry the Tech team and its supporters to the game. This was quite a rivalry as both Tech and Auburn were in the Southeastern Conference at the time and the outcome frequently had a bearing on which team became the conference champion.

Because of this intense rivalry, it was considered great sport to play practical jokes on, and generally harrass, the opposition, with the bulk of the pranks being played by the home team on the visitors.

Around 1948, the game was in Auburn, and the West Point Route, as was its custom, ran a football special to the game. All went well until Engineer Bill Keeler applied his brakes to slow for the Auburn station. Nothing happened. The Auburn students had greased the rails for a considerable distance on either side of the depot, and the train slid, despite the efforts of Keeler, about a mile past the Auburn station before finally shuddering to a stop.

Conductor Cy Roberts walked forward, and after conferring with Keeler regarding the situation, offered this comment: "If I had a boy in Kilby Prison and a boy in Auburn, damned if I wouldn't work to get the boy out of Auburn first!"

D. K. Freeman

RELIEF AGENT

It was the practice of the West Point Route to hire a few college students as relief agents for the summer vacation season in order to allow the agency staff at the various depots to take vacation in the summer. As a rule, the students performed admirably, a few of them coming to work for the railroad full time after graduation. Some, however, were less than stellar in their performance.

In the mid-1960's, one of these students was assigned to the agency at West Point while the agent took his vacation. While his intentions may have been good, his performance was not.

For openers, he billed cars out on West Point and Western bills indiscriminately, not taking note as to whether they originated on the West Point or the Western.

He had cars ordered by one firm spotted at another. These were woodracks and at the time they were in short supply, so this was not a minor error.

He sold a ticket to New York on a Southern Railway form, rather than the Pennsylvania RR form, causing the passenger in question to run out of ticket at Washington, DC. This was corrected by wires from the passenger department to the conductor on Southern 38 explaining the situation and authorizing him to correct the error without collecting any additional fare.

When the traveling auditor visited the agency to clear up the chaos, he inquired, along with his report, as to the status of the relief agent. The response from the operating department was a terse, " Mr. So-and-so is no longer with the company."

RHH from Traveling Auditors file.

TICKET AGENT'S PUZZLE

A young lady stepped up to the ticket counter in Newnan a number of years ago and asked the clerk on duty for a ticket for Magnolia.

The clerk, relatively new to the job, consulted his local tariff and discovered that there was no such station listed on the West Point Route. He then looked in the Official Guide and discovered, to his dismay, that there were several stations named Magnolia listed, on several railroads, and in several states. This would never do.

He then returned to the counter and said to the young lady, "Ma'am, there are several stations named Magnolia. I'll need to know the one that you wish to purchase the ticket for before I can issue the ticket and charge the proper fare."

The lady responded, "I don't know what the problem is. I need a ticket for Magnolia, and yonder she sits, right over there!"

D. K. Freeman

Only one Supplement to this tariff may be in effect at any time.

I. C. C. No. 529
(Canceling I. C. C. No. 475)

ATLANTA AND WEST POINT RAIL ROAD COMPANY
THE WESTERN RAILWAY OF ALABAMA

LOCAL PASSENGER TARIFF
No. 17
(CANCELING LOCAL PASSENGER TARIFF NO. 16)

ONE-WAY FARES

GOOD FOR TRANSPORTATION IN SLEEPING OR PARLOR CARS
—Also—
GOOD FOR TRANSPORTATION IN COACHES ONLY
and Mileages
BETWEEN ALL STATIONS

ISSUED NOVEMBER 1, 1956
EFFECTIVE DECEMBER 15, 1956

This tariff contains changes in fares, resulting in increases, reductions or no change, specific indication of which as required by Rule 28(b) of Tariff Circular No. 18-A, is omitted under Permission of the Interstate Commerce Commission No. 69497, dated July 6, 1956.

The fares authorized herein are in compliance with order of the Interstate Commerce Commission dated February 28, 1936, in Docket No. 26550, as subsequently modified, and as further modified by its order dated May 11, 1956, in Docket No. 31992.

This tariff contains fares that exceed the aggregate of the intermediate fares subject to the Interstate Commerce Act. Such departure from the terms of the amended Fourth Section of the Act is permitted by authority of Interstate Commerce Commission FOURTH SECTION ORDER No. 14500, dated January 21, 1942 (as amended) and Supplemental Fourth Section Order No. 18325, dated May 11, 1956.

Write or Stamp Here

Date Received
File 18221-A.

Issued by
W. W. SNOW,
Passenger Traffic Manager,
4 Hunter Street, S. E.,
ATLANTA, GA.

Try as he might, the ticket agent could not find "Magnolia" in the tariff. (Author's collection)

X

PASSENGER TRAINS

ATLANTA & WEST POINT RAIL ROAD
THE WESTERN RAILWAY OF ALABAMA

The following is a summary of passenger trains operated by the Atlanta & West Point Rail Road and The Western Railway of Alabama at various times.

The West Point Route apparently did not assign train numbers until the mid-1880's, and only those trains with assigned numbers are covered in this summary. It is interesting to note that originally, westbound trains bore even numbers and their eastbound counterparts were assigned odd numbers. This was reversed to conform to conventional practice in the mid-1890's.

Several numbers appear more than once for the same time period, particularly in the case of locals. Please remember that these are two different railroads and it may be possible to have an A&WP train of a particular number running between Atlanta and LaGrange or West Point and another train of the same number running between Montgomery and Selma or Opelika. Also, the Montgomery-Selma portion was operated as a separate division, and numbers could be duplicated between Selma and Montgomery and the Montgomery to West Point portion of the road.

It should be remembered that this list covers only the West Point Route. Dates of dieselization, discontinuance, etc. will differ on other railroads for some trains.

Train No.	Service offered
3-4	Atlanta-Opelika locals. Inaugurated around 1889, these trains did not last very long, being discontinued prior to 1893.
5	Montgomery-Opelika local, eastbound only. Inaugurated after 1888, this train was gone by 1893.
5-6	Montgomery-Opelika locals. Operated from mid-1890's until around 1900. Not shown in the March 1901 Official Guide, or thereafter. Years later these numbers were assigned to Montgomery-Opelika local freights.
7-8	Montgomery-Selma locals. Gone by March 1890.
11-12	Atlanta-College Park suburban trains. The A&WP operated a fairly extensive suburban service around 1900. The majority of the suburban trains operated between Atlanta and College Park, although service was offered by at least one train each way to Palmetto and La Grange. All suburban service operated on a daily-except-Sunday basis. The service was inaugurated on January 31, 1897 and discontinued June 8, 1902, after being rendered unprofitable by the extension of the streetcar line to College Park.
13	Selma-Montgomery local, eastbound only. Operated in the mid-1890's.

13-16	Atlanta-College Park suburban trains.
14-23	Atlanta-LaGrange locals, 1898 to circa 1903. No. 14 had, for a brief period, run opposite No. 27 and originated at Newnan.
15-20	Atlanta-Palmetto suburban trains, daily except Sunday. Unlike 19-22, most suburban trains which terminated and originated at College Park, No.s 15-20 operated farther down the line to Palmetto. These trains appeared and disappeared with most of the other suburban service, 1897-1902.
17-18	Atlanta-Columbus trains, inaugurated in 1907.
19-20	Prior to November, 1928 this was an interline run with West Point crews handling the train to Newnan and CofG crews taking charge of the train beyond that point. After that time, these trains were strictly Central of Georgia trains using trackage rights to between Atlanta and Newnan. These trains were dieselized and equipped with light-weight equipment in 1947 and were named *Man O' War"* after the celebrated racehorse. No.17-18 were discontinued in December, 1955 and No.s 19-20 ran until May, 1970. A&WP tickets were honored on these trains between Atlanta and Newnan.
21-24	Atlanta-College Park suburban trains, daily except
25-26	Sunday(In the late 1890's. Mo. 27 originated at
27-28	Newnan and ran opposite No. 14.)
29-30	
31-32	All-stops locals inaugurated in 1923 when No.s 33-34 became through trains. No.31 operated Atlanta-Montgomery. No. 32 offered service from Selma to Atlanta until late 1932 and again from early 1934 until mid-1942, when the number of the Selma-Montgomery portion of the run was changed to No. 40. (During the period from late 1932 until early 1934 the schedule was abolished and the service was covered by Selma Division train 212 which was upgraded to mixed status for that period.) The Selma-Montgomery portion of the run was downgraded to mixed train status in 1931. Trains 31-32 were discontinued March 31, 1953.
33-34	All-stops Atlanta-Montgomery locals until 1923. These trains were inaugurated in the mid-1890's and operated as locals until 1923. At this time their schedules were assumed by No.s 31-32. The schedules of No.s 33-34 were radically altered and they became through trains, ultimately named the *Piedmont Limited* in June, 1925. No.s 33-34 were part of the through service between New York and New Orleans operated by the Pennsylvania Railroad, Southern Railway, the West Point Route, and the Louisville & Nashville Railroad. They were discontinued in Novermber, 1966.
35-36	Atlanta-Montgomery through trains. Inaugurated in the mid-1890's and called, at various times, the *United States Fast Mail* (1919-1932) and the *New York-Washington-Atlanta-New Orleans Express* (1932- 1936). These trains were also part of the through PRR-SOU-A&WP- WofA-L&N service and handled through cars until the mid-1950's.These trains were discontinued in August 1958.

36-37	Selma Division locals. Inaugurated circa 1903. No 36 connected with mainline 36 at Montgomery. No. 37 changed to No. 43 circa 1907. Downgraded to mixed train status in 1930. No.s of these trains changed to 41-42 in mid-1942.
37-38	The flagship. These trains were inaugurated in the mid-1890's as extensions of the Southern's *Washington and Southwestern Limited*, although I have found no evidence that they carried this name on the West Point Route. They originally were assigned No.s 50 and 53, but were assigned No.s 37-38, consistent with the Southern Railway's numbers by 1895. The trains were named the *New York-New Orleans Limited* in 1906. This name lasted until April 1925, when the trains were renamed the *Crescent Limited*. In June 1934, the name was dropped when the consist of the train was expanded to include coaches. Even with the loss of all-Pullman status, No.s 37-38 remained the flagship, occupying premier status in the timetable. The trains were renamed simply *The Crescent,* omitting the word "Limited" in 1938. They were streamlined and dieselized in 1949-50. Pullman and dining car services were discontinued on Feb. 15, 1968, and the train itself was discontinued on the West Point Route on January 7, 1970.
38-39	Montgomery-Selma locals. Inaugurated in the mid-1890's. While No. 39 ran strictly between Montgomery and Selma, "local" No. 38 connected at Montgomery with the "through" No. 38 to provide Selma-Atlanta service. It could be argued that the train was a through Selma-Atlanta train, but lacking any knowledge of the operating practices of the day, I am not willing to make the claim that the Western created a "silk purse" limited train out of a "sow's ear" local at Montgomery. The connection at Montgomery with "through" No. 38 was broken when the schedule of Selma division No. 38 was changed in 1908. Shortly thereafter the train was abolished and replaced with Train 40, whose schedule called for a connection with the Montgomery-Atlanta local of the same number.
40	Montgomery-Atlanta local, operated circa 1902-1930.
40	Selma Division local. Designation changed from No. 38, circa 1909. Replaced by Selma Div. No. 34, circa 1914.
40	Selma Division mixed. Designation changed from No. 32 in mid-1942. Became a local freight on March 13, 1955, when passenger service on the Selma Division was discontinued.
41-42	Locals. Inaugurated in the mid-1890's as Atlanta-La Grange trains, these schedules were extended to West Point in 1908. They were replaced by buses of the Georgia Highway Transport Company in 1930.
41-42	Montgomery-Selma Mixed trains. No.s changed from 43-36 in mid-1942. Became local freights March 13, 1955
43	Montgomery-Selma local. Number changed from No. 37 around 1907. Ran opposite Selma Division No. 36, 1907-1942. Number assigned to Selma Div. local freight, 1942-1948. Resumed mixed status from 1948 until passenger service was discontinued on March 13, 1955. Became a local freight at that time.

44	Atlanta-West Point local. Operated 1908-14.
50-51	All stops Montgomery-Atlanta locals. Originally assigned these numbers in the 1880's, this arrangement lasted until 1891. At that time number 50 was re-assigned to the West Point Route's southbound connection with the Richmond & Danville's *Washington & Southwestern Vestibuled Limited* (although it did not carry that name on the West Point Route). After that time No. 51 ran opposite a re-scheduled No. 52.
50-53	The West Point Route's connection with the Richmond & Danville's *Washington & Southwestern Vestibuled Limited*. These numbers were re-assigned from locals in 1891 when the Limited was inaugurated. Continued to run as a local between Montgomery and Selma until the mid-1890's.
51	Selma-Montgomery local, eastbound only. Inaugurated early 1890's, discontinued prior to 1897.
52	Atlanta-Selma local. No apparent eastbound counterpart from the 1880's, when train numbers were first applied, until the early 1890's. By February 1893, train 51 had been rescheduled to run opposite 52. The train lasted until the general renumbering of the mid-1890's.
53	Montgomery-Atlanta through train. Operated as a limited on the Western and a local on the West Point. Inaugurated circa 1885, this train had no apparent counterpart until the early 1890's, when the schedule of train 50 was changed to run opposite this schedule. No. 53 lasted only about ten years, being discontinued in the mid-1890's.
54-55	Atlanta-Opelika locals. Apparently operated only a few years during the 1890's. Inaugurated in the early 1890's and off the timetable prior to 1897.
56-57	Originally Atlanta-LaGrange locals, this service was inaugurated in the mid-1880's and extended to West Point by 1890. Operated briefly during the mid-1880's and early 1890's, being discontinued in 1893.
56-59	Opeilka-Montgomery locals. Operated very briefly being inaugurated after March 1890 and being discontinued in early 1893.
61	Palmetto-Atlanta local, eastbound only. Inaugurated early 1893, off the timetable by November 1897.
65-66	Atlanta-Palmetto locals. Inaugurated early in 1893 and off the time table by November, 1897.
97-98	Atlanta-Montgomery segment of the famous New York-New Orleans mail train. Although it carried no passengers on the Southern Rail way portion of the run, passengers were accommodated in a single coach on the Atlanta-Montgomery and Montgomery-New Orleans segments, as the schedules shown in the *Official Guide* indicate. On the West Point Route, 97 made stops in Newnan, LaGrange, West Point, and Opelika. The train operated from November 2, 1902 until January 6, 1907, when it was discontinued due to the failure of the United States Congress to appropriate funds for its continued operation.

Selma Division freight which was briefly a mixed train. This train covered the passenger schedule vacated when No. 32 was cut back to Montgomery-Atlanta between late 1932 and early 1934. When No. 32's schedule was restored in 1934, No. 212 resumed freight train status.

en-wheeler 161 leaves Atlanta with train 31 in 1934. This train was an all-stops Atlanta-Montgomery local. (Hugh M. Comer photo, author's collection)

The 161 with No. 31 again, this time at East Point on July 31, 1948. (R. D. Sharpless photo, F. E. Ardrey, Jr. collection)

In its later days, No.3[] was occasionally as[]signed a diesel unit, b[] as a rule, it drew stea[] power, almost up to i[] discontinuance. No 3[] is shown here, behin[] diesels, at Milstead, A[]abama, in 1952. (Ma[] Lawson Photo, C. H[] Marsh, Jr. collection)

No. 34 was an all-stops local until 1923, when the number was assigned to the eastbound run of the *Piedmont Limited*. It is shown here at College Pa[] behind ex-FEC Mountain type 187 on October 31, 1948. (Hugh M. Comer photo, author's collection)

Trains 35 and 36 were secondary through trains that carried various names at various times until 1936, when they became simply No.s 35-36 with no name. Pacific 280 is at Opelika with No. 35 in March of 1946. (Hugh M. Comer photo, author's collection.)

No.s . 35 and 36 drew diesels on a fairly regular basis after 1951. FP-7 503 and an unidentified GP-7 have No. 35 in tow west of Auburn in the summer of 1953. (J. Parker Lamb photo)

No.s 37-38 were the flagship of the West Point Route's passenger service. They ran under various names at various times (and briefly, in the 1930's, with no name), but the most common names were *Crescent Limited*, and after 1938, simply *The Crescent*. A&WP 38 is a few miles from its destination at Atlanta Terminal Station behind Mike 430 in one of its rare passenger appearances in this March 4, 1946 photo. (Hugh M. Comer photo, author's collection.)

A&WP 290 leads westbound No. 37 at Red Oak, Georgia, on October 31, 1948. With minor changes, A&WP 290 and WofA 190 were virtual duplicates of Southern Railway's famous Ps-4 Pacifics, both classes being based on the USRA heavy Pacific design. (Hugh M. Comer photo, author's collection)

The Crescent leaves Atlanta behind WofA Mountain-type 181 in 1940. While *The Crescent* was all-Pullman north of Atlanta, it carried coaches between Atlanta and New Orleans after 1934, as witnessed by the second car in this train. (Hugh M. Comer photo, author's collection)

ofA 503 leads No. 38 through Oakland City in December 1951. The volume of Christmas mail has necessitated the use of two RPO's to handle the traffic this particular day. (O. W. Kimsey, Jr. photo.)

thirteen-car *Crescent* passes Fort McPherson on May 6, 1952. Included in the consist are four heavyweight coaches and a heavyweight combine. (O. . Kimsey, Jr. photo)

In a publicists dream shot, a solid lightweight consist of No. 38, *The Crescent,* is handled by two spanking clean FP-7's near College Park in February 1952. (O. W. Kimsey, Jr. photo)

No. 41, the Selma Mixed, is shown pulling away from the train shed at Montgomery on February 9, 1947. Shortly after the photo was taken, the cut of freight cars at the left of the 261 was coupled behind the trailing coach to complete the train's consist. (F. E. Ardrey, Jr. photo)

XI

STATION LIST

ATLANTA & WEST POINT RAIL ROAD
THE WESTERN RAILWAY OF ALABAMA

What follows is a listing of all stations known by the writer to exist on the West Point Route. It is taken from the *Official Guide*, timetables – both public and operating – and company station lists. Many stations did not appear in all timetables and some vanished entirely, their purpose for being having been fulfilled or removed. The presence and capacities of passing tracks and other sidings changed over the years as tracks were laid, lengthened, shortened, and removed entirely over the years. The capacities shown are those which prevailed for the longest period. While likely not complete, this list will give the reader some idea of the location of the stations on the West Point Route.

Mile post numbers represent mileage on West Point Route operating timetables after the addition of the Atlanta Belt Line to the railroad and therefore represent mileage from Hulsey Yard, not Atlanta Terminal Station. To ascertain mileage from Terminal Station, subtract 3.5 miles from milepost figure. This will give a close approximation of the distance traveled by passenger trains.

Status as a station stop or a flag stop for various passenger trains changed from time to time throughout the years. The status shown is that which prevailed most commonly during the life of passenger service in the era covered (roughly 1915 until 1970 – 1955 on the Selma Division.) Also be aware that all stops on the Selma Division, except for Montgomery and Selma, became flag stops after about 1950.

Station	MP	Comments
Atlanta	0	Passenger trains arrived and departed Atlanta Union Depot (pre–1905) and Atlanta Terminal Station (1905–1970). Freight trains ran through the terminal trackage until the Atlanta Belt Line was leased in 1900. After that time, freights ran down the Belt line and avoided the passenger facilities entirely.
Ormewood	2.12	Called Ormewood Station in the Offical List of Open & Prepay Stations. Freight agency only (on the Belt Line.) Station established in the 1920's, closed in the late 1970's. Various sidings had 169–car capacity.
Grant Park	3.15	This station was apparently eliminated when the Ormewood agency was established. Sidings held 48 cars.
Lakewood	4.35	Called Lakewood Station in the Open & Prepay List. Various sidings here had a combined capacity of 521 cars. The only tunnel (under Southern Railway's Atlanta–Macon line) on the A&WP is located near here.
Ivorydale	4.75	20–car spur track.
L&N Junction	5.61	Junction with the belt line of the Louisville & Nashville RR.
Oakland Junction	6.55	Also called Oakland City. Junction of the Atlanta Belt Line with the main line of the A&WP, approximately 2.5 miles from Atlanta Terminal Station. Various sidings held 103 cars. 24–hour telegraph office.

East Point	9.95	Originally the eastern terminus of the Atlanta & West Point. From here, the A&WP entered Atlanta over the tracks of the Central of Georgia until 1889, when it built its own track parallel to that of the Central. After 1909, the two tracks between East Point and Terminal Station were jointly owned (one track each by the West Point and the Central) and were operated as double track. Trains were governed by a Central of Georgia timetable and operated under the jurisdiction of a Central of Georgia dispatcher. Various sidings held 109 cars. 24–hour telegraph office. Flag stop for No.s 33–34 until 1923, 31–32 thereafter.
College Park	11.78	Originally called Manchester. Name changed in 1895, when Cox College relocated there from La Grange. Water station. End of double track until 1919. Sidings held 38 cars. Daytime telegraph office. Agency open at merger.
Camp's Spur	12.81	Shown in station list published by the railroad in 1920. No idea of what, if any facilities existed there. Not listed on any timetable in the author's collection. Non–agency station.
Red Oak	15.72	66–car passing track (until double track was extended), various sidings held 14 cars. Flag stop for No.s 41–42, 33–34 (until 1923), 31–32 (after 1923.)
Johnson's Spur	16.75	Non–agency station. Listed in station list issued by the railroad in 1920. What, if any, facilities existed there is unknown to the writer. Not shown on any timetable in the writer's collection.
Mixon	17.53	Station established effective with Operating Time–table No. 1, December 3, 1961, designating the end of double track after the second main had been removed from Palmetto back to this point. Named for President J. Clyde Mixon. Non–agency station.
Stonewall	19.12	Side tracks held 67 cars. Flag stop for No.s 41–42, 33–34 (until 1923), 31–32 (after 1923).
Union City	20.46	The Atlanta, Birmingham & Coast RR (later ACL,SCL, et al) passes underneath the A&WP at this point. This is the basis for the name, Union City. It was at the union of the A&WP and the AB&A. Incorporated in 1908. Flag stop, at various times, for trains 7, 19–20, 39–40, 41–42, 33–34, and 31–32.
Fairburn	22.22	Daytime telegraph office. 76–car passing track(until double track was extended in 1919) 68–car sidings. Agency closed in 1970. Large Owens–Corning insulation plant located here in the 1960's.
Phillipsdale	23.30	Non–agency station. Industrial track held 9 cars.
Palmetto Mills	24.80	Non–agency station. Sidetrack held 19 cars.
Palmetto	28.60	Water station. Daytime telegraph office. End of double track, 1919–61. 43–car passing track, 30–car sidings. Agency closed in 1956.
McCollum	33.67	Sidings held 20 cars. Flag stop for locals 33–34, 41–42.
Madras	36.55	Passing track varied in length from 45 to 125 cars over the years. Various industry sidings held 13 cars.
McBride's	40.63	Flag stop for No.s 41–42. Non–agency station.

Newnan	42.48	Junction with the Central of Georgia Railway. Atlanta–Columbus passenger trains 17–18–19–20 left West Point rails and continued their trip to Columbus on the CofG. Water station, 24–hour telegraph office. Two passing tracks ultimately held 139 and 66 cars, Other cars held 116 cars. Agency open at merger.
Moreland	48.57	Named for Dr. John F. Moreland, first company physician for the A&WP. Settlement was originally called Mt. Zion, renamed Wright's Crossing in 1850, and Puckett Station in 1852. Present name adopted on September 1, 1888. Daytime telegraph office. Water station. 72–car passing track, 48–car sidings.
St. Charles	49.90	Flag stop for 33–34 and 41–42. No passing track at this location, but other tracks held 14 cars. Eliminated prior to 1931. Incorporated municipality ceased to exist in 1935.
Grantville	54.36	Named for Col. L. P. Grant, Chief Engineer (and later President) of the A&WP. Originally called Calico Corners, the name was changed in 1852. Daytime telegraph office. 73¬–car passing track, other tracks held 30 cars.
Trimble's	58.65	Non–agency station. No passing track, but other industry tracks held 14 cars. There was also located here a spur of undetermined length. Flag stop for 33–34 (the pre–Piedmont Limited locals). Station abolished prior to 1931.
Hogansville	61.08	Daytime telegraph office. Water station. Passing track held 56 cars. Station stop for all trains except 37–38.
Whitfield	65.00	Shown in Official Guide tables between 1897 and 1907. Station (?!) stop for No. 41.
Louise	67.64	Passing track held 84 cars, other tracks held 10 cars. Flag stop for locals 33–34, 39–40, 41–42.
Dixie	69.00	Shown on timetables in the Official Guide for about 10 years (1897–1907). Flag stop, at various times, for locals 14–23 and 33–34.
LaGrange	74.27	24–hour telegraph office. Water station. Junction with Macon & Birmingham (1891–1922), Atlanta, Birmingham & Atlantic (1908–1926), Atlanta, Birmingham & Coast (1927–1945), Atlantic Coast Line(1946–1967), and Seaboard Coast Line (1967–1982). The last four represent different incarnations of the same piece of railroad. Ultimately passing track held 255 cars and a small yard held 139 cars. Station stop for all passenger trains. Agency open at merger.
Cannonville	81.22	Flag stop for locals 33–34, 41–42. Non–agency station.
Gabbettville	83.49	Daytime telegraph office. 54–car passing track. Station stop for locals 33–34 and 40. Flag stop for locals 31–32, 39, and 41–42.
West Point, Ga.	89.52	Originally called Franklin, the name was changed to West Point on December 24, 1832. 24–hour telegraph office. Water station. Station stop for all passenger trains. Origin point for No. 42, terminal point for No. 41. 51–car passing track, 127–car capacity yard.
– – – – – –	91.35	Georgia/Alabama State Line
Lanett, Ala.	91.99	Non–agency station. Flag stop for locals 33–34.
Nelson	95.50	Non–agency station. 109–car passing track.

Cusseta	99.90	Daytime telegraph office. Station stop, at one time or another, for all passenger trains except for 37–38. 73–car passing track.
Varner's Spur	101.30	Non–agency station. Flag stop for locals 33–34. Side tracks held 20 cars.
Andrews	105.58	Non–agency station. Various sidings held 52 cars.
White's	106.61	Non–agency station. Listed in 1920 station list. Handled only LCL freight. Not shown on timetable.
Roanoke Jct.	108.54	Junction with Central of Georgia. Central of Georgia trains operated between here and Opelika over WofA rails.
Opelika	110.96	24–hour telegraph office. Water station. Junction with and crossing of the Central of Georgia. Junction, prior to 1881, with the Columbus Branch of the WofA. Station stop for all passenger trains. Passing tracks held 115 and 71 cars. Opelika also possessed a small yard.
Pepperill Mills	111.72	Non–agency station. Industrial tracks held 17 cars.
Auburn	117.22	Daytime telegraph office. Station stop for all passenger trains except 37–38, which also stopped here after 1957. Passing track held 58 cars, other tracks held 15 cars.
Adams Siding	121.24	Non–agency station. Not shown on the timetable. Listed in 1920 station list.
Loachapoka	124.22	Daytime telegraph office. Station stop for locals 33–34, 39–40. 64–car passing track, other tracks held 4 cars.
Notasulga	129.65	Daytime telegraph office. Water station. Station stop for locals 33–34, 39–40. Flag stop for 35–36. 45 car passing track. Other tracks held 34 cars.
Red Creek	134.77	Non–agency station. Not shown on timetable. Shown in 1920 station list. Shown in notes on timetable as flag stop for locals 33–34 and No. 39.
Chehaw	136.10	Daytime telegraph office in 1921 timetable, this station was a 24–hou telegraph office by 1930. Water station. Connection with Tuskegee Railroad, 1860–1963. Station stop for all passenger trains except 37–38. Station stop for 37–38 after 1943. Passing track held 78 cars, other tracks held 118.
Fuller	137.21	Non–agency station. Not shown on timetable. Listed in 1920 station list.
Cloughs	138.98	Non–agency station. Flag stop for locals 33–34, as well as through trains 35–36. Later flag stop for locals 31–32. No passing track, but other tracks held 30 cars.
Franklin	141.20	Flag stop for locals 33–34 and 39–40. No passing track, but various other spurs held 20 cars.
Baldwin Farms	143.00	Non–agency station. 98–car passing track. Flag stop for 33–34, 39–40, and later 31–32.
Hornady	145.17	Non–agency station. Flag stop for locals 33–34, 35-36. No passing track, but other spurs had a capacity of 32 cars.

Milstead	147.68	Daytime telegraph office. Junction, 1902–1911 with the Union Springs & Northern RR and 1911–1965 with the Birmingham & Southeastern RR (same railroad, different names). 93 car passing track. Station stop for all trains except 37–38 until 1923, then became a station stop for No.s 31–32 and 35–36.
Goodwyn's	149.64	Non–agency station. Water station. Flag stop for locals 33–34. No longer shown in the timetable by 1930.
Rice	150.65	Non–agency station. Not shown on the timetable. Listed on 1920 station list.
Shorter's	152.28	Daytime telegraph office. Station stop for all passenger trains except 37–38 until 1923, when it became a flag stop for 35–36 and a station stop for locals 31–32. 61–car passing track, other sidings held 9 cars.
Tysonville	154.33	Flag stop for all passenger trains except No.s 36, 37, and 38. No passing track, but other tracks held 21 cars.
Brassell	156.90	Non–agency station. Flag stop for locals 33–34. 6–car siding.
Oakview	158.85	Non–agency station. Flag stop for locals 33–34.
Mt. Meigs	160.77	Flag stop for 33–34, 39–40 until 1923, thereafter a flag stop for 31–32. 102–car passing track built in the 1920's.
Cook's	162.97	Daytime telegraph office until the mid–1920's. 43–car passing track, 172–car capacity on other tracks until the 1920's when they were removed.
Madison	168.12	Also called Madison Park. Non–agency station. 6–car passing track. 4–car capacity in other tracks. Flag stop for locals 33–34 until 1923.
Boyleston	171.53	Called Vandiver Park until the mid–1920's. Daytime telegraph office. 68–car passing track. Express stop for locals 33–34 until 1923, 31–32 thereafter.
Chester Yard	172.74	Freight yards for Montgomery. Named for Chester Wickersham Kitchings, grandson of Charles A. Wickersham, longtime president of the WofA. Constructed in the 1920's this yard was in use until the mid–1980's when freight classification was moved to the former L&N facility by CSXT. Freight interchange point for all railroads entering Montgomery.
Montgomery	175.00	Yard, Union passenger station. Passenger connection point, in the 1900's with Central of Georgia, Louisville & Nashville, Atlantic Coast Line, Seaboard Air Line, and Mobile & Ohio (Gulf, Mobile & Ohio after 1940). 24–hour telegraph office.
M & M Junction	175.70	End of double track out of Montgomery Union Station. Has nothing to do with chocolates that melt in your mouth, not in your hand, but is junction with Mobile & Montgomery RR, later L&N. Various sidings held 32 cars.
Reese's Spur	178.15	Non–agency station. Flag stop for No. 36 and 43.
Cobb's Spur	180.10	Non–agency station. Not listed on the timetable. Shown on station list of 1920.
Stone's	181.96	Non–agency station. Flag stops for all Selma Division passenger trains. No passing track, other tracks held 43 cars.

Chickadee	182.30	Called Mitchell's until the mid–1920's. Non–agency station. Side tracks held 8 cars.
Cantelous Spur	183.50	Called simply Cantelous after the mid–1920's. Non–agency station. Flag stop for all Selma Division passenger trains.
Manack	187.32	No passing track. Other tracks held 16 cars. Flag stop for all Selma Division passenger trains.
Burkeville	188.96	Non–agency station. No passing track. Other sidings held 14 cars.
Robinson's	190.45	No passing track. Other tracks held 4 cars. Flag stop for all Selma Division passenger trains.
Lowndesboro	193.77	Daytime telegraph office. 70–car passing track. 10–car capacity on other tracks. Water station until the mid–1920's. Station stop for all Selma Division passenger trains.
Latham	197.40	Non–agency station. 13–car spur.
Whitehall	199.36	Daytime telegraph office. No passing track. Other tracks held 41 cars. Station stop for all Selma Division passenger trains.
Hall's Spur	201.23	Non–agency station. Not shown on timetable. Listed in station list for 1920.
Edson's	203.23	Called Edson's Spur until the mid–1920's. Non–agency station. 6–car siding. Flag stop for all Division passenger trains.
Benton	205.88	Daytime telegraph office. No passing track, but other tracks held 23 cars. Station stop for all Selma Division passenger trains.
Minter's Tank	208.67	Non–agency station. Oddly enough, not a water station (apparently it was Minter's tank, not the railroad's). Flag stop for all Selma Division passenger trains.
Rolens	210.00	Non–agency station. 9–car spur.
Tyler	211.12	Water station. No passing track. Other tracks held 39 cars. Station stop for No.s 36, 43. Flag stop for other trains.
Casey	213.15	Non–agency station. Not shown on the timetable. Listed on station list for 1920.
Tarver	216.59	Non–agency station, LCL freight only. Flag stop for all Selma Division passenger trains.
Reidsville	217.63	Non–agency station. Not shown on the timetable. Listed on station list for 1920.
Western Jct.	219.00	Point where WofA trains entered L&N tracks for access to Selma.
Selma Yard	221.92	WofA yard in Selma. Freight interchange point with Louisville & Nashville and Southern Railway. 24–hour telegraph office.
Selma	222.62	Union Station. Passenger change point for trains of L&N and Southern Ry.

The General Offices of the Atlanta & West Point Rail Road Company, The Western Railway of Alabama, and the Georgia Railroad. Located at 4 Hunter Street, SE, in Atlanta, this building served as the headquarters building until 1975. (W. F. Beckum, Jr. photo, F. E. Ardrey, Jr. collection.)

West Point Route passenger trains operated out of Atlanta Terminal Station from 1905 until the discontinuance of passenger service in 1970. WofA 181 is shown at the terminal in 1934. The ornate Spanish-style towers on the terminal building were removed in 1942. (Hugh M. Comer photo, author's collection.)

The first depot building at Ormewood a photo taken in the 1920's. This fra structure was replaced by a larger, b building sometime around 1930. (Cou photo, author's collection)

This brick depot replaced the earlier frame structure at Ormewood around 1930. It is located about a quarter mile north of the previous site and apparently on the opposite side of the tracks. Because no regularly scheduled passenger trains called at this station, it lacks ticket offices, waiting rooms, platforms, and other amenities normally associated with passenger service. (O. W. Kimsey, Jr. photo)

WofA passes the tower at Whitehall Street, Atlanta, with what appears to be train 35. (Jay Williams Collection)

The depot at Oakland City, 1967. This agency was closed not too long thereafter. It was closed prior to the author's employment as Assistant Traveling Auditor for the A&WP in 1971. (C. K. Marsh, Jr. collection.)

East Point Tower, April 2, 1967. The tracks of the A&WP are closest to the camera, those of the Central of Georgia are behind the tower in this photo. The tower was closed and torn down circa 1969. The operations were moved to the Southern Railway building on Spring Street in Atlanta. (O. W. Kimsey, Jr. photo)

A&WP depot, East Point, Georgia, 1967. The agency operations here were combined with those at College Park and the depot was closed, circa 1968. The station building had been razed by 1971. (O. W. Kimsey, Jr. photo, C. K. Marsh, Jr. collection.)

The depot at College Park, July 17, 1970. The agency here was open at the merger in 1983. This agency was billing more business than any other on the railroad in the early 1970's. After 1970, it handled the business formerly handled by East Point and Fairburn, as well as that normally handled by College Park. (O. W. Kimsey, Jr. photo)

The Red Oak depot, photographe in the 1960's, after the agenc there had been closed. (O. W Kimsey, Jr., photo.)

The passenger station at Fairburn, December 24, 1966. The freight depot was a couple of hundred feet farther down the track (behind the camera). By the time this photo was taken, less-than-carload freight operations had ceased, passenger traffic had dwindled, and there was little need for separate facilities. As a result, all agency functions – freight and passenger – were performed in the former passenger station. (O. W. Kimsey, Jr. photo)

The depot at Madras, Georgia, on December 24, 1966. The agency here had been closed for some years prior to this time. (O. W. Kimsey, Jr. photo.)

The passenger station at Newnan stood at the crossing of the Atlanta & West Point and the Central of Georgia and served both carriers. December 24, 1966. (O. W. Kimsey, Jr. photo)

The A&WP freight depot at Newnan, July 17, 1970. (O. W. Kimsey, Jr, photo)

The neat little depot at Grantville was occupied by the police department after the agency was closed. The photo was taken on July 17, 1970. (O. W. Kimsey, Jr. photo)

Hogansville, Georgia, wa served by a fairly impressiv brick passenger depot. Th shot was taken in the ear 1970's, after passenger se vice was discontinued. (F. Roberts photo)

The freight station was at Hogansville was somewhat less impressive. By the time this photo was taken (July 17, 1970) agency operations had been consolidated with those at LaGrange. Note the concrete telephone poles. (O. W. Kimsey, Jr. photo)

he management of The West Point Route was an early advocate of concrete as a construction material. Coaling towers, water tanks, bridges, and even lephone poles were constructed of concrete. The water tank at Hogansville, long out of service, is shown in this July 17, 1970, photo. The diamond West oint Route photo on the side of the tank is cast metal. The tank still stands as of this writing (2005). (O. W. Kimsey, Jr. photo)

The LaGrange depot stood between the tracks of the A&WP and those of the Seaboard Coast Line Railroad. The A&WP tracks are in front of the depot, the SCL is on the higher embankment, just in front of the tractor-trailer rig in the background. Circa 1968. (B. F. Roberts photo)

his train shed covered the tracks at the epot at West Point, Georgia, around the rn of the twentieth century. (Post card, uthor's collection)

97

The train shed was long gone by the time this photo was made in 1970, and was replaced by a tile-roofed umbrella shed. (R. W. Young photo, C. L. Goolsby collection.)

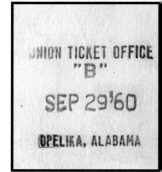

UNION TICKET OFFICE
"B"
SEP 29 '60
OPELIKA, ALABAMA

The depot at Opelika, Alabama, stood at the CofG-WofA crossing and served both carriers. A&WP FP-7 554 leads the westbound *Crescent* into the station in the summer of 1952. (J. Parker Lamb photo)

WofA 190 leads local No. 32 away from the depot at Auburn, Alabama, in December of 1952. (J. Parker Lamb photo)

Train 38, the eastbound *Crescent*, accelerates after exchanging mail sacks at the Loachapoka depot in the spring of 1955. (J. Parker Lamb photo)

he westbound *Crescent* approaches the depot at Milstead at approximately 45 MPH on November 18, 1959. On the opposite side of the platform, the otor car of the Birmingham & Southeastern awaits the mail. (David W. Salter photo)

Two WofA geeps lead a westbound freight train past the concrete coaling tower and water plug at Opelika in the summer of 1955. (J. Parker Lamb photo)

WofA 522 switches an unbelievable amount of head-end business on *The Crescent* at Montgomery Union Station on April 2, 1967. (O. W. Kimsey, Jr. photo)

Chester Yard was built in the 1920's and at the time was considered quite modern. It was used, with some modernization, until the early 1980's. The yard office is shown on June 18, 1970. (O. W. Kimsey photo.)

The coaling tower was a landmark at the Montgomery locomotive shop. It is shown here in the 1950's. (B. F. Roberts photo)

This frame structure served the town of Benton, Alabama, on the Selma Division of the WofA. (B. F. Roberts photo)

In one of the very few photos I've seen of action at Selma, a mixed train is approaching the Alabama River bridge as it leaves town for Montgomery, 1941. (B. F. Roberts photo)

XII

LOCOMOTIVE ROSTERS
MONTGOMERY RAILROAD

Name	Builder, Date	Wheel Arrang.	Driver Dia.	Disposition
Abner McGhee	Rogers, 1839	4-2-0	-?-	To Montgomery & West Point, Same name
West Point	Brooks, 1840	4-2-0	54"	To Montgomery & West Point, Same name
General J. Scott	D. J. Burr, 1841	4-2-0	54"	To Montgomery & West Point, Same name

MONTGOMERY & WEST POINT RAILROAD

No.	Name	Builder, Date	Arrang.	Dia.	Disposition
--	*Abner McGehee*	Rogers, 1839	4-2-0	-?-	Rebuilt to 4-4-0, Pre-Civil War
--	*Abner McGehee*	Rogers, 1839	4-4-0	54"	Rebuilt from 4-2-0, Condemned 1863; Repaired 1865, used in work train service in rebuilding the road following the war.
--	*West Point*	Brooks, 1840	4-2-0	54"	Condemned, 1863
--	*General J. Scott*	D. J. Burr, 1841	4-2-0	54"	Condemned, 1864
--	*J. E. Thompson*	Baldwin, 1844	4-2-0	-?-	
--	*John P. King (1st)*	Baldwin, 1845	4-2-0	-?-	
--	*James Madison*	Baldwin, 1847	4-2-0	-?-	
--	*Macon*	Baldwin, 1850	4-4-0	48"	Damaged by Federal troops, condemned 1865.
--	*Montgomery*	Baldwin, 1850	4-4-0	48"	Damaged by Federal troops at West Point, 1865; Rebuilt; Retired in 1869.
--	*Chambers*	Baldwin, 1852	4-4-0	54"	Burned by Federal troops at West Point, 1865, Not repaired.
--	*Russell*	Baldwin, 1852	4-4-0	60"	Damaged by Federal troops, 1865, Not repaired.
13	*Charles T. Pollard*	Norris, 1853	4-4-0	52"	Rebuilt following war damage, to WofA 13.
--	*William Taylor*	Baldwin, 1854	4-4-0	54"	Burned by Federal troops, 1865; not repaired.
--	*Thomas M. Cowles*	Baldwin, 1854	4-4-0	54"	Burned by Federal troops, 1865; not repaired.
14	*R. R. Cuyler*	Rogers, 1855	4-4-0	54"	Rebuilt following damage by Federal troops,1865; to WofA 14.
15	*Col. J. P. Taylor*	Rogers, 1855	4-4-0	54"	Burned, Columbus, by Federal troops, 1865, rebuilt; to WofA 15.
16	*W. B. S. Gilmer*	Baldwin, 1856	4-4-0	54"	Damaged by Federal troops at West Point, rebuilt; to WofA 16.
17	*James E. Besler*	Baldwin, 1856	4-4-0	54"	Damaged by Federal troops at West Point, rebuilt; to WofA 17.
18	*L. P. Grant*	Rogers, 1856	4-4-0	60"	Damaged by Federal troops at Columbus; rebuilt; to WofA 18.
19	*Samuel G. Jones*	Rogers, 1856	4-4-0	60"	Burned at West Point by Federal troops; rebuilt; to WofA 19.

No.	Name	Builder, Date	Wheel Arrang.	Driver Diameter	Disposition
20	*Native*	M&WP RR, 1858	4-4-0	60"	Damaged at Columbus by Federal troops; rebuilt; to WofA 20.
21	*B. S. Bibb*	Baldwin, 1859	4-4-0	54"	Burned at West Point by Federal troops; rebuilt; to WofA 21.
22	*Edward Hanrick*	Baldwin, 1859	4-4-0	60"	Damaged at Columbus by Federal troops; rebuilt; to WofA 22.
23	*Richard Peters*	Baldwin, 1859	4-4-0	54"	Damaged at West Point by Federal troops; rebuilt; to WofA 23.
24	*John Caldwell*	Baldwin, 1860	4-4-0	60"	Burned at West Point by Federal troops; rebuilt; to WofA 24.
25	*John P. King* (2nd)	Baldwin, 1860	4-4-0	60"	Damaged at West Point by Federal troops; rebuilt; to WofA 25.
26	--	M&WP RR, 1866	-?-	48"	Assembled from parts salvaged from condemned, war-damaged locomotives representing five different builders. To WofA 15.
27	*William M. Wadley*	Baldwin, 1866	4-4-0	56"	To WofA 27.
28	*R. D. Ware*	Baldwin, 1866	4-4-0	56"	To WofA 28.
29	*Uphaupee*	Rogers, 1866	4-4-0	60"	To WofA 29.
30	*Calebee*	Rogers, 1866	4-4-0	60"	To WofA 30.
31	*Savannah*	Rogers, 1869	4-4-0	60"	To WofA 31.
32	*Columbus*	Rogers, 1869	4-4-0	60"	To WofA 32.
33	*Selma*	Rogers, 1869	4-4-0	60"	To WofA 33.

THE WESTERN RAIL ROAD OF ALABAMA
THE WESTERN RAILWAY OF ALABAMA
LOCOMOTIVE ROSTER
1870-95

No.	Name	Builder, Date	Wheel Arrang.	Driver Diameter	Disposition
1	*A. M. McGehee*	Rogers, 1870	4-4-0	60"	Scrapped, 1893
2	*Montgomery*	Rogers, 1870	4-4-0	60"	Sold, 1891
2	*(2nd)* --	--	4-4-0	60"	Purchased from Mobile & Ohio RR, 1885; Off roster by 1894
3	*W. S. Holt*	Rogers, 1870	4-4-0	60"	Sold, 1890
3	*(2nd)* --	--	4-4-0	60"	Purchased from Mobile & Ohio RR, 1885; Off roster by 1894
4	*Opelika*	Rogers, 1870	4-4-0	60"	Scrapped, 1893
4	*(2nd)* --	Rhode Isl. 1887	4-6-0	54"	Orig. Western & Atlantic RR No. 61, acq. in 1891; Sold, 1904
5	*Alabama*	Baldwin, 1871	4-4-0	60"	Retired, 1895, disposition unknown.
6	*Georgia*	Baldwin, 1871	4-4-0	60"	Sold, 1900

7	*F. B. Clark*	Danforth, 1871	4-4-0	56"	Formerly No. 34, rebuilt, renumbered 1878; Converted to stationary boiler in 1886 due to inability to convert locomotive to standard gauge.
7	*(2nd) --*	Rhode Isl. 1888	4-6-0	54"	Sold, 1905
8	*Marchioness*	Baldwin, 1878	2-6-0	54"	Sold, 1900
9	*W. G. Raoul*	Rogers, 1879	4-4-0	54"	Sold, 1901
10	*E. P. Alexander*	Rogers, 1879	4-4-0	60"	Sold, 1902
11	*W. M. Wadley*	Baldwin, 1866	4-4-0	54"	Originally M&WP 27, to WofA 27; to WofA 11; Sold, 1889.
11	*(2nd) --*	Rhode Isl. 1889	4-6-0	54"	
12	*R. D. Ware*	Baldwin, 1866	4-4-0	54"	Originally M&WP 28, to WofA 28; to WofA 12; Sold, 1892.
12	*(2nd) --*	Rogers, 1890	0-6-0	44"	To WofA 6
13	*Charles T. Pollard*	Norris, 1853	4-4-0	52"	Originally M&WP 13; Condemned, 1871.
13	*(2nd) Columbus*	Rogers, 1869	4-4-0	60"	Sold, 1886.
13	*(3rd) --*	Rogers, 1890	4-6-0	54"	Sold, 1900
14	*R. R. Cuyler*	Rogers, 1855	4-4-0	54"	Originally M&WP 14; Condemned, 1878.
14	*(2nd) Selma*	Rogers, 1869	4-4-0	60"	Originally WofA 33; Sold, 1886.
14	*(3rd) --*	Rhode Isl. 1887	4-6-0	54"	Orig. Western & Atlantic RR No. 60; Acq. in 1891; Sold, 1904.
15	*Col. Jesse P.Taylor*	Rogers, 1855	4-4-0	54"	Originally M&WP 15; Off Roster by 1876.
15	*(2nd) --*	Rogers, 1884	4-4-0	66"	Originally WofA 30; Sold, 1905.
16	*W. B. S.Gilmer*	Baldwin, 1856	4-4-0	54"	Originally M&WP 16; Off Roster by 1876.
16	*(2nd) --*	Rogers, 1884	4-4-0	66"	Originally WofA 31.
17	*James E.Besler*	Baldwin, 1856	4-4-0	54"	Originally M&WP 17; Off Roster by 1876.
17	*(2nd) --*	Rhode Isl. 1887	4-6-0	54"	Originally Western & Atlantic No. 61; Acq. 1891; Re# 4; Sold, 1904.
18	*L. P. Grant*	Rogers, 1856	4-4-0	60"	Originally M&WP 18; Off Roster by 1876.
19	*Samuel G. Jones*	Rogers, 1856	4-4-0	60"	Originally M&WP 19; Sold, 1876, as part payment for 2nd hand locomotive No. 34.
19	*(2nd) --*	Rogers, 1895	4-6-0	-?-	Renumbered WofA 8.
20	*Native*	M&WP RR, 1858	4-4-0	60"	Originally M&WP 20; Off Roster by 1876.
21	*B. S. Bibb*	Baldwin, 1859	4-4-0	54"	Condemned, 1878.
22	*Edw. Hanrick*	Baldwin, 1859	4-4-0	60"	Originally M&WP 22; Rebuilt, 1878; Renumbered 29, 1884.
23	*Richard Peters*	Baldwin, 1859	4-4-0	54"	Originally M&WP 23; Sold, 1879.
24	*John Caldwell*	Baldwin, 1860	4-4-0	60"	Originally M&WP 24; Sold, 1879.
25	*John P. King*	Baldwin, 1860	4-4-0	60"	Originally M&WP 25; Condemned, 1876.

26	--	M&WP RR, 1866	-?-	48"	Originally M&WP 26; Off Roster by 1876.
27	W. M. Wadley	Baldwin, 1866	4-4-0	56"	Originally M&WP 27; Renumbered 11, 1882.
28	R. D. Ware	Baldwin, 1866	4-4-0	56"	Originally M&WP 28; Renumbered 12, 1882.
29	Uhaupee	Rogers, 1866	4-4-0	60"	Originally M&WP 29; Sold to Mobile & Girard RR in 1881.
29	(2nd) --	Baldwin, 1859	4-4-0	60"	Orig. M&WP 22; Sold, 1887.
30	Calebee	Rogers, 1866	4-4-0	60"	Originally M&WP 30; Sold, 1881.
30	(2nd) --	Rogers, 1884	4-4-0	66"	Re# WofA 15.
31	Savannah	Rogers, 1869	4-4-0	60"	Originally M&WP 31; Sold, 1881.
31	(2nd) --	Rogers, 1884	4-4-0	66"	Re# WofA 16.
32	Columbus	Rogers, 1869	4-4-0	60"	Originally M&WP 32; Renumbered 13, 1883.
32	(2nd) --	Rogers, 1864	4-4-0	60"	Orig. US Military RR 118; Acq. from Mobile & Ohio RR, 1885; Re# WofA 2.
33	Selma	Rogers, 1869	4-4-0	60"	Originally M&WP 33; Renumbered 14, 1883.
33	(2nd) --	Norris, 1864	4-4-0	54"	Orig. US Military RR 169; Acq. from Mobile & Ohio RR, 1885; Re# WofA 3.
34	F. B. Clark	Danforth, 1871	4-4-0	56"	Purchased 2nd hand,1876; Rebuilt and renumbered 7, 1878.
34	(2nd) --	Norris, 1864	4-4-0	54"	Orig. US Military RR 169; Acq. from Mobile & Ohio RR, 1885; Re# WofA 33, 1890.

THE WESTERN RAILWAY OF ALABAMA
STEAM LOCOMOTIVE ROSTER
1890-1954

Road No.	Wheel Arr.	Builder, Date	Builders Number	Driver Dia.	Tractive Effort Weight	Remarks
1	0-6-0	Rogers, 1906	40406	52"	25,490 118,000	Re# 101 in 1907.
2	0-6-0	Rogers, 1903	5975	52"	25,490 118,000	Re# 102 in 1907.
3	0-6-0	Rogers, 1903	5976	52"	25,490 118,000	Re# 103 in 1907.
4	0-6-0	Rogers, 1905	6259	52"	25,490 118,000	Re# 104 in 1907.
5	0-6-0	Rogers, 1896	5121	51"	-?-, 98,000	Sold to Georgia Car & Loco. Co., to Shelby Iron Co., Shelby, AL, #5, 5-25-17.
6	0-6-0	Rogers, 1890	4275	52"	-?-, 89,000	Sold to Ga. Car & Loco. Co., 1912; to New Orleans, Mobile & Chicago RR, 3-26-12
8	4-6-0	Rogers, 1895	5050	54"	-?-, 115,000	Sold to Ga. Car & Loco. Co., to Gainesville Midland Ry, No. 101, 9-1907.
9	4-6-0	Rogers, 1903	5898	61"	34,400 180,800	Re# 126 in 1907.

No.	Type	Builder, Year	Serial	Drivers	Weight	Notes
10	4-6-0	Rogers, 1903	5899	61"	34,400 180,800	Re# 127 in 1907.
11	4-6-0	Rogers, 1904	6246	61"	34,400 180,800	Re# 128 in 1907.
12	4-6-0	Rogers, 1900	5617	67"	25,070 162,500	Rebuilt to No. 175 in 1926.
15	4-6-0	Rogers, 1906	40202	78"	26,900 193,200	Mis-lettered A&WP at builder, re-lettered WofA; Re# 160, 1907.
16	4-4-0	Rogers, 1892	13063	66"	15,784 108,000	Sold to Ala., Tenn. & Northern RR.
17	4-6-0	Rogers, 1899	5472	72"	23,300 154,000	Re# 170 in 1907.
18	4-4-0	Baldwin,1895	14337	72"	14,688 103,000	Scrapped, 1923.
19	4-6-0	Rogers, 1903	5977	72"	23,300 159,000	Re# 171 in 1907.

Locomotive classifications were assigned with the 1907 general renumbering.

Class E 52 19/24 25.5

No.	Type	Builder, Year	Serial	Drivers	Weight	Notes
100	0-6-0	Rogers, 1907	43023	52"	25,490 118,000	Scrapped, 7-31-47.
101	0-6-0	Rogers, 1906	40406	52"	25,490 118,000	Sold, 1945, to Atlanta, Stone Mountain & Lithonia RR
102	0-6-0	Rogers, 1903	5975	52"	25,490 118,000	Retired 7-11-50.
103	0-6-0	Rogers, 1903	5976	52"	25,490 118,000	Scrapped 7-31-39.
104	0-6-0	Rogers, 1905	6259	52"	25,490 118,000	Sold, 1948, to Milstead RR. On display, Conyers, GA, as Milstead RR No. 104.
105	0-6-0	Cooke, 1910	48023	52"	25,490 118,000	Scrapped, 3-25-47.

Class G 52 25/28 50.0

No.	Type	Builder, Year	Serial	Drivers	Weight	Notes
115	0-8-0	Pittsburgh,1918	61036	51"	51,040 214,000	Retired, 7-1-54.

Class C 53 23/28 45.1

No.	Type	Builder, Year	Serial	Drivers	Weight	Notes
120	2-8-0	Richmond, 1913	53278	53"	45,134 205,000	Purchased from Birmingham Southern RR (No. 387), 1943; Retired, 7-31-51.

Class A 61 21/28 34.4

No.	Type	Builder, Year	Serial	Drivers	Weight	Notes
125	4-6-0	Rogers, 1907	43022	61"	34,400 180,800	Sold to Meridian & Bigbee River RR (No.125), 1936.
126	4-6-0	Rogers, 1903	5898	61"	34,400 180,800	Scrapped, 2-25-38.
127	4-6-0	Rogers, 1903	5899	61"	34,400 180,000	Rebuilt with piston valves; retired, 2-25-52.
128	4-6-0	Rogers, 1904	6246	62"	34,400 180,800	Rebuilt with piston valves; retired, 7-31-51.
129	4-6-0	Richmond, 1911	49686	61"	34,400 180,800	Destroyed, 1-31-45, in wreck.
130	4-6-0	Richmond, 1912	50959	61"	34,400 180,800	Retired, 12-31-45.
131	4-6-0	Richmond, 1913	52945	61"	34,400 180,800	Rebuilt with piston valves; retired, 7-28-52.

Class P 72 22/28 32.0

No.	Type	Builder, Year	Serial	Drivers	Weight	Notes
150	4-6-2	Rogers, 1907	43025	72"	32,000 212,000	Rebuilt, 1922, Re# 152.
151	4-6-2	Richmond, 1910	48868	72"	32,000 220,000	Rebuilt, 1923, same number.

Class P 72 23/28 35.0

| 151 | 4-6-2 | Richmond, 1910 | 48868 | 72" | 35,000 | 236,300 | As rebuilt; Sold to Georgia RR (No. 252), 1934. |
| 152 | 4-6-2 | Rogers, 1907 | 43025 | 72" | 35,000 | 236,300 | Ex-No. 150; Sold to Georgia RR (No. 253), 1934. |

Class A 78 21/28 26.9

| 160 | 4-6-0 | Rogers, 1906 | 40402 | 78" | 26,900 | 193,200 | Rebuilt, 1924; Re# 161. |

Class A 74 22/28 31.2

| 161 | 4-6-0 | Rogers, 1906 | 40202 | 74" | 31,200 | 198,500 | Retired, 3-11-53. |

Class A 72 20/26 23.3

| 170 | 4-6-0 | Rogers, 1899 | 5472 | 72" | 23,300 | 158,000 | Rebuilt, 1928. |
| 171 | 4-6-0 | Rogers, 1903 | 5977 | 72" | 23,300 | 158,000 | Rebuilt, 1924; Re# 173. |

Class A 72 21/26 27.1

170	4-6-0	Rogers, 1899	5472	72"	27,072	185,000	As rebuilt, 1928; Retired, 2-28-38.
173	4-6-0	Rogers, 1903	5977	72"	27,072	185,000	Ex-No. 171; Retired, 2-28-38.
175	4-6-0	Rogers, 1903	5617	72"	27,072	185,000	Ex-No. 12, as rebuilt, 1926; Later rebuilt for freight service.

Class A 61 21/28 34.4

| 175 | 4-6-0 | Rogers, 1903 | 5617 | 61" | 24,400 | 186,000 | As rebuilt for freight svc. Retired, 2-25-52 |

Class M69 27/28 47.8

| 180 | 4-8-2 | Richmond, 1920 | 62594 | 69" | 47,800 | 316,000 | Retired, 7-1-54. |
| 181 | 4-8-2 | Richmond, 1920 | 62595 | 69" | 47,800 | 316,000 | Retired, 2-25-52. |

Class M 73 26/28 44.1

185	4-8-2	Schen., 1924	65749	73"	44,079	315,200	Purch. from Florida East Coast Ry (No. 402), 1936; Retired, 7-1-54.
186	4-8-2	Schen., 1924	65766	73"	44,079	315,200	Purch. from Florida East Coast Ry (No. 419), 1936; Retired, 7-1-54.
187	4-8-2	Schen., 1924	65765	73"	44,079	318,500	Purch. from Florida East Coast Ry (No. 418), 1936; Equipped with Worthington Feedwater Heater; Retired, 7-1-54.

Class P 74 27/28 46.9

| 190 | 4-6-2 | Lima, 1926 | 7009 | 74" | 46,900 | 303,500 | Retired, 7-1-54. |

Class F 63 27/30 53.1

300	2-8-2	Lima, 1918	5691	63"	53,100	283,000	Renumbered 350 to avoid conflict with GaRR 300 which might be operating on the West Point Route.
301	2-8-2	Lima, 1918	5692	63"	53,100	283,000	Renumbered 351 to avoid conflict with GaRR 301 which might be operating on the West Point Route.
350	2-8-2	Lima, 1918	5691	63"	53,100	283,000	Retired, 7-1-54.
351	2-8-2	Lima, 1918	5692	63"	53,100	283,000	Retired, 7-1-54.

Class F 63 26/30 54.7

375	2-8-2	Lima, 1923	6731	63"	54,700	292,000	Retired, 5-28-53.
376	2-8-2	Lima, 1923	6732	63"	54,700	292,000	Retired, 7-1-54.
377	2-8-2	Lima, 1925	6930	63"	54,700	292,000	Retired, 5-5-52.
378	2-8-2	Lima, 1925	7005	63"	54,700	292,000	Retired, 7-1-54.

Class F 63 27/32 63.0

380	2-8-2	Baldwin, 1944	70888	63"	63,000	333,800	Retired, 7-1-54.

ROGERS LOCOMOTIVE WORKS,

ofA 5 was delivered by Rogers in 1896 and sold to Georgia Car & Locomotive Co. in 1917. (Harold K. Vollrath collection.)

ofA 12, shown here in Atlanta in June, 1916, was built by Rogers in 1900. (Earl E. Schlachter photo)

WofA 16 was sold to the Alabama, Tennessee & Northern Railroad, which renumbered the engine to No. 91 simply by rotating the number plate 180 degrees. The engine is shown here at York, Alabama, July 23, 1937, years after h glory days on the point of mail train 97. (William Monypeny photo, author's collection)

WofA 101 switches an L&N Jim Crow combine at Selma, 1939. This locomotive was sold to the Atlanta, Stone Mountain & Lithonia RR in 1945. (B. F. Roberts photo)

0-6-0 No. 103 was built by Rogers in 1903 and scrapped in 1939. Shown here at Selma, July 7, 1938. (George Votava photo)

WofA 104 was sold to the Milstead RR in 1948. The locomotive is shown here at work for that carrier at Milstead, GA, October 12, 1956. It is now on display near the former Georgia Railroad depot at Conyers, GA. (W. F. Beckum, Jr. photo.)

Switcher 105 was delivered by Cooke in 1910, and scrapped in 1947. (Author's collection)

WofA 115 was one of two USRA 0-8-0's on the West Point Route. Delivered in 1918, the locomotive was retired July 1, 1954. Photographed in Montgomery, November, 1950. (Harold K. Vollrath collection)

Name	Builder, Date	Wheel Arrang.	Driver Dia.	Disposition
Joel W. Terrell	Norris, 1851	4-4-0	54"	To A&WP Joel W. Terrell
E. Y. Hill	Norris, 1852	4-4-0	54"	To A&WP E. Y. Hill
F. C Arms	Norris, 1852	4-4-0	54"	To A&WP F. C. Arms
Patriot	Norris, 1852	4-4-0	53"	To A&WP Patriot
West Point	Rogers, 1854	4-4-0	60"	To A&WP No. 1
E. L. Ellsworth	Rogers, 1854	4-4-0	60"	To A&WP No. 2
Telegraph	Rogers, 1855	4-4-0	60"	To A&WP No. 3
Post Boy	Rogers, 1855	4-4-0	60"	To A&WP No. 4
George R. Gilmer	Rogers, 1856	4-4-0	54"	To A&WP No. 5
A. J. Berry	Rogers, 1857	4-4-0	60"	To A&WP No. 6
J. McLendon	Rogers, 1857	4-4-0	60"	To A&WP No. 7
John E. Robinson	Rogers, 1858	4-4-0	54"	Delivered after change of name to Atlanta & West Point RR; to A&WP No. 8

Consolidation type No. 12 was the only example of wheel arrangement on the West Point Route. It was purchased from the Birmingham Southern Railroad 1943 and was retired June 31, 1951. It is shown here in Montgomery in December 1950. (F. E. Ardrey, Jr. photo)

WofA 152 was rebuilt from No. 150 in 1922 and sold to the Georgia Railroad as their No. 253. Hulsey Yard, Atlanta, 1934. (Author's collection)

No.	Name	Builder, Date	Wheel Arrang.	Driver Dia.	Remarks
-	Joel W. Terrell	Norris, 1851	4-4-0	54"	Off Roster by 1868
-	E. Y. Hill	Norris, 1852	4-4-0	54"	Off Roster by 1868
-	F. C. Arms	Norris, 1852	4-4-0	54"	Off Roster by 1868
-	Patriot	Norris, 1853	4-4-0	54"	Off Roster by 1868
1	West Point	Rogers, 1854	4-4-0	60"	Off Roster by 1880
2	E. L. Ellsworth	Rogers, 1854	4-4-0	60"	Off Roster by 1880
3	Telegraph	Rogers, 1855	4-4-0	60"	Off Roster by 1881
4	Post Boy	Rogers, 1855	4-4-0	60"	Off Roster by 1881
5	George R. Gilmer	Rogers, 1856	4-4-0	54"	Off Roster by 1880
6	A. J. Berry	Rogers, 1857	4-4-0	60"	Off Roster by 1880
7	J. McLendon	Rogers, 1857	4-4-0	60"	Off Roster by 1879
8	John E. Robinson	Rogers, 1858	4-4-0	54"	Ordered by A&LaG but delivered to A&WP; Off Roster by 1880.
9	P. Stovall	Norris, 1859	4-4-0	54"	Off Roster by 1880
10	O. A. Bull	Baldwin, 1859	4-4-0	54"	Off Roster by 1880
11	Atlanta	Norris, 1860	4-4-0	54"	Off Roster by 1881
12	Dr. Thompson	Rogers, 1860	4-4-0	54"	Off Roster by 1881
13	F. Phinizy	New Jersey, 1866	4-4-0	60"	Off Roster by 1884
14	R. Peters	New Jersey, 1866	4-4-0	60"	Off Roster by 1884
15	Newnan	Rogers, 1869	4-4-0	56"	Sold, 1888
16	LaGrange	Rogers, 1870	4-4-0	56"	Retired, 1886
17	Gate City	Baldwin, 1870	0-4-0	48"	Off Roster, 1888
18	Fulton	Rogers, 1870	4-4-0	56"	Off Roster, 1888
19	Troup	Rogers, 1870	4-4-0	56"	Off Roster, 1888
20	Dr. John F. Moreland	Grant, 1873	4-4-0	56"	Retired, 1897
21	L. B. Lovelace	Grant, 1873	4-4-0	56"	Sold to Chattahoochee Valley Railway, 1898.
22	John P. King	Baldwin, 1879	4-4-0	48"	Rebuilt, 1897; Re# 23 (2nd)
23	L. P. Grant	Baldwin, 1879	4-4-0	48"	Off Roster, 1895
23	(2nd) -----	Baldwin, 1879	4-4-0	51"	No. 22, as rebuilt; Sold, 1902, to Aberdeen & Ashboro #23; to Ga. Car & Loco. Co.; to Fellsmere RR,#101, Sebastian, Fla., 4-20-12.
24	W. P. Berry	Baldwin, 1880	4-4-0	51"	Sold, 1899
25	B. C. Yancy	Baldwin, 1880	4-4-0	51"	Off Roster, 1900
26	J. S. Bigby	Baldwin, 1881	4-4-0	57"	Sold, 1904, to Flowers Lbr. Co.
27	W. P. Orme	Baldwin, 1881	4-4-0	57"	Sold to S.S. Betts Co.
28	D. N. Speer	Baldwin, 1881	4-4-0	57"	Sold to Geneva Lbr Co.
29	-----	Rogers, 1890	4-6-0	54"	Sold, 1902
30	-----	Rhode Isl.1888	4-6-0	48"	Sold, 1906, to Ga. Car & Loco. Co., to Birmingham & Atlantic #17, 8-1907.
31	-----	Rhode Isl. 1888	4-6-0	48"	Sold, 1904
32	-----	Baldwin, 1891	4-4-0		Retired, 1916
33	-----	Norris, 1864	4-4-0	54"	Orig. US Military RR 171; Acq. from

33	(2nd)-----	Baldwin, 1891	4-4-0	66"	Mobile & Ohio RR, 1885; Re# 34 (1st) Retired, 1923
34	-----	Norris, 1864	4-4-0	54"	Orig. US Military RR 171; Acq. from Mobile & Ohio RR 1885; previously numbered A&WP 33; Re# 36 (2nd).
34	(2nd)-----	Baldwin, 1891	4-4-0	66"	Retired, 1912
35	-----	Norris, 1864	4-4-0	54"	Orig. US Military RR 177; Acq. from Mobile & Ohio RR 1885; Re# 37 (2nd)
35	(2nd)-----	Baldwin, 1891	0-6-0	44"	Retired, 1911
36	-----	Rhode Isl. 1888	4-6-0	48"	Re# A&WP 30
36	(2nd)-----	Norris, 1864	4-4-0	54"	Orig. US Military RR 171; Acq. from Mobile & Ohio RR, 1885 as A&WP 33; (1st); Re# 34 (1st) then Re# 36 (2nd) off roster in 1894
37	-----	Rhode Isl. 1888	4-6-0	48"	Re# A&WP 30
37	(2nd)-----	Norris, 1864	4-4-0	54"	Orig. US Military RR 177; Acq. from Mobile & Ohio RR, 1885 as A&WP 35 (1st), Re# 37 (2nd); Off roster, 1894.

Ten-Wheeler 161 was rebuilt from No. 160 in 1924 and retired in 1953. Shown here at Montgomery Union Station in 1940. (Hugh M. Comer photo, author's collection)

ATLANTA & WEST POINT RAILROAD
STEAM LOCOMOTIVE ROSTER
1895 – 1954

West Point Route steam locomotive classification designation carried on each locomotive cab side just below the road number. It consisted of a letter designation of the wheel arrangement, the driving wheel diameter, the cylinder bore and stroke stated as a fraction, and the tractive effort, stated in thousands of pounds. It was similar but not identical to a system used by the Missouri Pacific Railroad.

The letter codes were as follows:

A – 4-6-0   (Ten-Wheeler)
B – 2-6-0   (Mogul)
C – 4-4-0   (American), also 2-8-0 (Consolidation)*
E – 0-6-0   (Six-wheel Switcher)
F – 2-8-2   (Mikado)
G – 0-8-0   (Eight-wheel Switcher)
P – 4-6-2   (Pacific)

Thus, a locomotive with the designation A61 21/28 34.4 would be a Ten-Wheeler with 61 inch driving wheels, a 21-inch bore, a 28 inch stroke, and 34,400 pounds of tractive effort.

The only 2-8-0 on the West Point Route, WofA 120, was acquired long after all 4-4-0's had been retired, making the "C" classification available for this engine.

Road No.	Wheel Arr.	Builder, Date	Builder's Number	Driver Dia.	Tractive Effort	Weight	Remarks
15	4-6-0	Rogers, 1906	40402	78"	26,900	193,200	Mislettered A&WP by the builder. Changed to WofA by the railroad.
20	4-6-0	Rogers, 1896	5140	58"	20,315	126,000	Retired 2-12-17.
21	4-6-0	Rogers, 1900	5616	67"	25,070	162,500	Rebuilt 1924, to No. 275.
22	4-6-0	Rogers, 1896	5141	52"	-?-	124,000	
23	4-6-0	Rogers, 1903	5900	54"	34,400	180,800	Renumbered 1907, to No. 226.
24	4-6-0	Rogers, 1903	5901	54"	34,400	180,800	Renumbered 1907, to No. 227.
25	0-6-0	Rogers, 1900	5615	44"	-?-	98,000	
27	4-6-0	Rogers, 1906	40404	61"	34,400	180,800	Renumbered 1907, to No. 228.
28	4-6-0	Rogers, 1906	40405	61"	34,400	180,800	Renumbered 1907, to No. 229.
29	4-6-0	Rogers, 1904	6247	61"	34,400	180,800	Renumbered 1907, to No. 230.
36	4-6-0	Rogers, 1899	5473	72"	23,300	158,000	Renumbered 1907, to No. 270.
37	4-6-0	Rogers, 1899	5479	72"	23,300	158,000	Renumbered 1907, to No. 271.
38	4-6-0	Rogers, 1906	40403	78"	26,900	193,200	Renumbered 1907, to No. 260.

Locomotive classifications were assigned with the general renumbering of 1907.

Class E52 19/24 25.5

200	0-6-0	Richmond, 1912	50958	52"	25,490	121,000	Sold to Atlanta, Stone Mountain & Lithonia RR 1945
201	0-6-0	Richmond, 1912	52944	52"	25,490	121,000	Scrapped, 4-4-50
202	0-6-0	Richmond, 1913	54039	52"	25,490	121,000	Scrapped 7-11-50

Class B57 20/26 31.6

210	2-6-0	Richmond, 1912	50957	57"	31,600	162,000	Retired 7-1-54.

Class G52 25/28 50.0

215	0-8-0	Pittsburgh,1918	60135	52"	50,060	214,000	Retired 5-29-50.

Class G58 25/30 49.5

218	0-8-0	Schen.,1923	64282	58"	49,500	233,100	Ex-Detroit Terminal RR Acq. 1943; Retired, 7-1-54.

Class G53 25/30 54.1

219	0-8-0	Schen., 1925	66321	53"	54,100	233,100	Ex-Detroit Terminal RR, Acq. 1943; Retired, 7-31-51.

Class A61 21/28 34.4

225	4-6-0	Rogers, 1907	43021	61"	34,400	180,800	Rebuilt with piston valves. Scrapped 7-11-50
226	4-6-0	Rogers, 1903	5900	61"	34,400	180,800	Rebuilt with piston valves. Retired, 7-1-54.
227	4-6-0	Rogers, 1903	5901	61"	34,400	180,800	Sold, 1923, to Birmingham & Southeastern RR.
228	4-6-0	Rogers, 1906	40404	61"	34,400	180,800	Rebuilt with piston valves. Retired, 3-11-53
229	4-6-0	Rogers, 1906	40405	61"	34,400	180,800	Rebuilt with piston valves. Retired, 3-11-53
230	4-6-0	Rogers, 1904	6247	61"	34,400	180,800	Rebuilt with piston valves. Retired, 1-28-53
231	4-6-0	Richmond, 1912	50960	61"	34,400	180,800	Retired, 9-30-36

Class P72 22/28 32.0

250	4-6-2	Rogers, 1907	43024	72"	32,000	212,000	Rebuilt 1923, to No. 251.

Class P72 23/28 35.0

251	4-6-2	Rogers, 1907	43024	72"	35,000	236,300	Sold, 1934, to Georgia RR.

Class A78 21/28 26.9

260	4-6-0	Rogers, 1906	40403	78"	26,900	193,200	Rebuilt 1923, to No. 261.

Class A74 22/28 31.2

261	4-6-0	Rogers, 1906	40303	74"	31,200	198,500	Retired, 7-1-54.

Class A72 20/26 23.3

270	4-6-0	Rogers, 1899	5473	72"	23,300	158,000	Rebuilt, 1925, to No. 272.
271	4-6-0	Rogers, 1899	5479	72"	23,300	158,000	Rebuilt, 1924, to No. 273.

Class A72 21/26 27.1

272	4-6-0	Rogers, 1899	5473	72"	27,072	185,000	As rebuilt. Retired, 2-28-38
273	4-6-0	Rogers, 1899	5479	72"	27,072	185,000	As rebuilt. Later rebuilt for freight service.

Class A61 21/28 34.4

273	4-6-0	Rogers, 1899	5479	61"	34,400	186,000	As rebuilt for freight service. Scrapped, 1-31-45

Class A67 20/26 25.1

275	4-6-0	Rogers, 1900	5616	67"	25,070	162,500	Rebuilt, 1924, same No.

Class A72 21/26 27.1

275	4-6-0	Rogers, 1900	5616	72"	27,072	185,000	As rebuilt. Scrapped, 3-22-47.

Class P74 24/28 37.1

280	4-6-2	Brooks, 1913	54037	74"	37,100	258,000	Retired, 2-28-53.
281	4-6-2	Brooks, 1913	54038	74"	37,100	258,000	Sold, 1940, to Georgia RR, No. 281.

Class P74 27/28 46.9

290	4-6-2	Lima, 1926	7008	74"	46,900	303,500	Presented to the City of Atlanta, 1958; To Atlanta Chapter, NRHS, 1973. Leased by New Georgia RR and Restored by them to operating Condition. Operated by NGRR for several years, circa 1990. Now at Southeastern Railway Museum, Duluth, GA.

Class F63 27/30 53.1

400	2-8-2	Lima, 1918	5694	63"	53,100	282,000	Retired, 2-25-52.
401	2-8-2	Lima, 1918	5693	63"	53,100	282,000	Equipped by RR w/Elesco feedwater heater. Retired, 7-31-51.

Class F63 26/30 54.7

425	2-8-2	Lima, 1923	6730	63"	54,700	292,000	Equipped by RR w/Elesco feedwater heater. Retired, 7-1-54.
426	2-8-2	Lima, 1925	6929	63"	54,700	292,000	Retired, 7-1-54.
427	2-8-2	Lima, 1925	7004	63"	54,700	292,000	Retired, 7-1-54.

Class F63 27/32 63.0

430	2-8-2	Baldwin, 1944	70887	63"	63,000	333,800	Retired, 7-1-54.

WofA 180 was leased to the Georgia Railroad for a number of months in 1949. Forrest Beckum caught the engine on film while it was on the point Georgia Railroad train No. 1 at Union Point, Georgia, on November 6, 1949. (W. F. Beckum, Jr. photo, F. E. Ardrey, Jr. collection)

WofA 175 was rebuilt from No. 12 in 1926 and was later rebuilt for freight service. Atlanta Terminal Station, July 24, 1934. (B. F. Roberts photo)

4-8-2 No. 181 was built by Alco's Richmond works in 1920 and retired in 1952. Opelika, Alabama, 1940. (Author's collection)

cific 190 was built by Lima 926 for use on the *Crescent Limited*. Here it awaits highball at Auburn, Alabama, with local passenger n No. 32 in December, 52, having been bumped No.s 37-38 by diesels years before. (J. Parker mb photo)

WofA 187 was one of three Mountain-types purchased from the Florida East Coast Railway in 1936 and the only one of the three equipped with a Worthington feedwater heater. Shown here leaving Atlanta with No. 37 in the late 1940's. (Hugh M. Comer photo, author's collection)

WofA No. 350 was built by Lima in 1918 and retired July 1, 1954. Montgomery, February 9, 1947. (F. E. Ardrey, Jr. photo)

Mikados 350 and 351 were modernized to some extent over the years. The improvements included disc main drivers and cast steel pilots, among other things. The 351 is shown here leading an eastbound freight at Union City, Georgia on May 2, 1949. (R. D. Sharpless photo, F. E. Ardrey, Jr. collection)

VofA 378 was leased to the Georgia Railroad for a period during 1941. Forrest Beckum's camera caught the engine on the point of second 12, a through freight, at Bel-Air, Georgia, while in service on the Georgia Railroad. (W. . Beckum, Jr. photo, F. E. Ar-rey, Jr. collection)

Built by Baldwin in 1944, Mikado 380 was the last steam power purchased by the WofA and, with A&WP 430, was the last locomotive of its wheel arrangement constructed in the US for domestic use. Red Oak, Georgia, March 1948. (Hugh M. Comer photo, author's collection)

A&WP 202 was built by Alco's Richomnd works in 1913 and scrapped in 1950. Shown here at Montgomery in 1940. (C. K. Marsh, Jr. collection)

No.	Builder	Model	Bldr. No.	Date	Eqt.	HP	Remarks
551	EMD	FP-7	8020	8-49	SG	1500	To GaRR 1005:1,1969; Burned,t-i to EMD on GaRR GP-40 order, 1970.
552	EMD	FP-7	8021	8-49	SG	1500	T-i to EMD, 1967.
553	EMD	FP-7	13569	2-51	SG	1500	T-i to EMD, 1969.
554	EMD	FP-7	13570	2-51	SG	1500	T-i to EMD, 1968.
571	EMD	GP-7	8868	2-50	SG	1500	Steam generator removed prior to 1962; To GaRR 1019, 6-70; to SBD 703, 1983; to PNC for scrap, 6-83.
572	EMD	GP-7	11876	8-50	SL	1500	To GaRR 1020, 6-70; to Naparano Iron & Metal for scrap, 8-83.
573	EMD	GP-7	13026	1-51	SG	1500	Retired 1980; Disp. Unknown
574	EMD	GP-7	13027	1-51	SG	1500	Wrked 8-29-70 on L&N (runaway); wrked again in 1-76; Ret. 1-76.
575	EMD	GP-7	17557	10-52	SL	1500	Sold to PNC for scrap, 8-83.
576	EMD	GP-7	12090	11-50	--	1500	Orig. SAL 1732 to SCL 912; to A&WP 576, 9-77; rebuilt by SCL Uceta (Tampa) Shop to "GP16" 4976, 6-81.
676	BLW	DS44-10	74596	4-49	--	1000	Ret. 8-69; Sold to SCL for parts 1969; Scr. by SCL at Jacksonville, FL, 1970.
677	BLW	DS44-10	74597	4-49	--	1000	Ret. 1971; Sold to Jacksonville Port Authority (#102) shortly thereafter; to SCL 235, 1974; Ret. 1976; to Buckeye Cellulose 235, Foley, FL, 1977. Final Disp. unknown
678	BLW	S-12	75280	7-51	--	1200	Ret. 1965; t-i to EMD, 1967.
726	EMD	GP-40	33099	5-67	DB	3000	To SBD 6646, 1-83. Ret. 8-1-86
727	EMD	GP-40	33883	7-68	DB	3000	To SBD 6647, 1-83.
728	EMD	GP-40	34750	1-69	DB	3000	To SBD 6648, 1-83.
729	EMD	GP-40	34751	1-69	DB	3000	To SBD 6649, 1-83.
730	EMD	GP-40	36171	5-70	DB	3000	To SBD 6650, 1-83.
731	EMD	GP-40	36172	5-70	DB	3000	To SBD 6651, 1-83.
732	EMD	GP-40	36173	5-70	DB	3000	To SBD 6652, 1-83.
733	EMD	GP40-2	73681-1	11-74	DB	3000	Wrked, 1-78; To SBD 6645; Re# SBD 6391, 5-86.
4976	EMD	"GP-16"	11915	5-50	--	1600	Orig. AWP 576; Reblt. to "GP-16" 4976 by SCL's Uceta (Tampa) Shop, 6-81; To SBD 4976, 1-83; to SBD 1857, 1986

4978	EMD	"GP-16"	14964	10-51	--	1600	Reblt. from SCL GP-7 777 (orig. ACL 246), 11-82, acq. by AWP at that time. To SBD 4978; 1-83; to SBD 1859, 1986
6007	EMD	GP38-2	786206-1	4-79	DB	2000	To SBD 6007, 1-83; to SBD 2658, 1986.
6008	EMD	GP38-2	786206-2	4-79	DB	2000	To SBD 6008, 1-83; to SBD 2659, 1986.

ROSTER NOTES:

EMD - Electro-Motive Division, General Motors
T-i - Traded in
disp. - Disposition
ACL – Atlantic Coast Line Railroad
SAL - Seaboard Air Line Railroad
PNC - Precision National Corp. (dealer)
SL - Steam Line
Reblt. – Rebuilt

BLW - Baldwin Locomotive Works
Acq. - Acquired
GaRR – Georgia Railroad
SBD - Seaboard System Railroad
SCL - Seaboard Coast Line Railroad
SG - Steam Generator
DB - Dynamic Brake
Wrkd. - Wrecked

Mogul 210 was the only specimen of its type on the roster of either of the members of the West Point Route. Built in 1912, the engine was used primarily in transfer service around Atlanta. Although it is shown here in storage (note the covered stack) in Montgomery, the 210 was not retired until July 1, 1954, dieselization day on the West Point Route. (Richard E. Prince photo, F. E. Ardrey, Jr. collection)

A&WP 215 was the on[l] USRA 0-8-0 on the rost[er] of that carrier. (Sister e[n]gine 115 was owned by th[e] WofA.) A builders plate fro[m] this engine (Alco-Pittsburg[h] 60135, 1918) occupies [a] place of honor in the author['s] memorabilia collectio[n.] Switching at Hulsey Yar[d,] Atlanta, in 1934. (Hugh [M.] Comer photo, author's c[ol]lection)

w-drivered Ten-Wheeler 225 was used in freight service. The engine was built in 1907 and rebuilt with piston valves in the 1920's. Montgomery, April 1938. (C. E. Rutledge photo, author's collection.)

WP 229 was built in 1906 as No. 28 and was renumbered to 229 in 1907. Much modernized through the years, the engine sits in Montgomery in this ril 24, 1938, portrait. (C. E. Rutledge photo, author's collection)

A very shiny A&WP 230 sits in Mo
gomery on November 5, 1937.
E. Rutledge photo, author's colle
tion)

Ten-Wheeler 261 was rebuilt from No. 260 in 1923 and was retired July 1, 1954. Montgomery, September 2, 1938. (George Votava photo.)

A&WP 271 was built by Rogers in 1899 and was rebuilt to No. 273 in 1924. It is shown here just outside the trainshed at Atlanta Terminal Station in Ju
1916. (Karl E. Schlachter photo, John B. Allen collection.)

No.	Builder	Model	Bldr. No.	Date	Eqt.	HP	Remarks
1	BLW	VO1000	71965	10-44	-	1000	To WofA 621, late 1940's
2	BLW	VO1000	71966	10-44	-	1000	To WofA 622, late 1940's
3	BLW	VO1000	71967	10-44	-	1000	To WofA 623, late 1940's
4	BLW	VO1000	70316	12-44	-	1000	To WofA 624, late 1940's
501	EMD	F-3	7604	9-48	SG	1500	Upgraded to F-7 rating, 1950; retired 4-68; t-i to EMD.
502	EMD	FP-7	8018	11-49	SG	1500	To GaRR 1005:2, 10-69; t-i to EMD, 5-70.
503	EMD	FP-7	8019	11-49	SG	1500	t-i to EMD, 1969.
520	EMD	GP-7	12092	11-50	-	1500	Orig. SAL 1734, to SCL 914, to WA 520, 9-77; ret. 1982.
521	EMD	GP-7	8869	2-50	-	1500	Ret., sold for scrap, 8-83.
522	EMD	GP-7	9082	8-50	-	1500	Retired, 1981
523	EMD	GP-7	9083	8-50	-	1500	Wrecked near Montgomery, AL, 1-76; to SBD 738; ret. 1983, sold to PNC, 8-83.
524	EMD	GP-7	15625	10-52	-	1500	Rebuilt by SCL/Uceta Shop (Tampa) to WA 4977, 7-81.
525	EMD	GP-7	18282	4-53	SG	1500	Retired, 1981
526	EMD	GP-7	18283	4-53	SG	1500	Retired, 4-82
530	EMD	GP-9	18724	5-54	SL	1750	Retired, 1980.
531	EMD	GP-9	18725	5-54	SL	1750	To SBD 1004, Sold to Caney Fork & Western 531, 12-83.
621	BLW	VO1000	71965	10-44	-	1000	Orig. #1, Re# 621, late 40's; Ret. 1970, t-i to EMD, mid-1970.
622	BLW	VO1000	71966	10-44	-	1000	Orig. #2, Re# 622, late 40's; Ret. 1970, t-i to EMD, mid-1970.
623	BLW	VO1000	71967	10-44	-	1000	Orig. #3, Re# 623, late 40's; Ret. 1967; t-i to EMD, 1967.
624	BLW	VO1000	70316	12-44	-	1000	Orig. #4, Re# 624, late 40's; Ret. 1970; t-i to EMD, 1970.
630	BLW	DS4-4-1000	74233	10-48	-	1000	Ret. 1969, to SCL 91:2, 1969; to B'ham Rail & Loco., 1978; to Indiana & Ohio 91.
701	EMD	GP40	33098	5-67	DB	3000	To SBD 6790, 1983.
702	EMD	GP40	33881	7-68	DB	3000	To SBD 6791, 1983.
703	EMD	GP40	34748	2-69	DB	3000	To SBD 6792, 1983.
704	EMD	GP40	34749	2-69	DB	3000	To SBD 6793, 1983.
705	EMD	GP40	36174	5-70	DB	3000	To SBD 6794, 1983.
706	EMD	GP40	36654	5-70	DB	3000	To SBD 6795, 1983.
707	EMD	GP40	36655	5-70	DB	3000	To SBD 6796, 1983.
708	EMD	GP40-2	73681-2	11-74	DB	3000	To SBD 6642, 1983; Re# 6388, 1986.
4977	EMD	"GP16"	15625	10-52	-	1600	Orig. WA 524; rebuilt by SCL/Uceta to 4977, 7-81; to SBD 4977, 1983; to SBD 1858, 1986.
4979	EMD	"GP16"	13926	2-51	-	1600	Orig. ACL GP-7 141; to SCL 729; rebuilt by SCL/Uceta to

							WA 4979, 11-82; to SBD 4979, 1983; to SBD 1860, 1986.
6045	EMD	GP38-2	796312-1	6-79	DB	2000	To SBD 6045,1983; Re# SBD 2696, 1986.
6046	EMD	GP38-2	796313-1	8-79	DB	2000	To SBD 6046, 1983; Re# SBD 2697, 1986.

The 271 as rebuilt by the Montgomery shops in 1924. Renumbered 273, the engine now possesses piston valves, a steel cab, and a more modern head light. Montgomery, May 13, 1939. (C. E. Rutledge photo, author's collection.)

A&WP 275 was built by Rogers in 1900, rebuilt in 1924, retaining the same number, and scrapped in 1947. Shown here at Atlanta Terminal Station May 9, 1936. (B. F. Roberts photo)

cific No. 280, shown here in Montgomery on September 3, 1939, was built by Alco's Brooks works in 1913 and retired February 28, 1953. (C. E. Rutledge oto, author's collection)

A&WP 281 was built in 1913 and sold to the Georgia Railroad in 1940 where it retained the same number. Photographed in Montgomery, February 20, 1935. (Author's collection)

A&WP 290, possibly the most noted of all West Point Route motive power due to its use in excursion service the late 1980's and early 1990's on the N[...] Georgia Railroad, is shown in Atlanta in 1934. The Terminal Hotel, shown in the background, burned in a spectacular fire in 1938 with an appalling loss [...] life. (Hugh M. Comer photo, author's collection)

Mikado-type locomotive 400 was built by Lima Locomotive Works in 1918 and was the first of its wheel arrangement on the A&WP. The locomotive wa[...] retired February 25, 1952. Shown here in Montgomery in 1946. (C. K. Marsh, Jr. collection)

Car No.	Type	Length	Builder	Date	Remarks
WofA 5	Baggage-Coach	63' 5"	St. Charles	1898	Rebuilt from coach 27, 1920; Retired 1929.
WofA 8	Baggage-Mail	64' 8"	Jackson & Sharp	-?-	Rebuilt with steel underframe 10-26-12.
WofA 9	Baggage-Mail	58' 0"	Jackson & Sharp	1901	Rebuilt with steel underframe 7-24-14. Retired 1929.
WofA 10	Baggage-Mail	64' 10"	Jackson & Sharp	1901	Steel underframe applied 11-21-15.
WofA 11	Baggage	53' 0"	Jackson & Sharp	1898	Retired 1922
WofA 12	Baggage	53' 0"	Jackson & Sharp	1884	Retired 1923
WofA 13	Baggage	53' 0"	Pullman	1890	Retired 1923
WofA 14	Baggage	64' 3"	Pullman	1894	Converted from Postal car Opelika, 1896. Retired 1922.
WofA 14	Coach	72' 2"	Unknown		Originally Reading Co. #1061, to Tallulah Falls Ry #16. Purchased by WofA, 1943.
WofA 15*	Baggage-Mail	-?-	Jackson & Sharp	Pre-1888	
WofA 15*	Coach	-?-	Ohio Falls	1892	Retired 1910
WofA 15	Coach	74' 6"	AC&F	1911	
WofA 15	Coach		Jackson & Sharp	1892	
WofA 16	Coach	74' 6"	AC&F	1912	Retired 4-56
WofA 17	Coach		Co. Shop	1893	
WofA 17	Coach	74' 6"	AC&F	1911	Retired 4-56
WofA 18	Coach		Ohio Falls	1892	
WofA 18	Coach	74' 6"	AC&F	1912	Retired 4-56
WofA 19	Coach		Jackson & Sharp	1888	
WofA 19	Coach	74' 6"	AC&F	1911	Retired 4-56
WofA 20	Coach		Co. Shop		
WofA 20	Postal		Pullman	1894	
WofA 20	Coach	74' 6"	AC&F	1911	Destroyed on GaRR 2-16-50.
WofA 21	Coach				Destroyed by fire, Cowles, Ala., Dec. 10, 1895.
WofA 21	Coach	59' 0"	St. Charles	1896	
WofA 22	Coach		Ohio Falls	1889	
WofA 23	Coach		C of Ga Ry	1886	Sold 1900
WofA 23	Coach	62' 8"	Ohio Falls	1900	Retired 1922
WofA 24	Coach		C of Ga Ry	1886	Sold 1900
WofA 24	Coach	62' 8"	Ohio Falls	1900	
WofA 25	Coach	59' 0"	St. Charles	1900	
WofA 26	Coach	63' 5"	St. Charles	1897	
WofA 27	Coach	63' 5"	St. Charles	1897	Rebuilt by St. Charles in 1898 following a wreck at the Cubahatchie Creek Bridge. Rebuilt by Co. Shop into baggage-coach 5 in 1920.
WofA 28	Coach	63' 2"	AC&F	1900	
WofA 29	Coach	63' 2"	AC&F	1900	
A&WP 30	Baggage	64' 3"	Pullman	1897	Retired 1925. Rebuilt as Baggage car 352, 1926.
A&WP 31	Baggage	53' 0"	Ohio Falls	1892	Retired 1923.
A&WP 32	Baggage	53' 0"	Jackson & Sharp		1884 Retired 1923.
A&WP 33	Baggage	-?-	Co. Shop		1890 Retired 1903. Converted to MofW service.

A&WP 33	Baggage	63' 8"	St. Charles	1903	Retired 1924. Rebuilt to Baggage car 351, 1924.
A&WP 34	Baggage	64' 4"	St. Charles	1898	Retired 1925.
A&WP 35	Baggage-Mail	64' 3"	Ohio Falls	1899	Converted Baggage Car 35, 1914.
A&WP 35	Baggage	64' 3"	Ohio Falls	1899	Orig. Bagg-Mail car 35. Rebuilt to straight baggage configuration, 1914. Retired 1926. Rebuilt as Baggage car 354, 1926.
A&WP 36	Baggage	-?-	Co. Shop	1888	Retired, converted to MofW service, 1902.
A&WP 36	Baggage-Mail	74' 6"	Co. Shop	1906	Rebuilt w/steel underframe, 2-18-13.
A&WP 37	Baggage-Coach		Jackson & Sharp	1888	Retired 1903.
A&WP 37	Baggage-Mail	66' 4"	Ohio Falls	1899	Rebuilt w/steel underframe, 8-27-13.
A&WP 38	Baggage-Coach	-?-	-?-	1902	Off Roster, reason unknown, by 1907.
A&WP 38	Baggage-Coach	74' 5"	St. Louis Car	1909	Rebuilt to straight baggage configuration with steel underframe, 1913; Ret. 12-31-65.
A&WP 38	Baggage	74' 5"	St. Louis Car	1909	Originally Baggage-coach 38, rebuilt to straight baggage configuration with steel underframe, 1913. Retired 12-31-65.
A&WP 40	Coach	-?-	Ohio Falls	1895	Retired 1911.
A&WP 40	Baggage	64'10"	Barney & Smith	1903	Rebuilt from postal car 92, 1916; Retired 1924.
A&WP 41	Coach	-?-	Pullman	1888	Retired 1911
A&WP 42	Coach	-?-	C of G Ry	1886	Retired 1905
A&WP 43	Coach	-?-	AC&F	1895	Retired 1922; Rebuilt into Office car 97, 1923.
A&WP 44	Coach	-?-	-?-	-?-	Retired 1906
A&WP 45	Coach	59' 0"	Jackson & Sharp	1896	Retired 1922
A&WP 46	Coach	-?-	Co. Shop	1886	Retired 1907
A&WP 47	Baggage-coach	-?-	Jackson & Sharp	1888	Retired 1902
A&WP 48	Coach	-?-	Ohio Falls	1892	Retired 1912
A&WP 49	Coach	63' 2"	St. Charles	1895	Retired 1926
A&WP* 50	Coach	63' 2"	St. Charles	1895	Destroyed in foreign line accident,1908
A&WP* 50	Postal	61' 0"	Pullman		1894
A&WP* 51	Postal	63' 0"	Pullman		1897
A&WP* 51	Coach	63' 5"	St. Charles	1897	Rebuilt by St. Charles in 1898 following a wreck at the Cubahatchie Ck. bridge. Retired 1935.
A&WP 52	Coach	63'5"	St. Charles	1897	Retired 1935.
A&WP 53	Coach	67'10"	Pullman	1899	Retired 1926, Conv. to Camp car 8101.
A&WP 54	Coach	67'10"	Pullman	1899	Retired, Converted to Foreman's Car 8100, 1925.
A&WP 55	Coach	74' 4"	St. Louis	1906	Retired 1929
A&WP 56	Coach	74' 4"	St. Louis	1906	Rebuilt w/stl. underframe, Renumbered 75, 1930
A&WP 57	Coach	74' 4"	St. Louis	1906	Retired 1929
A&WP 58	Coach	74' 4"	St. Louis	1906	Rebuilt w/stl. underframe, renumbered 76, 1930.
A&WP 59	Coach	74' 4"	St. Louis	1906	Retired, 4-56
A&WP 60	Coach	74' 4"	St. Louis	1906	Retired, 4-56
A&WP 61	Coach	74' 6"	AC&F	1912	Retired, 4-56
A&WP 62	Coach	74' 6"	AC&F	1912	Retired, 4-56
A&WP 63	Coach	74' 5"	AC&F	1914	
A&WP 64	Coach	74' 5"	AC&F	1914	

A&WP 65	Coach	74' 5"	AC&F	1914	
A&WP 66	Coach	78' 5"	AC&F	1915	
A&WP 67	Coach	78' 5"	AC&F	1915	
A&WP 68	Lt. Wt.Coach	85' 0"	Budd	1949	Destroyed, Nov. 25, 1951, on Sou. Railway, Woodstock, Alabama.
A&WP 69	Lt. Wt. Coach	85' 0"	Budd	1949	Destroyed, Woodstock, Ala. Nov. 25, 1951, on Sou. Railway.
WofA 70	Chair Car	65' 1"	Dayton Car Co.	1901	Originally Chicago & Alton Cafe-Observation 672. Puchased by WofA, 1902; Renumbered 401, 1903; Converted to Chair Car 70, 1906; Rebuilt to Office Car 99, 1910.
A&WP 70	Combine	72' 9"	Co. Shop	1930	
A&WP 71	Combine	72' 9"	Co. Shop	1930	
A&WP 75	Coach	75' 0"	St. Louis	1906	Rebuilt from coach 56, 1930.
A&WP 76	Coach	75' 0"	St. Louis	1906	Rebuilt from coach 58, 1930.
WofA 81	RPO-Baggage	64' 7"	AC&F	1911	Converted to baggage car 203, 1948.
WofA 82	RPO-Baggage	64' 7"	AC&F	1911	Retired 12-28-61
WofA 85	RPO-Baggage	74' 2"	AC&F	1930	Retired 1-7-70
WofA 86	RPO-Baggage	74' 2"	AC&F	1930	Retired 1-7-70
WofA 87	RPO-Baggage	85' 0"	Pullman	1949	Retired 7-16-69, converted to Co. Material/Tool car 7421.
A&WP 93	RPO-Express	64' 7"	AC&F	1911	Retired 7-16-69
A&WP 94	RPO-Express	64' 7"	AC&F	1911	Retired 12-28-61
A&WP 95	RPO-Express	74' 2"	AC&F	1930	Retired 1-7-70
WofA 96	Inspection	18' 8"	Cadillac	-?-	Cadillac auto, used as an inspection car; sold 7-11-41.
A&WP 97	Office Car	-?-	-?-	1895	Rebuilt from coach 43, 1923; Dismantled, 7-25-35.
WofA 99	Office Car	65' 1"	Dayton Car Co.	1901	Built as Cafe-Lounge 672 for the Chicago & Alton RR, purchased by WofA, 1902. Renumbered 401, 1903; Converted to Office Car 99, 1910; Retired, 9-30-54, sold to Charles Davidson of Lithonia, Ga., 1955; Purchased by Mills B. Lane in 1959 and donated to the Atlanta Chapter, NRHS, 1965. Severely damaged by fire while in storage, 1969, car deteriorated beyond restoration and was scrapped, 1992.
A&WP 100	Diner	-?-	St. Charles	1896	Renumbered 400, 1901; Retired 1926.
WofA 100	Office Car	-?-	Pullman	1894	Originally named *Alabama*. Name dropped number applied, 1902. Retired 1910.
WPR 100	Office Car	83' 6"	St. Charles	1902	Acquired 1908, 2nd hand. Sold 11-3-70. Owned jointly by the A&WP and the WofA
WofA 101	Coach	74' 5"	AC&F	1914	Retired 12-28-61
WofA 102	Coach	75' 6"	AC&F	1921	Retired 2-21-67
WofA 103	Coach	75' 6"	AC&F	1921	Retired 2-21-67
WofA 104	Coach	75' 6"	AC&F	1921	Retired 1-7-70
WofA 105	Coach	75' 6"	AC&F	1921	Retired 10-23-68
WofA 106	Coach, Lt.	Wt.85' 0"	Budd	1949	Retired, sold to Georgia RR as their No. 106, 1-7-70.

A&WP 120	Coach, Lt.	Wt.85' 0"	Budd	1953	Replacement for coaches 68-69 destroyed in 1951. Retired, sold to Georgia RR as their 120, 1-7-70.
A&WP 188	Office Car	-?-	Co. Shop	Pre1897**	Originally named *Georgia*. Name dropped and No. 188 applied, 1902. Retired, 1909.
WofA 200	Baggage	73' 0"	AC&F	1921	Retired, 7-16-69
WofA 201	Baggage	73' 0"	AC&F	1921	Retired, 1-7-70
WofA 202	Baggage	73' O"	AC&F	1921	Retired, 5-13-68
WofA 203	Baggage	64' 7"	AC&F	1911	Converted from RPO-baggage car 81, 1948. Retired 5-13-68.
WofA 205	Baggage	74' 1"	AC&F	1940	Retired 1-7-70
WofA 206	Baggage	74' 1"	AC&F	1940	Retired 1-7-70
WofA 207	Baggage	74' 1"	AC&F	1945	Retired 1-7-70
WofA 208	Baggage	74' 1"	AC&F	1945	Retired 1-7-70
WofA 221	Baggage	64' 9"	-?-	1914	Acquired 2nd hand, rebuilt, 1949. Retired 6-21-68.
WofA 222	Baggage	64' 9"	-?-	1914	Acquired 2nd hand rebuilt, 1949. Retired 1-7-70.
WofA 223	Baggage	64' 9"	-?-	1914	Acquired 2nd hand rebuilt, 1949. Retired 2-21-67.
WofA 231	Baggage	71'11"	-?-	1911	Acquired 2nd hand circa 1950, Destroyed by fire on L&N RR 1-28-69
A&WP 300	Baggage	74'10"	Bethlehem Shp.	1923	Retired 7-16-69
A&WP 301	Baggage	74'10"	Bethlehem Shp.	1923	Retired 1-7-70
A&WP 350	Baggage	62' 0"	Co. Shops	1924	Retired 7-31-65
A&WP 351	Baggage	64' 3"	St. Charles	1903	Rebuilt from baggage car 33 in 1924. Retired 1959.
A&WP 352	Baggage	61' 8"	Pullman	1897	Rebuilt from baggage car 30, 1926. Retired 1965.
A&WP 354	Baggage	62' 0"	Ohio Falls	1899	Rebuilt from baggage car 35, 1926. Retired 1965.
A&WP 400	Diner	-?-	St. Charles	1896	Renumbered from 100, 1901. Retired, 1926.
WofA 401	Cafe-Obs	65' 1"	Dayton Car Co.	1901	Purchased from Chicago & Alton RR, 1902; Renumbered 401,1903; Rebuilt to Office Car 99, 1910.
A&WP 402	Diner	80' 0"	St. Louis Car	1908	Converted to Cafe-Parlor 402, 1914.
A&WP 402	Cafe-Parlor	80' 0"	St. Louis Car	1908	Converted from Diner 402, 1914; rebuilt to diner configuration, 1927.
A&WP 402	Diner	79' 3"	St. Louis Car	1908	Rebuilt from Cafe-Parlor 402; 1927. Retired 1950.
WofA 403	Diner	74' 6"	Pullman-Std.	1914	Purchased from Illinois Central RR,1948. Retired 7-16-69.
WofA 500	Diner	73' 0"	AC&F	1913	Retired 12-20-58.
A&WP 501	Diner	Lt. Wt.85' 0"	Budd	1949	Retired 7-16-69 sold to Amtrak (8026, 8529) 1973.
A&WP 600	Tourist Slpr.	83' 0"	Pullman	1925	Acquired from the Pullman Co. in 1949 as 12 Sec.1 DR sleeper *Henry Timrod*. Name dropped, No. 600 assigned, 12-16-59. Retired, 7-31-65.
WofA 610	Tourist Slpr.	83' 0"	Pullman	1925	Acquired from the Pullman Co. in 1949 as the 12 Sec.-1 DR sleeper *McCaskill*. Name dropped and No. 610 assigned, 12-16-59. Retired, 7-31-65.

WofA 672	Cafe-Obs.	65' 1"	Dayton Car Co.	1901	Purchased from Chicago & Alton RR, 1902. To chair car 70, 1906; Rebuilt to Office Car 99, 1910.
Alabama	Office Car	-?-	Pullman	1894	Name dropped, WofA 100 applied, 1902. Retired 1910.
Alabama River	Sleeper	85' 0"	Pullman Std.	1949	Lightwieght. River 10 Rmt. 6 DBR. Built for Crescent service. To SBD Research Car 774501, 1983.
Charles A. Wickersham	Observation	85'0"	Pullman Std.	1949	Lt. Wt. 5 DB-Lge-Obs. Built for Crescent service. Originally named Royal Palace. Renamed, 1953. Retired, sold to Joseph B. Lanier, 1958.
Chattahoochee River	Sleeper	85'0"	Pullman Std.	1949	Lt.wt.10 Rmt.6 River DBR. Built for Crescent service. Retired, 1983. Dispostion unknown.
General Forrest	Sleeper	83'0"	Pullman	1930	Heavyweight sleeper 10 Sec. Lge. Acquired from Pullman Co., 1-49. Retired, 1965.
General Polk	Sleeper	83'0"	Pullman	1930	Heavyweight sleeper, 10 sec. Lge. Acquired by WofA from Pullman Co., 1-49. Sold to GaRR, rebuilt to Office Car 300 by Montgomery Car Shop, 1955.
Georgia	Office Car	-?-	Co. Shops	Pre-1897**	Name dropped and A&WP 188 applied, 1902. Retired,1909.
Henry Timrod	Sleeper	82'11"	Pullman	1925	12 sec. 1 DR heavy-weight sleeper. Acquired from Pullman Co. by WofA, 1-49. Name dropped, No. 600 applied, 12-16-59. Retired, 7-31-65.
Lake Belanona	Sleeper	82'11"	Pullman	1926	10 sec.-1 DR-2 Cpt. heavyweight sleeper. Acquired by A&WP from the Pullman Co., 1-49. Retired, 1965.
Lake Benton	Sleeper	82'11"	Pullman	1924	10 sec.-1 DR-2 cpt. heavyweight sleeper. Acquired by WofA from Pullman Co., 1-49. Retired, 1965.
McCaskill	Sleeper	82'11"	Pullman	1925	12 sec.-1 DR Heavyweight sleeper. Acquired by WofA Pullman Co, 1-49. Name dropped and No. 610 applied, 2-16-59. Retired 7-31-65.
Opelika	Postal	64' 3"	Pullman	1894	Converted to WofA Baggage Car 14, 1896; Retired, 1922.
Royal Palace	Observation	85'0"	Pullman Std.	1949	Lt.Wt.5DB-Lge-Obs. Built for Crescent service. Renamed Charles A. Wickersham, 1953. Retired, sold to Joseph B. Lanier, 1958.

The presence on the roster of two pieces of passenger equipment bearing the same number cannot be explained. Both cars are present on the 1898 and 1903 rosters in the author's collection.

** Some sources indicate that the previous identity of this car may have been *Stranraer*, the private car of Helen Gould, the daughter of Jay Gould. The story goes that the West Point Route, while taking bids on an office car, was approached by AC&F with this vehicle, which had been received in trade and had rebuilt with an enclosed vestibule on the forward end (1902 being the rebuild date). Other than the persistence of this story, its consistency, the general veracity of its sources, and the possession, by the author, of a serving spoon bearing the name, *Stranraer*, found on the car after its retirement, the story cannot be absolutely verified.

Some sources show Office Car 188/Georgia as being built in 1894. However, a roster of equipment dated 1898 has the notation "Unknown" under the column headed "Date Built". It is likely that 1894 is the date that the car was converted from some unknown piece of equipment, as it is inconceivable to the author that the mechanical department could, in four years, lose all records as to when the president's office car was built. Also, given the thrifty nature of the West Point Route's management, it is unlikely that they would retire a piece of equipment after a service life of only 15 years when they have been known to operate equipment in excess of 50 years of age, albeit in a much rebuilt and modified state.

A&WP 400 and 401 received disc main driving wheels late in their careers. The 401 displays this feature in Montgomery on August 31, 1947. (R. J. Foster photo, Jay Williams collection.)

A&WP 425 built by Lima in 1923 and was the only member of its class to possess an Elesco feedwater heater. Montgomery, April 24, 1938. (C. Rtuledge photo, author's collection)

Coaled, watered, and ready to go, A&WP 426 displays the spit-and-polish pride of the Montgomery Shops. At Montgomery, April 7, 1938. (C. E. Rutledge photo, author's collection)

. Wickersham liked his engines ·an and the Montgomery roundhouse ·ces certainly worked to carry out his ·shes, as shown here by A&WP 427 ·Montgomery on April 4, 1938. (C. E. ·tledge photo, author's collection)

·fA 380 and A&WP 430 were the newest and heaviest steam power on the West Point Route. The 430 wheels a westbound freight near College Park, ·eorgia, on March 13, 1948. (R. D. Sharpless photo, F. E. Ardrey, Jr. collection)

FP-7 551, the first road diesel on the A&WP's roster, was a dual-service machine designed for both freight and passenger service (hence, the "FP" designation). The unit is operating in freight service as it leads a westbound freight at Read Oak, Georgia in January, 1953. (R. D. Sharpless photo, F. E. Ardrey, Jr. collection.)

A&WP 552 leads No. 38, *The Crescent*, into Atlanta Terminal Station on March 30, 1967. (O. W. Kimsey, Jr. photo)

FP-7 553 is shown at Atlanta Terminal Station in June, 1952, with the Southern Railway building the background. Note that the aluminum-colored band did not extend across the rear of the unit. (R. D. Sharpless photo, F. E. Ardrey, Jr. collection.)

&WP 554 shows years of service as it sits at Hulsey Yard, Atlanta, in 1968. The steam locomotive in the background is not a West Point Route engine, t Gainesville Midland 206, a Russian Decapod that was being stored at Atlanta Joint Terminal for the Atlanta Chapter of the National Railway Historical ociety. (O. W. Kimsey, Jr, photo, C. K. Marsh, Jr. collection)

A&WP 571, a GP-7, displays the solid blue scheme that most West Point Route units had received by the mid-1960's. It lacks the silver frame stripe that many units received with this scheme. Atlanta, 1966. (C. K. Marsh, Jr. collection.)

though the solid blue paint scheme had en adopted in 1959, the transition to the wer scheme was quite slow. GP-7 572 still re its as-delivered scheme in this Decem- r 6, 1964, photo. (J. H. Wade photo, F. E. drey, Jr. collection)

A&WP 573 was a dual service (freight and passenger) Geep equipped with a steam generator for train heat and additional tanks for water for this apparatus. The presence of water tanks under the frame forced the air tanks normally located there to be placed atop the cab body, resulting in the "torpedo boat" appearance. Milledgeville, Georgia (on the Georgia Railroad) October 15, 1966. (E. E. Ellis photo, author's collection.)

GP-7 574 was another of the "torpedo boat" Geeps. The unit is shown here in the solid blue scheme at Hulsey Yard, Atlanta, December 10, 1966. (O. W. Kimsey, Jr, photo, author's collection.)

A&WP 575 receives sand at the Montgomery service facility on September 2, 1967. This unit did not receive the solid blue scheme as the solid black scheme was already being applied to repainted units by this date. (J. H. Wade photo, F. E. Ardrey, Jr. collection.)

GP-7 576 displays the solid black paint scheme that superseded the solid blue scheme. Newnan, Georgia, August 17, 1977. (F. E. Ardrey, Jr., photo)

Baldwin switcher No. 676 was built in 1949 and retired in 1969. Atlanta, 1966. (C. K. Marsh, Jr. photo)

A&WP 678 is shown in the blue and aluminum scheme as applied by the railroad. Atlanta, 1959. (T. G. King photo, C. K. Marsh, Jr. collection)

A&WP 727 was delivered 1968 and became Seaboa System 6647 in 1983. Atla ta, March 16, 1969. (E. A. E lis photo, author's collection

GP-40 728 was one of two units delivered to the A&WP in January 1969. The unit became Seaboard System 6648 in 1983. (O. W. Kimsey, Jr., photo, author's collection.)

scar Kimsey caught brand-new GP-40 No. 730 on film in Augusta, Georgia (on the Georgia Railroad) in 1970. (O. W. Kimsey, Jr. photo, C. K. Marsh, collection)

A&WP 731, delivered in May 1970, sits at Hulsey Yard, Atlanta, in October 1976. (Tom Sink photo, C. K. Marsh, Jr. collection.)

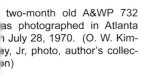

two-month old A&WP 732 as photographed in Atlanta n July 28, 1970. (O. W. Kimey, Jr, photo, author's collecon)

A&WP 6008 was the last new diesel locomotive purchased by the Atlanta & West Point Rail Road. Delivered in April 1979, the unit is shown here leading Georgia Railroad train 103 (the Augusta-Atlanta mixed train) at Union Point, Georgia, in 1982. (C. K. Marsh, Jr, photo)

F-3 501 was the first road diesel purchased by either of the partners of The West Point Route and was delivered by EMD in September 1948. Shown here (missing the air intake grills) in Atlanta in the early 1960's. (Authors collection)

WofA 502 was the first of the FP-7's on the WofA, delivered in November of 1949. By the time of this photo (February 14, 1968), the unit was nearing the end of its career. On the Georgia Railroad at Augusta, Georgia. (E. A. Ellis photo, author's collection)

WofA 503 displays a very grimy solid blue paint scheme in Montgomery on September 2, 1967. The stainless steel air intake grills were sometimes re- moved as a short-term solution to engine cooling problems. (J. H. Wade photo, F. E. Ardrey, Jr. collection)

GP-7 522 is shown here working the yard in Montgomery on September 2, 1967. The unit was delivered by EMD in 1950 and was retired in 1981. (O. W. Kimsey, Jr. photo)

WofA 523 was delivered by EMD in August of 1950 and was retired in 1983. Shown at Hulsey Yard, Atlanta, December 6, 1966. (J. H. Wade photo, F. E. Ardrey, Jr. collec- tion)

WofA 524 is at East Point, Georgia, in this July 27, 1967, photo. The unit is wearing the solid blue paint scheme and has the silver frame stripe applied some units. (O. W. Kimsey, Jr. photo, F. E. Ardrey, Jr. collection.)

GP-7 525 wears the then-new solid black paint scheme at Montgomery in this September 2, 1967, photo. (J. H. Wade photo, F. E. Ardrey, Jr. collection

148

WofA 525 and 526 were "torpedo boat" Geeps, equipped with steam generators for passenger service. The 526 is shown in Atlanta on March 18, 1967.(O. W. Kimsey, Jr., photo, author's collection)

-9's 530 and 531 were last first-generation units rchased by either partner The West Point Route. e 530 is shown in Atlanta December 5, 1964. (J. H. de photo, F. E. Ardrey, Jr. ection)

WofA 531 became Seaboard System 1004 in 1983 and was sold that same year to the Caney Fork & Western where it regained its original number. Atlanta, December 10, 1966. (O. W. Kimsey, Jr, photo, author's collection.)

WofA 621 was delivered as WofA 1 in 1944 and was the first diesel locomotive of any type on the West Point Route. Shown in Montgomery, October 1967. (J. H. Wade photo, F. E. Ardrey, Jr. collection)

Baldwin VO-1000 No. 622 was delivered as WofA 2 in 1944 as part of the Western's first diesel order. The unit was retired in 1970. Montgomery, September 2, 1967. (J. H. Wade photo, F. E. Ardrey, Jr. collection.)

WofA 623 was the shortest-liv the original Baldwins, being retir in 1967, three years prior to t reitrement of the other three uni Shown here in Montgomery, Ju 28, 1967. (J. H. Wade photo, F. Ardrey, Jr. collection)

Baldwin switcher 624 is shown at the Montgomery shop on September 2, 1967. This unit was delivered slightly later than the other three VO-1000's, arriving on the property in December, 1944 rather than with the other three in October of that year. (Author's collection)

~~P~~-40 701 was part of a two-~~uni~~t order delivered in May of ~~19~~67. (A&WP 726 was the ~~oth~~er unit in the order.) Atlanta, ~~Se~~ptember 30, 1967. (O. W. ~~Ram~~sey, Jr, photo, author's col~~lec~~tion.)

~~W~~ofA 703 is shown in Milledgeville, Georgia , (on the Georgia Railroad) September 15, 1969. The unit was delivered earlier that year and became Sea-~~bo~~ard System 6792 in 1983. (E. A. Ellis photo, author's collection)

151

WofA 705 is only a few weeks old a[s] it sits in the Augusta engine facil[ity] of the Georgia Railroad on Augu[st] 4, 1970. The unit was delivered [in] May of that year and became N[S] 6794 with the Seaboard System r[e-] numbering in 1983. (O. W. Kimse[y,] Jr. photo, author's collection)

The GP-40's were delivered in a[n] almost painfully plain black pai[nt] scheme, relieved only by white le[t-] tering, a white frame stripe, and [a] red diamond herald. WofA 706 [is] shown in Atlanta on July 18, 197[0.] (O. W. Kimsey, Jr. photo)

WofA 707 sits in the Georg[ia] Railroad engine servicing facil[ity] in Augusta on June 5, 1970. Th[e] unit has had only a few assig[n-] ments, having been delivere[d] only the previous month. (O. [W.] Kimsey, Jr. photo, author's colle[c-] tion.)

GP38-2 6045 was one of only two of its model on the roster of the WofA. The unit was delivered in July of 1979 and retained its number after the Seaboard System merger in 1983. Shown in Atlanta, 1982. (O. W. Kimsey, Jr. photo)

ofA postal car 20 was built by Pullman in 1894. It is
own at the builder. (Frank Moore collection)

A&WP postal car 50 was built by
Pullman in 1894 and was off the
roster prior to 1902. Shown at the
builder. (Frank Moore collection)

WP railway post office (RPO)
51 was built by Pullman in
97. By this time the A&WP
d gone to enclosed ends on
RPO's and away from open
tforms. Shown at the build-
(Frank Moore collection)

WP coach 59 was built by the St. Louis Car Company in 1906 and was retired in April of 1956. Shown in Montgomery, July 24, 1938. (George Votava
oto)

WofA RPO-baggage-expre[ss] car 87 was renumbered [to] materials car 7241 after [its] retirement from revenue s[er]vice. The car is now part [of] Chinese restaurant in Sm[yr]na, Georgia, called the O[ri]ental Express. Milledgevi[lle,] Georgia, August 15, 19[__] (E. A. Ellis photo, auth[or's] collection)

A&WP heavyweight RPO-Express car 95 was built by American Car & Foundry in 1930 and retired at the end of passenger service on January 7, 19[__] Shown here in Atlanta on April 28, 1968, the car has already been removed from RPO service as evidenced by the absence of a pickup arm on the rig[ht] hand door in this photo. (O. W. Kimsey, Jr. photo, author's collection)

WofA office car 99 was built as café-lounge car 672 for the Chicago & Alton RR in 1901. After its purchase by the WofA in 1902, was converted to an off[ice] car in 1908 and retired in 1954. It was donated to the Atlanta Chapter, NRHS in 1965 and was severely damaged by fire while in storage in 1969. It furth[er] deteriorated to the point that it was deemed beyond restoration and was scrapped by the Atlanta Chapter in 1992. Shown here shortly after donation [to] the chapter in 1965. (C. K. Marsh, Jr. photo)

West Point Route office car 100 was owned jointly by the A&WP and the WofA and had sublettering for both carriers on the letterboard. The car was purchased second-hand in 1908 and was retired in 1970. A much-modernized (steel underframe, steel sheathing, air conditioning) 100 was photographed by Oscar Kimsey in Augusta, Georgia, in February, 1970. (O. W. Kimsey, Jr. photo)

avyweight coach WofA 3 was built by American r & Foundry in 1921 d was retired February 21, 1967. It wears paint scheme of dark e sides, a dark gray f and imitation alumi- m lettering in this photo en in Atlanta, date un- wn. (W. C. Thurman oto)

ofA coach 104 was built in 1921 and lasted until the end of passenger service in 1970. It is shown here in Georgia Railroad service parked outside the orgia Railroad/West Point Route General Office Building at 4 Hunter Street, SE, in Atlanta on November 10, 1969. The office building is the brick build- to the right, the Georgia State Capitol is in the background. (O. W. Kimsey, Jr. photo)

WofA lightweight coach 106 was built for *Crescent* service by the Budd Company in 1949. It outlasted passenger service on the West Point Route and was sold to the Georgia Railroad in 1970, where it won fame of a sort in service on the Atlanta-Augusta mixed train. The car is shown here in the consist of the *Piedmont Limited* of the Southern Railway at Altavista, Virginia in April of 1957. (Author's collection)

A&WP coach 120 was purchased in 1953 to replace coaches 68 and 69 that were destroyed on Southern Railway in 1951. The story goes that it was paid for by the Southern but the author has seen nothing to substantiate this story. Atlanta, April 9, 1968. (C. L. Goolsby photo)

WofA 203 was built by American Car & Foundry in 1911 as RPO-baggage car 81 and was converted to a baggage-express in 1948. The car was retired in 1968. Shown here approaching Atlanta Terminal Station in the consist of train 38 on March 20, 1967. (O. W. Kimsey, Jr. photo)

WofA 221 was purchased second hand in 1949 and served the company until it was retired in 1968. Oscar Kimsey caught it in Atlanta, April 28, 1968, not long before it was retired. (O. W. Kimsey, Jr. photo.)

AWP 301 was built by Bethlehem Shipbuilding in 1923 and retired with the discontinuance of passenger service in 1970. Photographed in New Orleans, 1949. (Elliott Kahn photo, K. Marsh, Jr. collection)

...ner 501 was part of the West Point Route's contribution to the lightweight *Crescent* pool of cars. It was built by the Budd Company in 1949 and retired in 1969. It was sold to Amtrak in 1973 and is in service as of this writing. In Atlanta, March 2, 1969. (O. W. Kimsey, Jr. photo, author's collection.)

The Pullman *Alabama Riv[er]* was a 10 Roomette-6 Doub[le] Bedroom sleeping car built [as] part of the lightweight *Cre[s]cent*. It was owned by t[he] WofA and, after use as an e[x]ecutive sleeper (in conjuncti[on] with an office car) followi[ng] the end of passenger servic[e] went to the Seaboard Syste[m] in 1983 and was converted [to] Research Car 774501. Pho[to]graphed in storage at Huls[ey] Yard in Atlanta, November [13], 1969. (O. W. Kimsey, Jr, pho[to, author's collection)

The 5 Double Bedroom-Lounge-Observation *Charles A. Wickersham* was owned by the WofA and was part of the lightweight *Crescent* pool of cars. It w[as] built as the *Royal Palace* and renamed for the late longtime president of the A&WP-WofA in 1953. The car is shown here carrying the markers for No. 3[8] the northbound *Crescent*, out of Atlanta on Southern Railway in 1953. (Author's collection)

The Pullman *Chattahoochee River* was owned by the A&WP and was the sister car to the WofA's 10-6 sleeper *Alabama River*. Although used very lit[tle] after 1968, the car was not officially retired until 1983. (Jay Williams collection)

158

CHAPTER
XIII

FREIGHT EQUIPMENT

A&WP 8309 was used in company service. It is shown here in Atlanta , March 18, 1967. (O. W. Kimsey, Jr. photo, author's collection.)

A&WP 37418 was an outside-braced box-car that was obviously on its last legs when it was photographed at Camak, Georgia, by Oscar Kimsey in February, 1970. (O. W. Kimsey, Jr. photo, author's collection)

ofA 17625 was in assigned service haul-
g fertilizer when it was photographed in
hens, Georgia, on February 2, 1970. (O.
. Kimsey, Jr. photo)

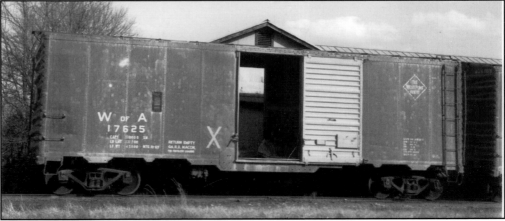

A&WP 32516 was a 40-foot fl car, one of 24 such vehicles the roster in the 1960's. Th photo was made at Hulsey Ya Atlanta, November 18, 1970. (W. Kimsey, Jr. photo, author collection)

A&WP 50005 was a 50-foot box car built by Pullman-Standard in 1960 and equipped with Spartan Easy Loader load restraint devices. Newnan, GA, July 17, 1970. (O. W. Kimsey, Jr, photo, author's collection)

A&WP 38210 was a 40-foot, wa fle side boxcar. These cars we painted "boxcar red" with whi lettering. The car was new whe photographed in Milledgevil Georgia, in May of 1973. (O. Kimsey, Jr, photo)

A&WP pulpwood car ("wood rack") 32903 was one of 83 similar cars on the roster in the early 1970's. Augusta, Georgia, June 6, 1973. (O. W. Kimsey, Jr, photo)

50-foot box car 39004 was built by Pullman-Standard in March of 1956. The car was painted silver with black ends and lettering. (Pullman-Standard photo, Mark Purvis collection)

ofA 17254 was an identical car to A&WP 39004 , was built part of the same order, and was painted in the same man-r. (Pullman- Standard photo, Mark Purvis photo)

A&WP 51129 was built in 1965 and was one of the last such cars to be built for the road with roof walks. Photographed in Augusta, Georgia in February, 1975. (O. W. Kimsey, Jr. photo)

ofA 18250 was a 40-foot box car built in June of 1956 and as painted in the same manner as the 50-foot cars built at the me time. (Pullman-Standard photo, Mark Purvis collection)

A&WP 38009 was a 40-foot box built in 1956 and carried the black/silver scheme. (Pullman-Standard photo, Mark Purvis collection)

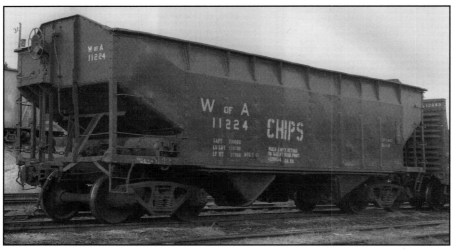

It doesn't take a rocket scientist to figure out that WofA 11224 was assigned to wood chip service when it was photographed at Camak, Georgia, in February, 197? (O. W. Kimsey, Jr. photo)

WofA 18119 was a 40-foot box car and was in assigned service to Covington, Georgia. It was spotted at the Atlanta Broom Company when photographed on March 15, 1969. (O. W. Kimsey, Jr. photo)

WofA woodrack 16539 was photographed under load at Hulsey Yard in Atlanta, May 1? 1970. (O. W. Kimsey, Jr. photo)

Coupla-type caboose WofA 150 was photographed in Atlanta on June 21, 1969. (E. A. Ellis photo, author's collection)

WofA 154 is exactly what it looks like – a converted box car. Montgomery, June 18, 1970. (O. W. Kimsey, Jr. photo, author's collection)

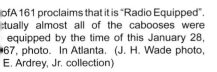

ofA 161 proclaims that it is "Radio Equipped". ctually almost all of the cabooses were equipped by the time of this January 28, 67, photo. In Atlanta. (J. H. Wade photo, E. Ardrey, Jr. collection)

A&WP cab 550 was photographed at Chester Ya[rd] Montgomery, on June 18, 1970. (O. W. Kimsey, Jr. ph[o]to, author's collection)

A&WP 551 displays an earlier lettering scheme used on West Point Route cabooses. Atlanta, 1962. (T. G. King photo, C. K. Marsh, Jr. collection)

Caboose 560 has still another lettering schem[e] The lettering went from "Atlanta & West Point R[R]" to "Atlanta & West Point", to "A&WP". In Atlan[ta] 1967. O. W. Kimsey, Jr. photo, C. K. Marsh, Jr. c[ol]lection.)

A&WP cab 561 was photographed in Montgomery on June 18, 1970. The small "safety first" slogans are wrapped around white diamonds similar to those in the West Point Route herald. (O. W. Kimsey, Jr. photo, author's collection)

C H A P T E R

XIV

THE FLIGHT OF THE MIDNIGHT MAIL

A N D   O T H E R   S T O R I E S

These stories are accounts of some of the more spectacular operations on the West Point Route around the turn of the 20th Century. The first four are contemporary accounts and originally appeared in various Atlanta newspers at the time. They were reprinted by the West Point Route's passenger traffic department in 1930 and distributed in a oklet titled The Flight of the Midnight Mail from which they are reprinted.

The last story, "Wild Ride of the 97", is the result of a late 1961 interview by Hugh Park of the Atlanta *Journal* with the ggage master on one of these runs and appeared in his column on January 3, 1962.

THE FLIGHT OF THE MIDNIGHT MAIL

By Roscoe W. Gorman
The Atlanta *Constitution*, circa 1905

A few nights ago No. 97, the fast mail on the Southern Railway dropped down the Atlantic seaboard and reached Atlanta considerably late. It had done its work well. Leaving the great metropolis, it skimmed the Jersey marshes and thundered through towns and cities. Gathering Momentum with each hour, it hurled itself through space like a catapult until the Gate City of the South was reached. Here, panting and quivering, it came to a stop, while the dust settled slowly around the wheels.

Engine No. 16 of the West Point Route, lithe and keen, stood under the west end of the old shed, and in the gloomy glimmering of the electric lights among the iron girders it looked like an iron greyhound. It stood about sixteen feet above the water line of the worm-eaten floor, and breathed like a thing of life. Back behind it, like the tail of a kite, there stretched four cars.

In the mail cars all was confusion. Brawny negroes hurled themselves dozens of sacks of mail into the open doors, while the clerks worked rapidly. L. D. McDonald, a big blonde Scotchman, with clean blue overalls, oiled the mammoth machinery and caressingly wiped away a bit of grease here and there that interfered with the beauty of the 16. Jackson, the faithful fireman, touched up bolts and stirred around getting ready for the 175 miles down to the first capital of the Confederacy. Up and down the shed Conductor John Harrison stirred, hurrying up everything and everybody, for the schedule was then thirty minutes to the bad, and he knew that the dispatcher was worried an that the train sheet of No. 97 was the first that went under the president's eye in the morning. In the hands of these two men, McDonald and Harrison, lay the honor of the company that night. Strong, honest and handsome, they looked like the men such a company would select for such arduous and responsible duties. The schedule must be made. The mail must to into Montgomery and same the company the forfeit, and then, too, there were a number of passengers hurrying southward who had spent the last minute in Atlanta and the East and then took the last train.

There is a last hurried rattle of the mail trucks, a conglomeration of noises, and "All aboard" – the least jar, a puff of white smoke out of the 16's stack, a glimmer of steel in the electric light, and Montgomery was eighteen feet nearer.

Down there a half asleep hostler backed a Louisville & Nashville engine on the turntable and began getting ready for 97 over the Louisville & Nashville for New Orleans. The Montgomery dispatcher was calling East Point, and then College Park, to know if 97 had passed, but it was winding through a mystic maze of green, red, and white lights through the Central railroad yard. A lone policeman on the Mitchell Street viaduct watched the electric light on the engine come into sight and fade into the red light on the rear end in another moment, and the city slipped suddenly away. High up in the air, the red light changed to white at McPherson, when the 16 called for the semaphore, and the throb of the engine rose to a higher note.

East Point flared up in the darkness and a cloud of dust at the street crossing and all was still, while the calliope whistle asked the operator at College Park if all was well.

Off of the double track and out in the open 97 slipped into the night, Captain Harrison took up the tickets in the back coach, and the mail clerks worked with prodigious energy assorting the great pile of mail. The immense driving wheels were hammering the fish plates and the exhaust had grown into a titanic hum. The headlight cast ghostly glances athwart the landscape and the train seemed to be standing still, with the entire territory in front of it rushing toward it with feverish haste.

Andy opened the furnace door and dropped in a few shovels of coal and the glow from the furnace door lit up the whole country in the rear. The heavy rails and the ballast held the cars steady, but the pace now and then threw the conductor or the mail clerks to one side or caused a piece of mail to miss the sack thrown at. There was a low hum of the calliope and 97 dropped into and out of Red Oak like a bird swoops through the air. The little tombstones of the country cemetery glimmered a moment in the light and disappeared, and the 16 settled down like a horse with a good road and loosened bit until Fairburn, Palmetto and Coweta were passed and with a whir the train hustled into Newnan with a smoking hot box on a Pullman car and a record of 39 miles in 43 minutes. Jacks and lever and brasses were thrown out. Willing men went to work. The train dispatcher at Montgomery was impatiently calling the operator at Newnan – "See that those fellows get a move on them and get out of there, at once." Newnan's eastbound freight trains were seeking sidings down the road. The station master at Montgomery was marking up 97 half an hour late. The 133 miles of silence that lay between Newnan and there were oppressive with their great distance. McDonald and Harrison worked as hard as men ever worked. The possibilities of missing connections were great. The United States Mail was being delayed. Passengers were fretting. Armed with a permit from the proper officer, I climbed up into the fireman's seat and watched McDonald, serious and cool, climb into his, I saw his hand reach over and release the airbrakes, drop the lever forward and with hand on the throttle lean out of the window and watch the gloom behind the signal. At last the light stabbed the air as it waved him forward, the 16 jumped like a frightened bird. Newnan was slipping by!

The time card called for 97 to be in Montgomery in 135 minutes and it was 133 miles away. When 97 does not make the schedule, the cause for it must be shown on the president's desk the next morning. We slowed at the Carrollton crossing and in a moment whirled past the Pearl Springs park. As we took the curves, I leaned heavily inward to help balance the engine, which seemed to be instinct with life. Back in the night, the green light glowed like the ghosts of stars and the dust there kept time to the general roar. All at once a bright light flashed into my face, there was a crash like a broken glass and Moreland went by to eastward. The switch light had destroyed my peace of mind with a jar that took my nerve. The momentum grew terrific. I tried to speak to the fireman, but my voice made no sound. I saw a twinkling of light, like fireflies on a dark background, or the moving of a man of war, and wondered, but the whistle told me it was Grantville. With three fingers on the throttle and his body half out of the window, McDonald leaned into the darkness and the whirlwind of sound and dust and leaves eddied into lovely little Hogansville and swept again into the outer world.

There seemed to grow in the darkness vast and fantastic shapes as forests or farms whirled into view and disappeared to make room for others. I felt some one looking at me, and McDonald was looking at his watch by the one small light. He smiled at the time card hanging in front of him and caressed the throttle seriously, looked at the fireman and the steam gauge and back into the night. Afar I saw the twinkling of many stars, as I thought, but in a moment LaGrange seemed to be coming madly up the hill and at us. I watched the brass handle turn and heard the hiss of the air, and saw the sparks flying from the wheels, and lurching half over, I caught myself as we drew up at the depot. There was a hurried alighting from the train, a few trunks off and on, and into the night 97 went again like a mad charger. Twelve minutes later we were peacefully getting water at West Point, and twenty minutes later Conductor Harrison was registering at Opelika, 22 miles away. Then again we were off, but I was in the back coach. Sixty-six miles away at Montgomery, the station master climbed up to the board and marked down the half hour sign to ten minutes. Down into Auburn 97 was falling like the stars fall in the sky. Its whistle awoke the echoes in the hills and startled the night birds from their haunts. Loachapoka was passed in a few moments, leaving a long freight and wondering crew looking after the apparition. Then Notasulga and Chehaw and Milstead came sliding up the steel rails toward 97, while the pace grew more furious. There was no time to talk. The coaches rolled uneasily as they took the curves, the whistle moaned uneasily above the hurricane of sound, while the roar was as of a great battle. And it was. It was the battle of business, where the diligent alone succeed. Down the hill at Chehaw we rushed, while under the engineer's call the red light was turned to white and the miles were rolled up under the 16 like tread on a spool. Thirty-nine miles in thirty-seven minutes was the record, and around the long curves leading into Montgomery this thing of steam and steel and human endurance swept, while the astonished depot employees could hardly believe their senses. The long night's ride was over and one of the world's records had been made. Every night over this superb road one of the mighty engines and brave engineers, with a gallant crew, makes exceptional speed, and here and there some phenomenal record is made.

Only the finest roadbed and the best rolling stock can stand the strain, and the West Point Road is not egotistical when it claims the best.

When an ordinary passenger and mail train, without any preparation, puts its speed up to 5,280 feed every fifty-two seconds and holds it there for hours, it is something to talk about, and this record is in black and white on the train sheet in Montgomery, which tells the story of the lives and work of the heroes who make and keep the reputation of the midnight mail.

HOW ENGINEER MCWATERS MURDERED THE LOST HOUR

By Alan Rogers
The Atlanta *Constitution*, circa 1905

This is the story of "97", an engine, an engineer, and the murder of an hour in the making up of lost time.

Your Sunday-school teacher, if you have one, will tell you that it is impossible to take the moments that are gone and live them over again. It is quite possible that she will also draw some beautiful similes about improving each shining hour, etc.

But while it is true that the present never returns in this world for the correcting of the mistakes that were made at that time, there is one exception. This is the Atlanta & West Point Railroad and its midnight mail train, No. 97, which has for its very mission this correcting of the mistakes that are bound to be a part of one of the fastest schedules in the world, and the elimination of the past for the present, which, if an impossibility, is an actual accomplishment on the part of 97. Or perhaps, to put it more plainly, if an hour is lost by the mail train before it reaches Atlanta, No. 97 has for her mission the making up of as much of that hour is possible in order that the letters entrusted to her care may be delivered on time and within the contract specifications provided by the government.

It is a very wonderful and a very difficult mission, is that, and it takes a rock ballast roadbed, a nicety of elevation in the matter of curves, grades that will permit, rolling stock and equipment that have reduced the delays of friction and other obstacles to lowest terms, and, most of all, a man at the throttle who knows and understands these things, and is on sufficiently intimate terms with each to enlist their help whenever the fight with time, and the making up of an hour that is lost, is imperative and immediate.

Incidentally there is another time feature in connection with the story of 97. She runs from the capital city of a nation of the present to a capital city of a nation of the past; from the stars and stripes that ripple with every passing breeze in Washington to the stars and bars that are furled with a "lost cause" in Montgomery. It is certainly the most historic train that runs today, connecting the Union of the present with the Confederacy of the past in those close ties of commerce and brotherly love which have long since swept sectional feeling into that oblivion where only such obsolete and worthless things as last year's schedules and yesterdays newspapers are relegated.

A Fight with Father Time

A few nights ago, the fast mail on the Southern dropped into Atlanta considerably late. She had encountered many obstacles, and while she had fought a good fight with Father Time, she had lost an hour in the struggle with the old gentleman. With the transfer of the mail sacks, Engineer John F. McWaters saw that the work of a hard night was cut out for him He didn't run around wildly or expostulate loudly with the decrees of fate. Engineers are not made of that kind of material. They are quiet men almost invariable, and quiet looking as well, as quiet looking as the plain blue overalls and jumper which constitute their official uniform of active service. But they are as strong as the great driving wheels they control and as true as the materials of highly tempered metal that are all around them. Such as one is Mr. McWaters.

Standing watching the transfer of the mail sacks was the writer and General Passenger Agent Joseph B. Billups, of the West Point road. "Get on that engine," said Mr. Billups, "and run down to Montgomery with Mr. McWaters. He's going on a trip tonight where there will be murder, battle and sudden death. It's a great chance for you as a war correspondent of peace to get close to the methods of railroad warfare where regular schedules are reduced to lowest terms and the making up of lost time demands the strongest of nerves, the best of equipment and a roadbed that is never afraid of the severest strain."
"You'll see engineer McWaters murder lost time, do battle with grades, curves and the elements, and if you don't pull into Montgomery on time, there'll be sudden death in that engine cab or McWaters had changed a whole lot lately – which I know he has not."

So the newspaper man climbed on board, and he found it all that Mr. Billups had said – quite that much, if not more so.

Mr. McWaters has been with the road thirty-six years, and, as Mr. Billups remarked, "what he doesn't know about that run, is sure torn out of the books." Of medium height, the engineer's figure is rather stocky, suggesting all kinds of strength, but is the light in his eye that labels him for the kind of man he is. Those eyes are as clear and as clean as polished crystal, and yet a light burns there that is indescribable, a something in the way of expression that has come with thirty-six years of leaning out of a cab window, always looking ahead for the care and safety of others. And it is very strange that the expression should be such a gentle one, and still it is always so with those who know not fear.

Giant Cobweb of Solid Steel

With noisy remonstrance, big engine No. 16 pulled out from the great turtle-backed trainshed, and seemed to feel its way through the darkness of the yards outside, where little green and red and white switch lamps were scattered in what seemed to be a promiscuous profusion. But somewhere away out in the darkness a train dispatcher was manipulating these winking, blinking little switch lamps, and telegraph operators, night men in the switch towers, engineers and trainmen were following instructions, and out of the labyrinth of intermingling strips of steel that looked like giant cobwebs in the reflection of the headlight, order was brought out of apparent chaos by means of a system that is as perfect in its accomplishment as it is incomprehensible to the average sleepy passenger struggling with refractory trousers in the narrow confines of a sleeping car compartment.

Slowly the engineer continued to pick his way through the great steel-spun web, on below viaduct bridges, with their network of superstructure that looked like great curtains thrown out of darkness; on below skyscrapers of solid black, except for the single light left burning on every floor by the night watchman, that seemed to stare a sleepy good-night message to 97 as she crawled on her way, aching to jump forward and show her strength, but held impatiently in leash by the speed ordinances of a city government and the hand of Engineer McWaters.

Slowly the speed was increased until the sleeping barracks at Fort McPherson seemed to rush past in the opposite direction before the sentinel on guard could wave a welcome out of the glare of the headlight for this sudden interruption to his lonely vigil. But is was not until beautiful College Park, the gem suburb of the South, was reached that the man at the "trots", looking out on the long line of track that stretched on and on into the darkness, like the colossal finger of destiny pointing the way of the narrow path, struck the spurs into the sides of his charger with a single motion of his hand, and the race of the night was on.

From that time the murder of an hour of lost time by Engineer McWaters was perpetrated on the unsuspecting sleepers of Georgia, and all that was left as a clue for the assault on a mail train schedule was a broad track of smoke that was seen lost in the darkness. But all along this trail of the murder of an hour was the excitement of battle and sudden death; battle with grades and curves and the death of seconds which counted for much in the making up of the lost time. It was certainly war from College Park to Montgomery, and all the hell that Sherman painted and practiced.

Jumping Through Georgia

Jumping through Georgia by night carries with it many sensations. To some it may mean trepidation and uncertainty until they fell the solic rock of the roadbed underneath, the unseen influence of strict discipline, akin to military, and the governing hand of thirty-six years' experience above. After that knowledge, the sensations may ben ovel, but they are hardly dangerous enough in the nature of things to breed excitement.

Next to his engine, the roadbed with its grades and elevations of track are the creeds of an engineer to which he pins his faith. For his engine he has a sentiment that appears in his conversation, sometimes in a way that is apt to cause confusion.

"No, she ain't the least bit cranky. She's never gone back on me since I've been with her. Of course, you take someone who don't know her and it might be different, but I understand her ways an' we haven't had any real trouble yet."

No, gentle reader, if by chance you have read this far, he is not speaking of his wife or his sweetheart. he is simply referring to his engine as you will know when he adds: "Of course, you got to keep her fire clean. A dirty fire will make any of 'em stir up trouble, but give her a clean fire and her steam'll hold up as steady as possible."

Some ministers of the gospel place much stress on immersion or the foreordination or infant baptism, all of which beliefs lead to the maikng of denominations. These matters may also concern the enginerr when he is at home, but when he is on duty it its the roadbed and all that goes with it from which he draws his text for the preaching of a sermon that all who ride may read. If it is a soft roadbed with old ties and light rails, he will preach caution and restrain his temptation to pull her wide open, and he will practice what he preaches. But if the roadbed is of the rock ballast kind, with new ties and ninety-pound rails to the yard, he will come out boldly with these as his text and for full salvation and the saving of souls even when the schedule requires running at high speed to make up for lost time. For while eginneers may differ as to the matter of a fulcrum of the trailing wheels or as to the proper limits of boiler pressure, they all believe in rock ballast as the only sure means of saving grace and time, which is equally essential.

And because that was kind of a roadbed Engineer McWaters had, the theme of his unpreached sermon was perfect faith and confidence, and he dashed around curves and down grades secure in the knowledge that the road on which he traveled had been builded upon a rock, which according to bothe the scriptures and the scientific teaching of the best civil engineers.

Engineers of Fiction

It would be very pleasant to write something in the way of a characteristic interview with Mr. McWaters, but while he was just as pleasant as thousands of Atlantans know him to be, he was also on duty. And the only really talking engineers a railroad man ever meets are those he sometimes stumbles on fiction. Of course when a stop I reached the engineer will get out and make a careful scrutiny of his "pride and joy" in much the same way as will a horseman who is in love with his animal. But if he says something, which is seldom, it will be to the effect that the forward truck is equipped with simple swing hangers; or if he thinks you are really interested, he will tell you confidently that the trailing truck has a radius bar which is equlized with the rest pair of drivers, from which the equalization extends continuously through to the front pair or drivers.

At which confidence you will to frown intelligently and remain silent in the hope that he will think you understand what he has said, which you do not in the least possible. So, while it would be most pleasant to fake up and alleged interview, this is a true story and will not permit it.

There was only one accident that happened, and this was almost at the end of the run, when away to the east the sky was pregnant with that pecular shade of gray that promises the birth of a new dawn. It was on a straight stretch of track, which has gained for the West Point the name of the "Pennsylvania of the South", and the actual running time was between 80 and 90 miles, for Engineer McWaters was murdering the lost hour with frightful stabs that gave the telegraph poles the appearance of a picket fence and made the cab rock like a double-reefed schooner listing with every wave in the trail of a northeaster.

A rather young and somewhat dissipated looking dog who should have been home at his own kennel fireside looking after wife and four small children, who were crying for dog biscuit, came skulking across the green fields of Georgia. He started to cross the track. The schedule showed that 97 had the right of way. The following moment also showed that some 40 pounds of dog was indiscriminately sown on those same green fields of Georgia for a circumference of about 150 feet, and his canine soul was started toward Nirvana or the Brimstone Springs, according to whether he was a Buddist or a Presbyterian.

The end came at Montgomery, and when Engineer McWaters stepped down from his cab there was still that peculiar gentle light in his eyes. Perhaps no one suspected it, but at least one tired and stiffened newspaper man knew that this same pleasant-looking man had done just what he started out in cold blood to do. And this was the murder of a lost hour, or to be more exact, in this remarkable run Engineer McWaters had made up forty-seven minutes between Atlanta and Montgomery.

"HOW FAR IS IT TO NEWNAN?"

By Smith Clayton
In the Atlanta *Journal*, circa 1905

Didst ever ride on a locomotive, familiarly called the iron horse?

I didst.

It was a night ride, too, between Atlanta and Montgomery, and there was something doing every moment. Jack Wilson says it's going like going into a new world when a man rides on a locomotive the first time. That's no mistake. My impression was quite vivid that we would be in a new world before reaching Newnan, but, to my surprise, we did not. It was this way. My friend, John McWaters, was at the throttle. His engine, No. 16, is the monster machine which pulls the fast train on the Atlanta & West Point Railroad. This is said to be one of the fastest trains in the country. She leaves Atlanta at 11:15 in the evening and at 3:15 a.m. she rolls into Montgomery. The distance is 175 miles. She makes only five stops of one minute each. The points are Newnan, Moreland, where she takes water, LaGrange, West Point and Opelika.

I had taken water long before we reached Moreland, and am ready to swear that this is the fastest train on earth.

My original idea was to ride all the way on the engine, but John discouraged me. "No," said he, "you will, probably be a little tired when we make the first stop, Newnan. You can go back in the car and rest when you get there and return to the engine at Opelika. From that point we run 66 miles without a stop, into Montgomery. This is a smooth run through a level country." As John has been with the old Atlanta & West Point thirty-five years, and is one of the best engineers who ever pulled a throttle, I was guided by him – that is, to some extent. The start was splendid.

We crawled along under the viaduct, the fireman feeding the red mouth with shovels of coal. The bells were ringing, the steam hissing, the lights dancing on trains all around us. It was glorious.

John was seated on the box; I right behind him, hugging a friendly part, and enjoying the sparkling, shadowy scene. Suddenly the monster groaned heavily and stopped. This gave me a queer feeling, and of course, I thought something had occurred. It had – but it was only a train crossing our track ahead. Three minutes later we crawled on down to the Mitchell Street viaduct, then we walked. At Peters Street we struck an easy jog trot. The smoke was passing into the second and third volumes, the breeze blew stiff, and pretty soon, John pulled a cord and a blast was blown that rather startled me. We then struck a canter; the monster snorted, and the flashing headlight showed the open country ahead, with the track looking as if the rails were about a foot apart.

It was exhilarating, but not quite as glorious.

John looked back over the rumbling train, the fireman shoveled coal into the inferno faster, the sparks spangled the smoke, the lever was pulled back several notches – and we were running. I tried to think I was having a good time, but did not entirely succeed.

169

In a few minutes – it seemed to me a quarter of an hour – I timidly glanced ahead and was a light seemingly on the track.

What if it was the headlight of an approaching train? That thought popped into my mind. We slowed up a little. It must be! No – we swept past – it was a switch light at East Point.

What a relief! And yet I was not altogether happy. As we passed through the town I ventured to asked the fireman:

"How far is it to Newnan?"

He smiled grimly. "About 33 miles. You know its 39 miles from Atlanta to Newnan." Right there I developed an entirely new set of emotions when John carefully looked at his watch and casually remarked:

"We lost three minutes waiting for that train to get by at Atlanta." When he said that my imagination began to work overtime.

As we dropped below East Point he swung the lever away back, and, in a trice, we were roaring through the dark woods. He blew a blast that waked the echoes. This stimulated my imagination – but understand me, I was not exactly alarmed, only terribly interested. Everything was so fearfully new to me. I watched the fireman like a hawk. I watched John like two hawks.

Every motion made aroused my suspicions that something awful was about to happen. I began to freeze with intense interest. That's a good word – interest. Every time she shot around a curve it seemed a case of into the woods. Presently I asked the fireman:

"How far is it to Newnan?"

He looked worried. "Why, a long ways yet. We haven't passed Palmetto yet." That seemed to settle it. My mind was now eaten up with a single thought, to-wit: "Will we ever get to Newnan? IF so, at what precise hour?"

"Sit over there on the fireman's box – it's more comfortable – you can see better," remarked John.

Just a little remark like that not only renewed my imaginative power, but actually worked upon my feeling. It really startled me. Machanically, I waddled over, and the fireman helped me up. One glance ahead through the window not only satiated me – it glutted me. The headlight glared on a curve, the powerful reflection looking exactly like a headlight of and engine rounding that curve. All the collisions that I had ever heard of flashed through my mind in a second.

That was the last look ahead. My surprise was so great when we swept safely and grandly around that curve that it staggered me. The revulsion of feeling almost crazed me with joy – for about a sixteenth of a second. Then I snapped back.

John and the fireman were now talking in low tones, and as they talked, they smiled. They glanced at me. With a mighty effort, I vented a little two-by-four laugh.

But it sounded awfully like the hilarity of despair. Strange,

but a moment later, when a frightful blast announced our approach to Palmetto, and we slowed up, I felt as bold as a lion.

But this emotion was strictly temporary. Like whited ghosts the houses glide by, but the worst was to come.

As we struck the long grade the other side of that town the fireman came over and said: "Ever been on this schedule before?" With a vacant stare, I shook my head. "Well," said he, "you'll never strike a faster one. Now we go down hill." I felt as cheerful as a corpse.

It was all a mistake that we had been running before. The engine took wings now.

"That's a pretty flower garden there," he yelled.

"Where?" I asked without looking up.

"About two miles back," he replied, and he laughed.

A moment later when it seemed that all was over, I gasped:

"How far is it" – but could go no further.
"Oh, to Newnan?" he asked.
Nodding meekly, I murmured, "Now I lay me"-

"Three miles and a half."

For miles I had been limp as a dish rag. Now I was stiff as an icicle. My courage arose in exact proportion as the grade steepened, and when we rolled into Newnan, the first stop, the fireman helped me down. A whole relief corps never enjoyed such a sense of glorious relief. Almost idiotic with ecstacy, I exclaimed:

"I would never make an engineer."

"Come back when we make Opelika!" shouted John.

"Not for Stone Mountain if it was a diamond."

My hat is off to the locomotive engineers. Some men, at times in their lives, are heroes. But these, ah, these, the best of all the brave, are heroes all the time.

"WE MADE THE MAIL WITH A MINUTE TO SPARE!"

By Edwin Johnson

The Atlanta *News*, circa 1905

"There'll be something doing to-night," said Andrew Jackson, fireman, as I climbed aboard engine No. 16 on the Atlanta & West Point, to ride to Montgomery on the fastest engine south of the Pennsylvania Railroad.

"What's the trouble to-night, Andy?" I asked, although I knew that Engineer L. D. McDonald had already been delayed more than an hour and that he would have to make up considerable time on the run or cause his road to forfeit a large amount to the Government for missing the mail.

"When we leave late we most generally cuts the mustard," was the expressive language used by Andy in explaining the situation.

As for Engineer McDonald, I did not know how greatly worried he was until we pulled under the station in Montgomery with a minute and seven seconds to spare. He leaped from his box, jerked his watch from his overalls pocket, and then with a shout of delight clapped me on the back. Number 16 had completed one of the fastest runs ever recorded in the South. A total of twenty-seven minutes had been saved on a schedule which averages forty-four miles to the hour without allowing time for stops. Shortly before we left Atlanta, Engineer McDonald turned to me and said: "You won't want to ride on the engine any further than LaGrange or West Point, will you? I expect by the time we reach the latter place you will want to go back in the coach."

And ere the morning's light had made gray the eastern sky his prophecy had been fulfilled: I did want to go back in one of the coaches, for the ride through pouring rain on the swaying engine, and sometimes at the rate of seventy miles an hour, got on my nerves; but I lacked moral courage to confess to the man who sat at the throttle, as brave as a lion, that I was frightened. I valued the good opinion and praise of that man more than I did my personal safety, and when No. 16 pulled under the shed in Montgomery I was seated on the fireman's box, where I had hung with desperation throughout the trip.

Train No. 97 carries the mail from New York to New Orleans. It leaves New York over the Pennsylvania. At Washington it is taken by the Southern and brought to this city. From here it goes to Montgomery by way of the Atlanta & West Point, and from Montgomery to New Orleans over the Louisville & Nashville. When the government contracted with the railroads hauling this mail, the fastest trains secured the contract. Engineer McDonald pulled No. 16 on the trial trip. That was more than a year ago. Since that time the train has been run every night, with never an accident, despite the fact that she has to make more than an average of sixty miles an hour between Atlanta and Montgomery.

When I went down with Engineer McDonald we were an hour and nine minutes late. We lost time on the road on account of a series of mishaps over which the engineer had no control. There was a hot box on a second class coach. We lost eight minutes at West Point while the train crew was trying to put it out. We lost eleven minutes at Chehaw, where we had to kick it onto a siding. In addition to these delays, we stopped at Moreland for coal and water, which is contrary to the usual run.

Going out of Atlanta the switch lights danced merrily past us, bidding a coquettish farewell. The bell clanged incessantly. We gained speed after reaching West End. At East Point we were running at a high rate of speed. At College Park the bell stopped ringing, engine No. 16 settled herself, and as Engineer McDonald pulled the throttle wide he shouted across to me that "We are on our own tracks now and we will begin to run fast." Pride in the road was expressed in his remark, "On our own tracks." From that time on not twenty words were spoken.

The locomotive let out a derisive snort of restraint and leaped into the air as the throttle was opened like a thoroughbred horse leaps at the touch of a spur. As the steam seeped through the valves she rushed onward. We were gaining momentum at every revolution of the seven-foot drivers. We began to sway like a ship in a heavy storm. And then I knew the race against time was on.

Before we reached Fairburn the storm broke. Rain began to fall in torrents. The track had the appearance of a deep running stream. The rails resembled two gleaming knife blades. Just this side of Fairburn there is a long, straight stretch of track. We rounded the curve leading into it, and as I peered into the falling rain, down the track, I felt that the headlight was a streak of lightning to which we were attached, being dragged to certain death.

We were running now. I glanced across the Engineer McDonald. He was crouched like a jockey on a horse; his left hand was on the throttle, his right on the air brake. From time to time his left hand would feel among the valves, reaching true, but his eye never left the track. His jaw was hard set, his eyes gleamed in the half light as clear cut as diamonds. Every muscle was drawn and tense. His very attitude bespoke determination.

Andy was busy with the shovel. His steam gauge registered 160 pounds and did not vary five pounds the entire trip. Andy sustained his reputation for being a smokeless fireman. Over the top of the coaches a thin blue-white stream of smoke sped as if kissing them lightly here and there. There was no black smoke; the heat was too white, the pace too hot.

Into Fairburn the engine burst like a fiend incarnate. Before we reached the station I was a reflection of the headlight in the station window. My heart was in my mouth, for I felt sure that it was the headlight of a freight train. Before I had time to speculate on what kind of death I would meet we were past. On down the track and the switch light at the far end leaped toward us like a goblin. There was a clanging of the bell. I thought of Sir Henry Irving and "The Bells."

It was far past the fell hour of midnight. There was no sound save the roar of the engine, the pounding of the piston, and the grind of the drivers. Back in the mail cars the clerks were busy distributing the letters. They were too busy to think of the rate at which they were running. I tried to speak. Engineer McDonald never turned his head. He was busy watching the track. And the fascination of the track got into my blood. I gazed down it, expecting, yet dreading, every minute some frightful calamity. I tried to turn away to shut out of my mind's eye the visions of railroad wrecks, mangled limbs, and torn flesh; to stop my ears to the cries of the wounded. But the effort was useless. Every cell in my brain in which was pigeon-holed a memory of wrecks and disasters, gave up its pages, and I read them all over again.

The railroad track looked like a huge needle running to a point at the end. We seemed dashing to destruction. The telegraph poles on either side reminded me of a huge vice into whose grim jaws we were soon to be crushed. Life at that moment was dear to me. I thought of my folly in undertaking such a trip. I thought of how little the man at the throttle valued his life to run regularly this train. But was he running regularly? Andy had said there would be something doing. We were late. He was trying to make up time.

I have seen a man's life snuffed out by the crack of a revolver; have seen cold steel plunged into a heart; have seen the hangman's noose fitted snugly about the neck of some victim who was soon to be swung into eternity. None of these caused the feeling of dread I experienced on that night. It seemed something awful which one could not grapple.

Andy opened his furnace door and threw huge shovelfuls of coal into its yawning jaws. No. 16 hissed and snorted and plunged and rocked, like a drunken fiend whose blood had just been fired by and additional drink. Engineer McDonald had the reverse lever in the tenth notch. The throttle was side. We sped through Palmetto, Powell Station, and rushed into the switch leading to Newnan. There was a hissing of steam, a protest against restraint, and the panting monster came to a stop at the water tank.

Engineer McDonald was on the ground. With flambeau and oil can he was going around his iron horse touching the oil receivers, pouring oil here, rubbing with waste there, while Andy was back on the pile of coal in the tender filling the nine stomachs of the horse. I sat, wet and cold, on the fireman's box, looking longingly in the direction of the coaches.

About the time I had made up my mind to swallow my pride and go back where it was warm and comfortable, where sensible people were riding, there came up the squeak, squeak from Conductor Bellamy's cord. Mr. McDonald leaped to his box. Up went the water spout, and before Andy had reached the gangway, before I had time to swallow my pride, we were well under way and I was soon busy trying to swallow my heart.

We had reached Newnan, a distance of 39 miles, after a run of forty-seven minutes. I thought this remarkable time, especially when I remembered that we had run comparatively slow until we reached College Park. But this was not a circumstance. We began to run in earnest. The feats she had already performed, and many more, were enacted by No. 16 within the next nine minutes. We dashed around curves with a rapidity that made me believe we would take to the corn fields in spite of the excellent roadbed. We swayed to such an extent that I thought I could pick up a rock with which the road was ballasted.

The whistle began to toot, toot, toot in an alarming manner. I peered down the track with aching eyes, for I had been taught that when an engine gives that signal there is danger ahead. It was not hard to convince me that danger was lurking all around. I experienced a sinking sensation around my heart. Andy threw open his door and I caught a glimpse of my reflection in the glass in front of me. It appeared ghostly.

Suddenly there was a jerking, and application of the air, a slipping of the wheels on the wet tracks. More toots, and we came to a dead standstill.

"We coal up here," said Engineer McDonald, and he was on the ground again, oiling. The smell of the oil was in my nostrils. The feel of the coal was on my hands, the tinge of the smoke was over my face. I felt strangely alone up in that engine cab. I did not know until we were coming back on a slower train the next day why he had whistled so fiercely. He told me it was to signal the man who has the coal chutes in charge.

We lost three minutes at the coaling station. We stopped for water in LaGrange. We dashed away, sometimes rounding curves, sometimes going through a deep cut, sometimes on a long straight stretch. But we seemed going down grade all the time. That is the peculiarity about riding and engine at night. During the day it appears as if one is going up hill all the time, no matter how steep the down grade, but at night it appears that one is going down hill all the time, no matter how steep the up grade. Therefore, it appeared to me that we were rushing down hill to our death, and that the headlight was the eye of fate pointing out a dreadful doom.

At West Point we dashed onto the Chattahoochee River mammoth steel bridge. From a distance the structure looked to me like a cavern, within whose depths we were sure to meet our end. We passed safely over, however, and I breathed a sigh of relief, for the waters looked cold, and deep, and sinister, as if they might hold within their breasts many of such as we.

At West Point we took water again, and would have left within three minutes if had not been for that hot box. The train crew was at work on it. They poured oil over the brasses, crammed in more waste, and the flagman scalded his arm. But the box was not cooled. They could not miss the mail, however. Andy clanged the bell to hurry them up. The squeak, squeak from Conductor Bellamy told us we might pull out, and we were off, nine minutes delayed. From West Point to Opelika it is 23 miles up grade. We ran the distance in twenty-four minutes. We remained in Opelika five minutes. The first 24 miles after leaving Opelika we ran in 17 minutes. We were going at a breakneck speed where there came that squeak, squeak from Conductor Bellamy. Mr. McDonald glanced back for the smallest part of a second. The reverse lever was thrown forward, the throttle was closed at a bound, and the air was applied. We stopped with a rapidly which took my breath away, but there was not that jerking, jolting that one usually experiences when coming to a sudden stop.

"We are liable to lose the mail," said Engineer McDonald, but he was on the ground, oiling, wiping, before I could reply. In a few moments the flagman rushed forward and told him it was necessary to set the coach out; pull down to the switch. It was a middle coach and took more time. Mr. McDonald glanced uneasily at his watch.

"Minutes are precious at this stage of the game," he said, simply.

The coach was kicked out. We coupled on, and, after having lost eleven minutes, received the signal to "give 'em white!"

It is 39 miles from Chehaw to Montgomery. We had exactly forty minutes in which to run it. There are some grades and curves in the distance. There is also in progress some repair work. I did not know it then, but I did afterwards.

We pulled out of Chehaw, and were soon running at the rate of 72 miles per hour. The speed was cyclonic. The wind and rain dashed over my face. The bell-cord swayed over, cought my hat under the brim and dashed it to the floor of the gangway. Andy threw in his shovel of coal, and handed it to me. I turned loose long enough to place it on my head. It slipped. I passed my hand over my brow, and it was damp with cold perspiration.

But we made the mail. It was the talk of the railroad circle next day. The station master spoke of it; the train dispatcher commented on the run; old railroad men congratulated Mr. McDonald, who bore it all modestly.

"It was simply a case of have to," he told me, "so I got busy to do it!"

So long as I live I will never forget that mad flight of No. 16 as she plunged through the rain and darkness to make the mail. I will never forget Engineer McDonald, and the manner in which he attended his duties; the unselfish devotion to his work; his disregard of nervous strain; anything to save the mail; was his slogan, and he saved it.

I learned on this trip why engineers have strong faces; I also learned why the lines around their mouths are well defined and denote courage. No weakling, no ordinary man, need try to run an engine. I have often thought the work easy, but this man earns every penny paid him. I would not have the job for three times his pay. All honor to Mr. McDonald, that brave man who knows not the word fear, and whose nerves must be as the bands of steel which hold his engine together. When I retired that night I was more tired than if I had worked at ordinary labor for twelve hours without cessation. I appreciate the president's courtesy in furnishing the transportation, but I have had enough. It will be many a night before I cease to think of Mr. McDonald and wish him well on his trip.

THE WILD RIDE OF THE 97

By Hugh Park
In his "Around Town" column
In the Atlanta *Journal*
January 3, 1962

One Saturday night in the spring of 1903, the West Point and the L&N railroads made an emergency decision in favor of Sarah Bernhardt, the great French actress.

They agreed to hook her private, heavy steel car onto Mail Train 97 and haul it on their tracks from Atlanta to New Orleans so she could fill a 3 o'clock engagement there Sunday afternoon.

This was quite a concession for the times. Because mail trains, instead of passenger trains, were the jets of their day and hauled nothing but their mail coaches and a coach for the crew.

They were the crack outfits. Mail Train 97 was to make a run that few people remember, or even knew about. One of those aboard that horrowing night was Quillian E. Martin, of 877 Ashby Street, SW, its baggage master.

"Train 97 always had the right of track over anything in both directions," he said, who is a gentle, ruddy man of 78. "Freight trains wouldn't get to within 50 miles of 97 because they didn't know whether they could make to the next junction before 97 came pounding down the rails. Train 97 didn't have to look out for nothing – the rest had to look out for 97."

The mail train was something that people in Georgia, Alabama, Mississippi and Louisiana stayed up to see because it made the 496-mile trip to New Orleans in 12 hours. If a mail run was late, the government would fine the railroad or railroads responsible under the contract of the day. The fines began with $125 for the first five minutes a train was late and increased for each subsequent minute.

So you can see the concession the rail officials made for Miss Bernhardt. And then 97's engine was built for speed and not for the heavy haul because it had high drivers.

John McWaters Accepts the Challenge

Miss Berhnardt and her party were 15 minutes late arriving at the station (at 11:30 p. m.) from the Grand Theatre while the train crew waited anxiously.

"John McWaters was the engineer, as brave a man as ever had his hands on the throttle," said Mr. Martin. "He had to make up that time, although his high drivers were slow in pulling out from each station. We had Miss Bernhardt's car hooked onto our three mail coaches and crew's coach and its extra weight was telling."

We were still 15 minutes late at LaGrange but the government penalties wouldn't go into effect unless we were still late when we reached Montgomery where we were due at 3:17 Sunday morning. John McWaters, who was a good medium-sized man, told the dispatcher at Montgomery that he thought he could make up the time."

At Opelika they were still running late. And there was a sha[rp] message from the dispatcher which informed the blackhead[ed] engineer "that the tracks were wide open and he was looking f[or] him under the Montgomery depot at 3:17."

"John McWaters was a proud man," continued Mr. Mart[in]. "He didn't want anybody saying he couldn't make his schedu[le]. All he knowed was running an engine and he wasn't afraid."

"Ahead of us lay Notasulga Hill which was seven miles lo[ng] and had a dangerous curve right at its foot. McWaters told t[he] dispatcher that if we were not at Montgomery at 3:17 to send t[he] wrecker to the foot of Notasulga Hill and he would find us in t[he] woods.

"We were all in the crew's coach and Conductor Bob Ingra[m] took out his watch. You couldn't see anything but the night outsi[de] and hear the wheels running themselves to death. Then he to[ok] a deep, long breath. We had made the curve. We had gone dow[n] seven-mile Notasulga Hill in six minutes and we kept going. W[e] made Montgomery on time, running the 66 miles from Opelika [in] 64 minutes. Sarah Bernhardt and her party, asleep in their priva[te] car, never did know about their wild ride."

- Reprinted with permission from The Atlanta *Journal* and T[he] Atlanta *Constitution*

estern of Alabama 501 was the first road diesel on the West Point Route. It was delivered in a paint scheme of dark blue with an aluminum (silver) band ng in a "bow wave" on the nose and running along the side. (Tidwell-Couch Collection)

The 501 is shown here, in Atlanta Terminal Station circa 1961, in the solid blue paint scheme that replaced the blue and aluminum dress the unit wore at delivery. The West Point Route's F-units were used interchangeably in freight and passenger service. (Author's collection)

175

The last order of first generation diesels is represented here by WofA 530; a GP-9 delivered in May of 1954. These units were equipped with steam lines (but no steam generators) that enabled them to be used in conjunction with steam generator-equipped units in passenger service. (Author's collection)

WofA FP-7 503 leads two Geeps and another F units with a rather substantial train 37, the *Crescent*, into East Point, GA, in March of 1958. At this time it was a rarity to see Geeps on 37 and 38, but it became more common in later years. (Shelby F. Lowe photo, author's collection)

fA "Torpedo boat" GP-7 525 and two mates lead a through freight over the Central of Georgia diamond and past the depot at Opelika, AL. The air tanks
top of the units, moved there to make room for the steam generator's water tank, were similar in appearance to the torpedo tubes on a World War II PT
at, giving units so equipped the nickname "torpedo boats." (Author's collection)

FP-7 503 is shown in Atlanta Terminal Station in March of 1958. The yellow paint on the handrails and grab irons mandated by an Interstate Comm Commission order that such safety appliances be painted a contrasting color, preferably yellow. (Shelby Lowe photo, author's collection)

Western of Alabama Baldw VO-1000 switcher 623 w delivered with a solid bl scheme in 1944. It is shov here in Montgomery, AL, wea ing the blue and alumin (weathered to an off-wh or light gray) scheme that placed the original paint in t early 1950's. (Tidwell-Cou Collection)

WP FP-7 554 stands in Atlanta Terminal Station prior to heading south (railroad west) to Montgomery with No. 37, the *Crescent*. Once a week the train rried an express refrigerator car (immediately behind the locomotives) loaded with fresh cut flowers. (Howard L. Robins photo, author's collection)

A&WP 552 and friend lead a seemingly endless train 37 at Opelika, AL, in October of 1959. While it was all Pullman north of Atlanta at this time, the *Crescent* carried coaches (and considerably more head-end business) between Atlanta and New Orleans. (David W. Salter photo, author's collection)

A&WP 574 switches cars in Atlanta Terminal Station, circa 1955. At Terminal Station, each road handled its own switching as the terminal company owned no motive power or rolling stock. (R. D Sharpless photo, David W. Salter collection.)

Given the location (West End, Atlanta), season (winter – note the bare trees in the background), and time of day (shadows indicate either early AM or late PM) this is train 37, the *Crescent*, shortly after its 8:25 AM departure from Terminal Station. While the photo is undated, it appears to be winter of 1962 or '63. (Tidwell-Couch collection)

Atlanta Terminal Station is only about 40 minutes away as WofA 501 brings the eastbound *Crescent* past the depot at East Point and under East Point Tower in 1965. If the train is on time its 11:25 AM. (Marvin Clemons photo, Author's collection)

e lineup at Terminal Station on this late afternoon in the late 1950's includes (left to right) A&WP 553, preparing to depart for Montgomery with the *Pied-ont Limited* (No. 33), Seaboard Air Line 1710, a GP-7 waiting to switch SAL train 34, the *Silver Comet*, on its arrival, and Central of Georgia 805, an E-7 eparing to depart for Savannah with the *Nancy Hanks II*. (Howard L. Robins photo, Author's collection)

A pair of FP-7's leads an impressive westbound *Crescent* just north of Palmetto, GA, in 1952. Even at this relatively early date (for the moderniz
Crescent the lightweight consist had been infiltrated by a few heavyweight cars. (David W. Salter photo)

It's about 8:15 AM in this circa 1952 shot of the south side of Atlanta Terminal Station. Southern Railway E-8 2929 and an E-6B brought the *Crescent* in from Washington at 8:00 AM (assuming the train was on time) and A&WP 553 and two WofA passenger Geeps (525 and 526) will depart with the train for Montgomery at 8:35AM. (Tidwell-Couch collection)

In the mid-1970's, motive power of parent roads Louisville & Nashville and Seaboard Coast Line began running through on West Point Route freigh A&WP 728 and WofA 701 lead three L&N units on a through freight in early 1977. (W. B. Folsom photo)

A&WP 733 and WofA 08 were the last two locomotives delivered in the black paint scheme used by the West Point Route after 1967. They were built by EMD in November 1974 and delivered the following month. The 733 is shown here in Atlanta in 1978. (Jim Brown photo)

In later yeras motive power was used interchangeab and indiscriminately between the affiliated lines. Pri to that time the practice was forbidden by the cond tional sales agreements governing the purchase the units. By 1964, however, the first generation un were paid for and were no longer bound by the restr tion. WofA GP-9 530 is shown here on the Georg Railroad's Athens mixed on the north side of Uni Point, GA, on March 20, 1971. (W. B. Folsom phot

In the last several months of 1982, just prior to the formation of the Seaboard System, a number of units renumbered into the Seaboard System numbering series and received the Seaboard System paint scheme of French gray with a yellow and red "squiggle" logo and white lettering. Until the merger was completed (on January 1, 1983), the units carried the owning roads initials on the cab side under the road number. After the merger, the cabside initials were removed and the unit simply became a Seaboard System locomotive. WofA 4977, rebuild from WofA GP-7 524 at Seaboard Coast Line's Uceta Shop in Tampa, is shown here in Atlanta in December of 1982. (W. B. Folsom photo)

Western of Alabama heavyweight coach 104, shown here in Atlanta in November of 1963, illustrates the paint scheme and lettering arrangement used on the West Point Route's heavyweight passenger equipment in later (post 1945) years. Dark blue body, gray roof, black trucks, aluminum lettering and striping. The lettering and striping quickly weathered to a light gray or white. (Author's collection)

Western Railway of Alabama 10-roomette, 6 double bedroom Pullman *Alabama River* represents one-half of the West Point Route's sleeping car contribution to the modernized Crescent of 1950. The A&WP's *Chattahoochee River* of the same configuration represented the other half. The *Alabama River* is shown here in Atlanta in 1980, when it was being used as an executive sleeper. (W. B. Folsom photo)

Western of Alabama caboose 128, shown here in Montgomery in 1972, illustrates the basic paint scheme for West Point Route cabooses. Red body, white lettering and striping, yellow handrails and steps. This scheme made for a spiffy looking car. (Robert H. Hanson photo)

For its part of America's Bi-Centennial celebration in the 1970's each partner in the West Point Route had a special paint scheme applied to a caboose at the suggestion of W. P. Silcox of the engineering department. WofA cab 150, shown here in Atlanta in the Bi-Centennial month of July 1976, was chosen to wear the snappy red-white-blue scheme. (Lloyd Neal photo, author's collection)

The West Point Route built for permanence. This photo shows the corner of the Western Railway of Alabama office building in Montgomery, Alabama. The building was constructed in 1898, the photo was taken by Bill Folsom in 1997, and the building is still in use today (2004), albeit not by the railroad. (W. B. Folsom photo, Tidwell-Couch collection.)

BIBLIOGRAPHY

Books:

Avary, J. Arch, Jr., and Bowie, Marshall L., *The West Point Route,* Atlanta, 1954.

Black, Robert C., III, *The Railroads of the Confederacy.* Chapel Hill, NC, University of North Carolina; Press, 1952.

Bowie, Marshall L., *A Time of Adversity – and Courage.* Atlanta, 1961

Busby, T. Addison. *The Biographical Directory of the Railway Officials of America,* Chicago, 1906.

Garrett, Franklin M., *Atlanta and Environs.* 2 vol.s Lewis Historical Publishing Co., 1954. Athens; University of Georgia Press, 1969.

Gregory, G. Howard. *History of the Wreck of Old 97,* Danville, VA, 1981.

Hanson, Robert H., *History of the Georgia Railroad.* Johnson City, TN: The Overmountain Press, 1996.

Hanson, Robert P., ed. *Moody's Transportation Manual – 1980.* New York: Moody's Investment Service, 1980.

Harrison, Fairfax. *A History of the Legal Development of the Railroad System of the Southern Railway Company.* Washington, DC, 1901.

Kay, John L., *Directory of Railway Post Offices,* Chicago, Mobile Post Office Society, 1985.

Klein, Maury, *Edwin Porter Alexander,* Athens, GA: The University of Georgia Press, 1971.

Klein, Maury, *The Great Richmond Terminal.* Charlottesville, VA: University of Virginia Press, 1970.

Klein, Maury, *History of the Louisville & Nashville Railroad.* New York: The MacMillan Company, 1972.

Johnson, James Houston, *Western & Atlantic Railroad of the State of Georgia.* Atlanta: Georgia Public Service Commission, 1930.

Joubert, William H., *Southern Freight Rates in Transition.* Gainesville, Fla.: University of Florida Press, 1949.

Poor, Henry V., *Manual of Railroads of the United States for 1873-74,* New York: H. V. & H. W. Poor, 1873.

Poor, Henry V., *Manual of Railroads of the United States for 1878,* New York: H. V. & H. W. Poor, 1878

Poor, Henry V. *Manual of Railroads of the United States for 1886,* New York: H. V. and H. W. Poor, 1886.

Poor, Henry V. *Manual of Railroads of the United States for 1894,* New York: H. V. & H. W. Poor, 1894.

Poor's Manual of the Railroads of the United States, 1917, New York: Poor's Railroad Manual Co., 1917.

Prince, Richard E., *Steam Locomotives and History, Georgia Railroad and West Point Route,* Green River, WY, 1962.

Stover, John F., *Railroads of the South, 1865-1900.* Chapel Hill, NC: University of North Carolina Press, 1955.

Tavenner, C. B., ed. *Who's Who in Railroading in North America,* 13th edition. New York: Simmons Boardman Publishing Company, 1954.

Articles:

Edson, William D.,"The Norris Construction Record", *Railroad History* 150, Spring 1984, pp. 57-85

Moshein, Peter, and Rothfus, Robert R., "Rogers Locomotives: A Brief History and Construction List." *Railroad History* 167. Autumn, 1992, pp. 12-147

Sadler, Joseph P., "West Point Route", *Trains Magazine*, June, 1943, pp. 8-13.

Young, S. R.. "Automatic Block Signals and How They Operate." *The Courier*, December 1926, p. 15.

Periodicals:

Atlanta *Constitution*

Atlanta *Journal*

The Courier

Diesel Era Magazine

Extra 2200 South

Montgomery *Advertiser*

Official Guide of the Railways

Railway Age

Railway Gazette

Ties

Trains Magazine

West Point Route Materials:

Agreement Between The Central Rail Road & Banking Co. of Georgia and the Atlanta & West Point Rail Road Co. Covering the Operation of Double Track Between Atlanta and East Point, September 4, 1890.

Agreement Between The Louisville & Nashville Railroad Co., the Atlantic Coast Line Railroad Co., Lessees of the Georgia Railroad, The Atlanta & West Point Rail Road Company, and The Louisville & Nashville Railroad Co., Covering Joint Use of Terminal Facilities, Atlanta, Ga., April 1, 1907.

Agreement Between The Western Railway of Alabama and the Central of Georgia Railway Co. Covering The Joint Use of Facilities, Montgomery, Alabama, July 1, 1899.

Agreement Between The Western Railway of Alabama and the Central of Georgia Railway Co., Covering The Joint Use of Facilities, Montgomery, Alabama, April 6, 1927.

Annual Reports, Atlanta & West Point Rail Road Company, various dates, 1858-1977.

Annual Reports, Montgomery & West Point Rail Road, 1860-1867

Annual Report, Purchasers of the Western Railroad of Alabama, 1880

Annual Report, The Western Railroad of Alabama, 1876.

Annual Reports, The Western Railway of Alabama, various dates, 1889-1981.

Atlanta & West Point Rail Road Company, The Western Railway of Alabama, Georgia Railroad,

Condensed Roster of Equipment, various dates, 1962-1980.
Atlanta & West Point Rail Road-The Western Railway of Alabama, operating timetables, various dates, 1918-1982.
Atlanta & West Point Rail Road - The Western Railway of Alabama, public timetables, various dates, 1895-1969.
Atlanta & West Point Rail Road – The Consist and Make-up of Passenger Trains Operating into and out of Atlanta By The Atlanta & West Point Rail Road, Revised to July 1, 1960.
Atlanta & West Point Rail Road – The Western Railway of Alabama, Traveling Auditor's File, F-892
Charter, Bylaws and Amendments of the Atlanta & West Point Rail Road Company, Revised by Heyman, Howell & Heyman, General Counsel, 1948
Declaration of Incorporation, The Western Railway of Alabama, With Copies of Papers and Acts of the Legislature Relating Thereto, And To The Montgomery & West Point R. R. Co. and the Western Railroad Company of Alabama, To Whose Charter Privileges It Succeeded, no date.
Equipment Diagram Book, A&WP-WofA-GaRR, 1953.
The Flight of the Midnight Mail, promotional booklet.
"From Selma to Atlanta", Passenger Department, A&WP-WofA, 1905, promotional book.
Hale, L. D., "Historical Sketch of The Western Railway of Alabama, 1885-1946", Internal document.
The Heart of the South", Geo. C. Smith, President and General Manager, Atlanta & West Point Rail Road And Western Railway of Alabama, 1898, promotional book.
Locomotive Diagram Book, A&WP-WofA, 1945.
Macon & Western RR and Atlanta & LaGrange RR, Articles of Agreement Covering Joint Use of Track , November 26, 1849.
Statistics, Atlanta & West Point Rail Road, The Western Railway of Alabama, 1898-99, 1903.
Valuation of The Western Railway of Alabama, Office of the Chief Engineer, 1910.
Young, S. R., Letter to Dr. Rena M. Andrews, Winthrop College, Rock Hill, SC, September 10, 1945.

Other Sources:

"A Grand New Train with a Grand Old Name", Southern Railway promotional brochure, 1950.
Atlanta Historical Society, "Down the West Point Road", paper prepared for the First National Bank of Atlanta, no date.
Atlantic Coast Line Railroad, File 425 – Purchase of Equipment
Central of Georgia Railway Company, Contracts and Agreements, Volume I, Savannah, Ga., 1901. (Internal document, not published.)
Central of Georgia Railway Company, Contracts and Agreements, Volume XIV, Savannah, Ga., 1929. (Internal document, not published.)
Central of Georgia Railway, Macon Division, Atlanta District, operating timetables, various dates, 1900-1963.
Family Lines Rail System, Condensed Roster of Equipment, 1981, 1982.
Freeman, D. K., interviews with author, various dates.
Georgia Acts, 1857.
Georgia Public Service Commission, Annual Reports, various dates.
Georgia Railroad Commission, Annual Reports, various dates.
Interstate Commerce Commission, Corporate History of the Atlanta & West Point Rail Road Company, As Of the Date of Valuation, June 30, 1918. (ICC Valuation Document)
Interstate Commerce Commission, Finance Docket No. 24155, Atlanta & West Point Rail Road Company And Western Railway of Alabama – Discontinuance of Trains Nos. 33 and 34 Between Atlanta, Ga., And Montgomery, Ala., Decided October 14, 1966.
Interstate Commerce Commission, Forty-first Annual Report, Washington, DC, 1927
Lease, Georgia Railroad & Banking Company to William M. Wadley, May 7, 1881.
Louisville & Nashville Railroad Company, Ninety-seventh Annual Report, Year Ended December 31, 1947.
Seaboard System Railroad, Condensed Roster of Equipment, 1983, 1984.
Southern Railway Company File 6025, "Atlanta Terminal Company Incorporation Papers, Selection of Officers, etc." November 27, 1902-June 30, 1903.
Ward, A. A., Jr., interviews with author, various dates.